Punk Science

INSIDE THE MIND OF GOD

Dr Manjir Samanta-Laughton, MD

First published by O Books, 2006
O Books is an imprint of John Hunt Publishing Ltd., The Bothy, Deershot Lodge,
Park Lane, Ropley, Hants, SO24 0BE, UK
office1@o-books.net
www.o-books.net

Distribution in:
UK and Europe
Orca Book Services
orders@orcabookservices.co.uk
Tel: 01202 665432 Fax: 01202 666219 Int. code (44)

USA and Canada
NBN
custserv@nbnbooks.com
Tel: 1 800 462 6420 Fax: 1 800 338 4550

Australia
Brumby Books
sales@brumbybooks.com
Tel: 61 3 9761 5535 Fax: 61 3 9761 7095

Singapore
STP
davidbuckland@tlp.com.sg
Tel: 65 6276 Fax: 65 6276 7119

South Africa
Alternative Books
altbook@peterhyde.co.za
Tel: 27 011 792 7730 Fax: 27 011 792 7787

Text copyright Manjir Samanta-Laughton 2006

Design: Stuart Davies

ISBN-13: 978 1 905047 93 2
ISBN-10: 1 905047 93 2

A CIP catalogue record for this book is available from the British Library.

Printed in the US by Maple Vail

Punk Science

INSIDE THE MIND OF GOD

Dr Manjir Samanta-Laughton, MD

BOOKS

Winchester, UK
Washington, USA

Contents

Preface

In September 2003, I had a profound insight that would change my entire worldview and fuel the writing of this book. At the time, I had actually begun to write, not knowing how the book would end. Having decided on the content of the first few chapters, I turned my attention to some of the current problems that exist within cosmology. I had a sense that there was something missing, if only I knew what it was. It seemed to be on the tip of my mind!

One afternoon, I took a break and went for a walk in the Ashridge woods near my home. I found an oak tree with a low branch and sat so that my feet were left dangling. I remembered a video I had seen a few years back, featuring the cosmologist, Brian Swimme, in which he described how it is possible to sense the rotation of the Earth by simply becoming aware of it. So, whilst sitting suspended on an oak tree, I tried to feel the Earth's rotation.

Suddenly, I was thrust into an infinity of spinning orbs. In a moment that seemed to transcend space and time, conveying many books of information in just a few seconds, I understood what I now call the Black Hole Principle.

All the pieces of information I had been studying suddenly fitted together into a framework that is elegant and simple, but also allows for infinite, emergent complexity. This vision has formed the basis for this book and is nothing less than a new view of the cosmos.

What was also clear to me during this experience is how little we know about the universe. Even the Black Hole Principle is just a tiny part of an infinite design. The human race may never truly understand the full workings of the cosmos. All we can do is move from paradigm to paradigm.

Each scientific revolution refines and completes the one before it, but requires a total leap in consciousness. Hence Newton realized that the force that causes an apple to fall is the same one that keeps the planets in orbit. Einstein realized that space and time are not fixed, but relative. Heisenberg developed the idea of wave-particle duality. And now, in the early 21st century, we are ready to take another leap.

In our era, the situation in science is similar to that of the end of the 19th century. People are yet again announcing that all the laws of the universe have been found; there are no further conceptual leaps to be made. All we have left is to refine what we already know. In the book, *The End of Science*, John Horgan writes, "the great era of scientific discovery is over ... Further research may yield no more great revelations of revolutions, but only incremental, diminishing returns."[1]

The time is right for a change in science: for the next big discovery. This revolution will place consciousness at the very heart of an intelligent universe. This movement started to gain momentum in the early 1970s and every year sees a gathering of pace.

There are many who decry this movement as heresy and pseudoscience. Just as in all scientific revolutions that have come before, those firmly entrenched in the older paradigm will try to discredit the proponents of the new. Eventually, time provides the answer and the old guard will be dead and forgotten, leaving future generations incredulous at their lack of vision, just as we are amazed by the blindness of those who refused to believe that the Earth is round.

Before my visionary experience in the woods, I had set out to explain those aspects of life that are currently deemed unscientific and paranormal. I had realized, during my experience as a medical doctor and a practitioner of energy medicine, that the techniques used in energy medicine could greatly benefit patients within the orthodox system. However, one of the main barriers to the use of energy medical techniques within the mainstream is the lack of a scientific explanation as to how they work. I started to realize that developments in modern physics, such as the concept of non-locality, have direct parallels with energy medicine. So I began to explore these connections and uncovered many more links between esoteric knowledge and modern physics.

In fact, Horgan's statement, that there is nothing more to find in science, is an extraordinary one, as there are many aspects of life that we find inexplicable. Our current scientific establishment does not even deem these anomalies worthy of study, yet they have crept into the public consciousness and are gradually becoming mainstream interests.

The realms of mysticism and esoteric wisdom, including psychic abilities, distant healing, channeling, near death experiences and angelic encounters are becoming commonplace in our popular culture. The public interest in such subjects is growing. If this were mere fashion or fad, this growth would not be sustained. This genuine interest comes from the fact that many have had actual life experiences of the above. This has resulted in a personal under-standing of the reality of such phenomena. However, the scientific establishment tends to ignore such experiences and fails to explain them.

As more people have such experiences, a new science is called for. Amazingly, we have all the information we need to provide possible scientific explanations for many esoteric phenomena, but in many cases, these links have not been made. This is starting to change as we realize that the content of modern science looks remarkably similar to esoteric knowledge.

For example, by linking separate areas of science, the conclusions made about our universe, obtained by a branch of physics called quantum theory, can be applied to other areas of science. This can help us make sense of anomalies of Nature that have puzzled scientists for centuries. These conclusions also lay the foundation for the Black Hole Principle, a model of the universe that fits cosmological data and solves mysteries currently plaguing scientists such as the origin of high-energy cosmic rays.

This is how *Punk Science* was born: from a recognition that science needs to find a radical voice yet again. It has become lost in the quagmire of funding and bureaucracy and lost its spirit of adventure.

This book will take you on a journey exploring the importance of science itself in our modern culture and why it underpins our lives and shapes our paradigms. It will explore how science has lost its soul and how it is beginning to regain it.

Once the soul is put back into science, certain scientific conundrums become clear in the realms of biology, physics and those areas of life commonly known as paranormal. Hence we gain new perspectives on topics such as evolution, the origins of life and distant healing.

Once we have gained this understanding, we will then explore Black Hole Principle: a new vision of the cosmos that makes sense of astronomical data currently puzzling astrophysicists. This principle has applications in many areas of life from medicine to politics.

But first, we shall start with examining why such an exploration is necessary at all. We shall start by saying it like it is.

M S-L January 2006.

References for Preface

1. Horgan J. *The End of Science*. (Broadway) 1997.

Part I

Rocking the Foundations

Chapter 1

Saying it like it is

Science is sorted!

A s we start the 21st century, it seems that science has answered all the big questions about the universe. The human mind has conquered the world; there is little left to find. We have staked our claim on the moon and even Mars. We have cracked the genetic code, probed deep space and looked into the origins of the universe. We know how life began and how it continues. We can clone sheep and even humans, making us the creators of life itself.

Science is sorted and we are just filling in a few gaps. Or so many people believe. The reality is very different. We may know about the first few seconds after the big bang, but we don't know what banged and why. We have catalogued every single molecule of the body, but we don't know how they become organized. We have taught ourselves about every last part of the machine, but we don't know why it runs. We have been so busy with the tiny pieces that we have lost sight of the big picture.

The truth is that the big questions still remain: how did life arise; why did the big bang occur; what is consciousness? If science cannot answer these questions, then effectively we are only just beginning to discover our universe. Furthermore, we are increasingly discovering aspects of our universe that just don't seem to fit our current scientific models. Certain phenomena such as psychic abilities are seen as unscientific. Yet if science has not answered some of the basic questions about our universe then how can it be an authority on such issues? As people become more interested in such subjects, the demand grows for an explanation, which science has not provided so far. It is not enough to dismiss these aspects of human experience, when so many people are having them. Clearly, science is far from sorted, and there is much to be discovered.

Why science?

For most people, science was their least favorite subject at school. However, it has become the definitive authority in our world. This is because science is supposed to be objective and beyond the imperfections of the opinion of the individual. We use science to justify everything in our world, especially when we want to sell something.

We have advertisements for washing powders in which blue stains disappear faster with one particular brand. We illustrate any serious discussion with scientific facts, presenting charts and statistics. We may have dropped this subject at school, but science and the scientific method deeply influence our daily lives. The scientific method relies on solid, tangible objective results and seems to be an oasis of certainty in turbulent times.

Despite its underpinning of society, there is a rise of dissent against the cold, objective detachment that science represents. It has a bad reputation for many people and deservedly so. We are faced with reports of pharmaceutical companies experimenting on children in developing countries and biologists releasing genetically modified organisms into the wild, putting profit before public opinion.[1]

Such events have left many feeling that science is out of balance. As we move towards practices such as human cloning, this feeling intensifies: science is lacking something. The scientific establishment often ridicules this public sense of imbalance, dismissing these outcries as the opinions of people who do not know the facts. The implication is that irrational emotions are clouding the steps of progress and if people just knew enough about science they would feel differently. However, some learned scientists also speak out about these issues. There is a real sense that science has lost its way.

The Old School

So how did science get like this? How did it become so blind in the eyes of so many? Originally the scientific quest was no different from the questions that everyone asks of our universe. There was no separation between science, philosophy and mysticism, but a dichotomy eventually occurred. Science emerged as a separate discipline and concerned itself with the physical and the tangible and started to ignore matters of the soul and the mind.

The science that we know today, with its objective measurements and mathematics, has really only existed for a few centuries. Its ethos has been to eradicate subjectivity in our way of dealing with the world. This way, everyone has common ground; the same experiment done by separate people around the world should yield the same results. We see science as a way of finding the truth about our universe instead of relying on the opinions of mere, fallible human beings.

After the work of Isaac Newton and Rene Descartes, scientists started to see the mind as separate from the body. (Whether these men really meant to do this or not is another story.) We often talk about the Newtonian or Cartesian world when describing this scientific view.

The universe started to be seen as a big clockwork machine of many separate parts. These parts run to a universal, constant clock ticking away in the background, no matter where you are in the universe. Many people still view the world in this way because it seems obvious to us: we shall discuss why this is not the case later.

If the universe was seen as a machine in Newton's day, then so was everything in it, including us. The Newtonian view sees humans as machines of many parts too. When our parts break down, we take them to be mended by the doctor. Our innermost thoughts and feelings are seen as the results of little pieces of machinery or brain chemicals. Everything about us is determined by a molecule called Deoxyribonucleic acid (DNA) which exists in our cells and contains the complete code for who we are, how we behave and even which diseases we are likely to get. In the Newtonian view, it is the size of our brains that allows us to think, unlike animals. The bigger the brain, the better the machine.

This is the view many people have today and some scientists want to go further. They dream of the ultimate human machine and are trying to blend living cells with machinery to produce 'cyborgs' with artificial intelligence.

This view of a purely solid, material world has served us very well. It has allowed us to explore a lot of amazing technology that we take for granted today. Can we imagine a world where diabetics do not have access to insulin treatment, or a world without antibiotics? We have become used to air travel: the dynamics of which are researched using Newtonian principles.

But when is enough, enough? It seems that we are tipping over the edge of what is comfortable. The paradigm of life as a machine is drawing to a close. Many don't want us to build genetic nightmares; Dolly the sheep had many prototypes that were riddled with problems.[2] How do we bring science back to balance?

There is a new spirit of science emerging. Those who are at the cutting-edge are reflecting on what science is truly about: a continual adventure of discovery. Science is coming out of the old school and entering the new. The results are astonishing and point the way to a new science of the future. Science is finding its soul.

The New School

In all extreme situations, inevitably there has to be a swing back of the pendulum. This is the case in science too. It all really started in the early 20th century with that wild-haired rebel, Albert Einstein. Although we normally think of Einstein as an old man, when he first presented his theories he was in his twenties and a scientific outsider. His degree result had been so bad that he could not even get a job teaching physics. Despite this, his work managed to change the scientific worldview and the rest of the world.

Einstein showed that the universe does not have universal time, but instead, time runs differently according to what speed you are traveling. This was one of the major blows to the Newtonian view. Since then there have been more and more findings in physics and in biology that have changed our ideas about how our universe works. Some leading thinkers have been calling it the 'New Science' and have realized that if science underpins our society then we are about to have a major rethink about how we operate. We not only have whole new theories, but we have cutting-edge experiments too. All this is opening up a new unlimited world of possibilities and human potential.

This New Science is one that many don't hear about and is a far cry from those boring lessons at school. It is a science that goes beyond the mechanical view of reality and demonstrates that the universe behaves very differently from how we previously thought. With the advent of quantum physics, which emerged in the 1920s, we realized that the universe behaves very strangely indeed.

Where we had previously thought that the world is mechanical and solid, we now know that this is not how Nature operates. Some scientists have thought about what this means for us and have realized that all sorts of possibilities are opening up. Quantum physics introduced the notion that our own thoughts interact with matter. For many years it was thought that this principle only applies to very small, subatomic levels but researchers are showing that, under controlled conditions, it can be demonstrated that our own thoughts influence events. We shall further discuss this research in Chapter 6.

Some have gone further to reflect on what this truly means about the nature of reality and of consciousness from a logical perspective. Their conclusions can revolutionize our view of the cosmos, throwing new light on everything from the origins of life, to paranormal phenomena and the creation of the entire universe and ourselves.

It's not just about the PhDs

The true spirit of science is the spirit of adventure. Science is really about our exploration of our universe. It is about asking questions about how things work. What the word 'science' has come to be synonymous with is actually the application of science: technology. What most people think of when it comes to science is 'can we discover something useful so we can make some money out of it?' This is not the same as discovery for the sake of discovery, from truly knowing and experiencing how the universe works.

Science is now mainly confined within social structures, with aims to make discoveries that have applications to technology. This approach has proved to be very useful to society. Yet this is not the only path to make scientific discoveries. Einstein himself, as previously stated, was not actually in the system when he made his great insights.

We owe much in our lives to Michael Faraday, including our methods of daily transport. Until recently Faraday was featured on British twenty-pound notes, such is his recognized contribution to society. It may be surprising to some that such a prominent scientific figure was not actually formally educated in science and left school at around fourteen years of age.[3] It was Faraday's job as a bookbinder that led to his interest in science, sparked by the books he came across in his work.

This is not to say that education is not needed or useful to the furthering of human knowledge, of course it is. We have become so attached to the structures built up around knowledge that sometimes we forget the purity of the truth that we are searching for. Universal truths exist whether you have a PhD or not. It is up to us to take the time to find out what they are.

When trying to understand the universe, progressively new perspectives are needed. If you attempt to solve a problem with the same thinking as before, you run the risk of gaining similar results as before (to paraphrase Einstein). It is those sudden insights that appear to come out of nowhere that can be so revolutionary. An insight by itself is not much use without the backing of experiment or mathematical proof, but it is interesting to realize that some of the biggest ideas in science have emerged via this method. It does not depend on what academic job you hold.

This is where we stand at the beginning of the 21st century: at the brink of another scientific revolution. Far from being the end of science, a new paradigm is just beginning. Just as we are reaching the very edges of our discomfort with the current scientific model, it is starting to make a leap back to holism. A swell of radical voices can be heard across the world and this movement is gaining momentum. They are the ones who bridge science and 'spirit', until there is no longer any distinction. As this occurs, phenomena that were previously seen as paranormal suddenly have a scientific explanation.

Gradually the soul is being put back into science. So how exactly is this happening? For this we need to explore the central idea of this book, that is the fundamental nature of consciousness in our universe.

References for Chapter 1

1. Ready T. Pfizer in "unethical" trial suit. *Nature Medicine.* 2001; 7:1001–1077.

2.Wolf PL, Liggins G, Mercola D. The Cloning debates and progress in biotechnology. *Clinical Chemistry* 1997; 43:2019-2020.

3.Morus IR. *Michael Faraday and the Electrical century.* (Icon books Ltd) 2004.

Chapter 2

Putting the Soul back
into Science

Waking up the world

In all the headlines and political wrangles that make up our daily news there is an important story that often goes unnoticed. Something is happening to the human population; they are waking up to a new reality. There are no official surveys on how many or in what ways. This is not a subject discussed in the Sunday politics, yet it is changing the views of many.

The Western World, so long devoid of any discussion of soul, is starting to find it was there all along. It is expressing itself in many ways: children walking out of schools to protest against war, medical schools teaching complementary therapies due to public demand, weekend workshops to discuss angelic experiences, the growth of mediums on television. We seem to be growing in awareness that there is more to life: that human beings are more than just the obvious.

As many turn their attention to psychics and the 'paranormal', the skeptics have demanded proof. They claim that some of these practices are not scientific and therefore cannot be true. For many years there has not been a scientific explanation for distant healing, mediumship and other practices. But science has changed. Science has revealed that the universe is much stranger than we first thought. As science reveals these strange secrets, its parallels with esoteric knowledge are becoming clear.

The frontiers of science are revealing that the universe behaves as the mystics have told us all along. We are finally gaining a logical explanation for paranormal phenomena and in modern scientific language. We are finding that soul or consciousness is not only a part of science, it is fundamental to the universe.

The study of consciousness is becoming more common. We can divide those researching consciousness into two camps: those who believe that consciousness is a result of brain activity and those who believe that consciousness is more fundamental. In order to see how this divide came about we need to look back at history.

Losing our minds

A discussion of consciousness is largely absent from science. This absence is often ascribed to the philosopher, René Descartes, who decided that mind and body are separate. As the physical body is more easily understood and more obviously compared to the elusive mind, scientists preferred to focus on the body. The study of consciousness and the mind was relegated to the sidelines.

We started to view ourselves as machines composed of various parts. Our minds were simply side effects of the workings of the body. When discussing consciousness we called it an 'epiphenomenon' of the brain as if it were nothing more than an after-thought!

Not only did we see ourselves as machines, but we also saw the whole universe as a giant machine. This had been the way forward for science until the 20th century and remains the path of most scientific disciplines. This approach is often called *reductionism*. According to this approach, if you reduce a system into its component parts, then learn about the parts, you know all there is to know about that system. Reductionism only considers physical components that you can see, touch and feel, ignoring the possibility of any other qualities existing.

A universe made of mechanical parts can be easily predicted. As discussed in the last chapter, Newton is often seen as having been a great proponent of this view. He believed that if you had information on all the mechanical parts in the entire universe then the future of the universe could be predicted. The universe was a giant clockwork machine: predetermined, without soul or mind. Humans could be seen simply as parts in the machine.

This mechanical, soul-less view that made up the basis of 17th-century science became the starting point for all of the systems that now constitute modern Western life, from medicine to economics. We are still living with the legacy of reductionism and it touches every aspect of our lives.

This is easily seen by visiting any Western-style hospital. People are treated according to systems and parts and are likely to see a specialist such as a cardiologist to deal with heart problems. The rationale is that if all the various parts of the body that have broken down are dealt with, and then the person will make a recovery.

The idea of the body comprising separate parts does not stop at the level of major organs and tissues. With the growth of molecular medicine, parts of the machine of the body are just as likely to be molecules. The philosophy of reductionism applies here too. Pharmaceutical drugs are produced to correct any molecules that may have become imbalanced. Again this follows the philosophy of fixing the parts to heal the whole person. The reductionist system in medicine has worked very well for many years but people are now wishing to be seen as more than the sum of the parts, hence the rise of medical modalities that are seen as more holistic.

This holistic movement touches other areas of our lives too, such as economics and ecology. As we begin the 21st century, there is a rising disquiet regarding the view that our universe and ourselves are simply machines. There is a call for a science of holism: a science of more than the sum of the parts. So how do we put the soul back into science? Some may be surprised to find that this movement has already begun.

The conscious revolution

We have discussed that for many years, consciousness has been seen as an unimportant subject. Recently there has been a renewed interest in the subject of consciousness, with a growing number of books and television programs attempting to address this faculty.[1, 2]

It is an odd state of affairs: we make observations of our world, these very observations give us the foundations of science itself, yet we do not often explore that the common factor behind these observations is the fact that we are observing. It is amazing that science has thus far largely ignored this ubiquitous phenomenon.

Although we use the act of observation in science we do not ask *how* we are able to observe at all. It is generally agreed that observation requires an action by a conscious entity. The discussion of observation is, therefore the discussion of consciousness.

It was the birth of quantum physics in the early 20th century that changed this state of affairs. From then on, the phenomenon of consciousness could no longer be ignored by science.

The new reality

Many will have heard the term, 'splitting the atom'. Taken literally this is a phrase that does not make sense. The word 'atom' comes from the Greek word meaning 'indivisible'. It was thought for many centuries that all matter could be broken into constituent parts. It was envisaged that these parts were similar to tiny, solid, billiard balls.

When the atom was probed more deeply it became apparent that it was not solid. The atom was in fact predominately 'empty' space with just a speck of subatomic particles contained within. These are the particles that many will be familiar with from school science classes: the protons and neutrons in the center or nucleus with electrons occupying 'shells' in orbit around it.

Figure 1 – Classical picture of an atom

Originally it was thought these particles that existed inside the atom were also like solid billiard balls. Further probing of these particles revealed a very different reality. The early forefathers of quantum physics found something they were not expecting. These particles were not solid either.

Instead they found that these particles displayed a very strange type of behavior. It seems that a particle, such as an electron, exists as a wave of probability. This is a very odd concept indeed and one that the early quantum physicists found very difficult to grasp. It is as if when you really get to the fundamental of what an object consists of and reach this subatomic level, where you might expect to find a particle, all you actually find is a map of where that particle might be.

The electron seems to exist as a mere whiff of possibility, existing at this position or that position, until the act of measuring occurs. It is at that moment when its position can be determined. It is the very act of measuring which seems to bring it into the realms of reality and out of probable existence. This property of particles to be sometimes like a wave and sometimes like a point is called wave-particle duality.

Figure 2 – Wave-particle duality
The particle exists as a wave of probability until measurement occurs.

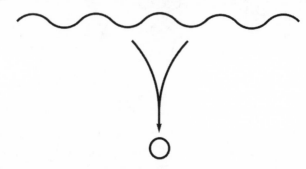

This strange behavior exhibited by particles moved Nobel Prize-winning physicist, Richard Feynman, to say in one of his lectures, "The theory of quantum electrodynamics describes Nature as absurd from the point of view of common sense. And it agrees fully with experiment. So I hope you can accept Nature as she is – absurd."[3]

Quantum physics introduced the idea that the act of measuring alters the nature of reality, much to the disturbance of those who discovered it. Suddenly we had progressed from passive observers of our universe to active participators. From seeing ourselves as soulless cogs in a clockwork machine universe, we realized that we are important. Our act of observation has an effect on matter. Furthermore, as we discussed earlier, our ability to observe depends on our faculty of consciousness. This means that consciousness is intricately entwined with reality.

This idea caused much upset and debate amongst the early 20th-

century physicists including Albert Einstein and Neils Bohr. It is interesting to note that we are almost one hundred years on, yet the concept of consciousness affecting matter at the subatomic level is not accepted by some physicists. Other scientific disciplines, such as biology, remain largely unaffected by the findings of the early 20th century. It seems that many people still ignore Feynman's plea to accept that Nature is absurd.

Our personal power

The reluctance to accept this could be due to the shock of realizing that as human beings we are not just at the mercy of fate and genetics; we have an influence on reality. But with that realization comes responsibility and that may be hard to accept. It is often easier for us not to accept responsibility for our lives.

I do not think it is a coincidence that the growing interest in quantum theory from the non-scientific public is occurring at the same time as the rise in interest in personal development. Personal development teaches the idea that a person's beliefs can affect their life and can include techniques to help examine beliefs and change them. This helps people take responsibility for their lives. As more people make the link between their personal beliefs and how these affect their lives, the findings of quantum physics gain acceptance.

There is much evidence behind quantum physics. It is not just a theory or confined to a laboratory, it also has practical applications. It is a principle called quantum tunneling, derived from quantum physics, that is used in most of the technology of modern life.[4] For example, quantum tunneling is used in the electronic microchips incorporated in most modern equipment from personal computers to televisions, to mobile phones. Although Nature seems to be absurd, we are happy to take advantage of this behavior in our daily lives.

We know that quantum physics is a more accurate description of reality than the Newtonian view. If we are to accept that our mobile phones are real, then we also have to accept the other consequences of quantum physics: that consciousness interacts with matter at a subatomic level. So what is consciousness?

Mind trek

As we start the 21st century, the scientific world is increasingly turning its attention to the problem of consciousness. Consciousness is generally associated with the brain; therefore this field of research is largely contained within neuroscience. Neuroscience is essentially a branch of biology that specializes in the brain and nervous system. Biology in general has been untouched by the revolution in physics, which has moved from reductionism to the quantum view of reality. As a consequence, biology, and therefore neuroscience, remains stuck in the billiard ball view of reality. It operates with the belief that the examination of every part of a system reveals all there is to know about it.

This is a logical conclusion from our observations of life; people with brain tumors or strokes that damage the brain can undergo personality changes. From this we can conclude that the mind exists in the brain and that the brain produces consciousness. This is an assumption so basic to modern neuroscience that it is rarely questioned.

The goal of neuroscience is to learn everything about the brain and its parts. It is expected that through this process the full workings of the mind will be revealed. Much of neuroscience focuses on mapping the parts of the brain and their various functions.

The assumptions made about the brain by neuroscience form the basis of neurological medicine. My medical training taught me that the mind was in the brain. (It also taught me not to worry too much about the whole concept of the mind.) I was shown the parts of the brain that controlled various parts of the body. As a doctor on a neurology ward, I would often examine patients who had suffered strokes. According to my findings, I would draw a conclusion as to which area of the brain had been affected by the stroke. I would then compare this conclusion with the results seen on the Computerized Tomography (CT) scans, which often show the damaged parts of the brain.

We have observed over time that damage to the brain affects various functions of movement, memory and personality. These qualities are all seen as aspects of mind and consciousness. It is no wonder that neuroscience looks for consciousness within the architecture of the brain. It is from this logical process that we have come to this fundamental assumption of neuroscience.

BRAIN = MIND = CONSCIOUSNESS

Now that functional brain imaging is available with techniques such as Positron Emission Tomography (PET) scans, researchers are asking what area of the brain is responsible for happiness.[5] Neuroscience is attempting to explain transcendent experiences, describing them as unusual activity of the hippocampus area of the brain. This area has even become known as the *God spot*.[6]

Naturally this type of questioning will give rise to the query; which part of the brain is responsible for consciousness itself? How is it that the mechanical firings of neurons give rise to the inner pictures, memories and thoughts that we all experience? How do flat, electrical processes give rise to our full, three-dimensional inner experiences?

Those who believe that all there is to know about consciousness comes from studying the brain, continue to pursue their current methods of investigation and research. Neuroscience views the brain as a machine and the various neurological chemicals as parts of the machine, interacting with structural parts: the neurons. Yet all these molecules are made up of atoms. Generally biology does not consider activity at the atomic or subatomic level. The molecule is the smallest part of the machine it considers. So what happens if we go deeper than the molecule to the level of the quantum physics and subatomic particles?

The paradox

As we have seen in our discussions on quantum physics, our own consciousness has an influence on reality at the subatomic level. Often this influence is dismissed as being unimportant to our daily lives. This is due to quantum effects only becoming obvious at the level of the very small, they are assumed to be irrelevant in daily life. To our perception, objects are solid and stable; we do not experience objects flipping in and out of existence.

Yet everyday objects are made up of atoms. If atoms interact with our consciousness, then does that mean that the objects around us do? Even though we may not be aware of it, at a deeper level, all matter behaves in this quantum fashion, even the objects that we see around us which seem so solid. They too, are made up of subatomic particles displaying wave-particle duality and interacting with consciousness. We can see from this logic that it is possible to say that our consciousness interacts with all matter.

In our earlier discussion on quantum physics, we had seen how quantum subatomic particles only exist as a wave of probability until the act of observation. Physicists say that 'consciousness collapses the wave function.' 'Collapsing' describes the way in which the probability wave gains qualities that are certain. Until then it remains in a strange, probable state. It seems that consciousness is the mechanism that collapses the wave function and brings the sub-atomic particle into being as opposed to just possibly being there. These particles make up the objects we see around us: matter. It could be said, therefore, that consciousness creates matter.

Amit Goswami, a conventionally trained physicist, started to worry about this in the 1960s. He recalls his journey and his conclusions in his books such as, *The Self Aware Universe* and *The Visionary Window*.[7,8] He started to realize that science contains a paradox.

He realized that consciousness is responsible for creating matter by collapsing the wave function. The current view in biology, however, is that consciousness emanates from the brain. Yet the brain itself is also made up of atoms that require consciousness in order to exist. The question is - which came first, brain or consciousness?

The way in which Goswami answers this question is by saying that consciousness is the 'ground of all being': that everything in the universe is consciousness. Matter emerges from some inherently conscious ground substance. In this way the paradox dissolves, consciousness came first. Consciousness is a fundamental quality in everything. Many other scientists and scholars are reaching this conclusion such as Peter Russell, Dale Pond, William Tiller, Fred Alan Wolf and Christian De Quincey.[9, 10, 11, 12, 13]

Have we found the 'mind of God' that Stephen Hawking famously left us pondering on at the end of his book *A Brief History of Time*?[14] Have we been looking in the wrong place for consciousness, as it is an inherent quality in everything, not just the brain?

Consciousness as the ground of all being is not a new idea at all. It is an idea found in many religions and spiritual traditions of the world. Peter Russell, as well as being a physicist, is also a student of Eastern philosophy. He gives some excellent evidence of this tradition in his book *From Science to God*.[15] For the first time, the same conclusion has been reached from a scientific perspective.

It is important to realize that the introduction of consciousness into physics is not one that was expected or welcomed. The methods used in making the discoveries of quantum physics were in the reductionist tradition. It is by following reductionism that these results were obtained. Science has led us full circle: by eliminating all discussion of consciousness, it has found that consciousness is inevitable in our universe and is inherent in all.

This idea lays the foundation for this book. There are many phenomena in Nature that are not easily explained such as psychic experiences and the origins of life itself. Physics has led us to the conclusion that consciousness is the ground of all being. How does this help us to understand the conundrums of life? What happens if we incorporate consciousness into science? What possibilities can this hold for us? What happens when we put the soul back into science?

We shall explore this line of questioning: looking at areas of mysticism, biology and cosmology. We shall see how we can gain new answers regarding the origin and workings of life and the creation of the whole universe.

In the next section, we shall be looking at an area of the universe that is most associated with consciousness: life. We shall be looking at the conundrums that have arisen in the scientific model and how these problems can be solved if we place consciousness at the heart of reality and put the soul back into science.

References for Chapter 2

1. Winston R. *The Human Mind.* (Bantam Press) 2003.
2. Carter R. *Mapping The Mind.* (Phoenix) 2000.
3. Feynman RP. *Q.E.D. The Strange theory of Light and Matter.* (Penguin Books Ltd) 1990.
4. Al-Khalili J. *Quantum: A Guide for the Perplexed.* (Weidenfeld & Nicolson) 2003.
5. Newberg A, D'Aquili EG, Rause V. *Why God Won't Go Away.* (Ballantine) 2001.
6. Persinger MA. Propensity to report paranormal experiences is correlated with temporal lobe signs. *Perceptual and Motor Skills.* 1984; 59: 583- 586.
7. Goswami A. *The Self-Aware Universe.* (Tarcher/Putnam) 1995.
8. Goswami A. *The Visionary Window.* (Quest Books) 2000.
9. Russell P. *From Science to God: Exploring the Mystery of*

Consciousness. (New World Library) 2005.

10. Pond D. ed. *Universal Laws Never Before Revealed.* (Infotainment world Books) 1995.

11. Tiller WA. *Science and human transformation.* (Pavior) 1997.

12. Wolf FA. *Starwave* (Macmillan) 1984.

13. De Quincey C. Nature has a Mind of It's Own. *Network.* 2002; 80: 6-9.

14. Hawking S. *A Brief History of Time.* (Bantam) 1995.

15. Russell P. *From Science to God: Exploring the Mystery of Consciousness.* (New World Library) 2005.

Part II

The Ghost in the Machine

Chapter 3

Dumb Molecules

Dumbed down

Whilst attending a lecture by a professor of quantum physics, I heard him describe the discoveries of the early quantum physicists, including how they found that their acts of observation collapsed the quantum wave function. Logically, in order to observe, there needs to be an observer. An observer must possess the quality of consciousness, so I decided to ask him about the importance of consciousness. He answered, "Consciousness has nothing to do with anything." I was very surprised, as I had assumed that the fact he was sitting on a chair giving a lecture to a group of people meant that he was very much alive and conscious!

His answer seems to reflect the fact that scientists want to avoid questions that are not easily answerable in the old school. Physicists seem to want to explore every question in the universe from the subatomic to deep space but are extremely reluctant when it comes to exploring their own inner space.

The interaction of consciousness with matter has not been eradicated by physics; some call it *the measurement problem*.[1] Some physicists do not accept the quality of consciousness as even worthy of consideration. However, as we discussed in the previous chapter, there are a growing number of physicists and scholars who say that consciousness is fundamental to matter and not the other way round.[2]

This is a far cry from the current scientific model. According to the old school, consciousness is a quality found only in the nervous systems of living systems, specifically humans. It is only bestowed to animals that display signs of self-awareness (although opinion may differ on what that means).

Effectively, only humans are credited with this quality of self-awareness; they also happen to be the only ones who can vocalize their thoughts. Science is only just starting to recognize that other animals, even flies, may have self-awareness and personalities.[3, 4] However, this is a radical shift away from the traditional idea that only a complex, highly evolved brain has the quality of consciousness.

According to this view, it was only when fully functional humans evolved that consciousness came into existence. Other animals have traditionally been seen as without minds. It has been out of the question that organisms without a nervous system, such as bacteria, have any quality of consciousness associated with them. Something so simple just does not have a mind. Or does it? Where can we say that consciousness begins? At what level of life does sentience start?

The most basic unit of life is usually regarded to be the cell. Before the days of advanced microscopy, the cell was seen to be rather like a building block. The cell, just like the atom, was seen as a solid part of a machine. Improved microscopy techniques have revealed that cells, all cells not just human cells, are a hubbub of complex communications and activity.

Despite all our modern technology, we have not managed to build a system as complex as a single cell.[5] According to science of the old school, it should be as simple as putting all the parts together. Cellular activity is extraordinarily precise and complex, but miraculously organizes itself. Cellular structures seem to be acting out a very particular dance, without a choreographer. Nobody knows how this self-organizing complexity exists and sustains itself. One has to wonder how do dumb molecules know what to do?

How do dumb molecules know what to do?

This seemingly simple question is actually extraordinarily profound as it reaches to the heart of the mystery of life itself. It is so simple that I asked the question of my biology teacher at school when she was teaching me about cell division.

Cell division is a process that can be easily observed with a light microscope. The sequence of events involved has been well documented. During the process, the DNA within a cell makes a copy of itself. It then wraps itself up and forms the structures we call chromosomes.

The chromosomes line themselves up along the middle of the cell. They are then pulled along by the cellular equivalent of guide-wires, which are created by structures called *centromeres*.

The centromeres are made up of a type of protein molecule. What is interesting is that they position themselves at the poles of the cells during this process. What I wanted to know in school was; how do the molecules know how to align themselves? How do they know which end of the cell is which? These dumb molecules perform such an intricate, ordered dance without brains or nervous systems. My biology teacher told me, "we simply do not know."

Questions like these are often brushed aside when studying biology. Instead, the student learns the steps of cellular and molecular processes in order to repeat them in exams. Questions about how the process is possible at all are ignored, as if they are not important. Yet within these questions lies a larger, fundamental question; how do molecules behave in an intelligent and ordered fashion when intelligence is associated only with a human being with a large brain?

The conventional view that all cellular control lies with DNA surely cannot apply, due to the fact that, at this stage of cell division, the DNA is tightly woven into neat little packages at the center of the cell in the form of chromosomes. The DNA is effectively inaccessible for its inherent information to be accessed.

Another view of conventional biologists is that messenger molecules, such as cytokines, tell molecules where to go. Many of these *cytokines* have been found by molecular biologists, but this does not give them the answer. They have found all the parts of the jigsaw, but are at a loss to explain how it assembles itself spontaneously.

If we take the view that centromeres are guided to the poles of the cells by messenger molecules then how do *they* know where to go? Cytokines are molecules too, so we have to return to the question: how do dumb molecules know what to do? There is a big difference between knowing which molecules are present in a cell and knowing why they are perfectly orchestrated.

This question arises again in the formation of an embryo. Even an animal as complex as a human being grows from a single cell. That cell contains a set of genetic material, which has the information for all the cells of the body. This solitary cell turns itself into a human by dividing itself into more cells. These cells divide until there are many more cells and somehow they all organize themselves into a human. Very early in the process of division, it is decided which cells will turn into liver, which into nerve tissue and so on. How this division of labor is determined is a mystery.

The original cell contains the information of the whole human. How is it that this one cell, which contains one set of genetic material, produces all the cell lines in a three-dimensional figure? How does a cell decide it is going to be an early liver cell? What is the original switching process? This is a question that our science has not yet answered.

Another conundrum facing reductionist biologists is what causes the three-dimensional shape of an organism? For example, how does an arm become arm shaped? For the last thirty years, biologists thought they had solved the issue, with the Progression Zone model. According to this model, an arm grows in three stages. As the arm grows to the first stage, certain molecules give information for the next stage to be grown and so on. This model also contains the concept of an internal clock inside the cell. When a cell has traveled a certain distance up the growing arm, the clock somehow tells the cell to stop moving and start becoming part of the arm. The exact nature of this clock has never been defined.

Recent findings have called this model into question.[6] Experimental data suggests that each part of the arm bud knows where it belongs from the start and does not need this type of prompting. Some of the cells know that they are destined to be a finger and so on. How is this information already available if all the cells are essentially the same to begin with?

Life: the fundamentals

I am certainly not alone in wanting to know the answers to these questions. Erwin Schrödinger, one of the early forefathers of quantum physics, was also curious as to why cell processes work as well as they do. He wrote a book called, *What is life?* highlighting these questions in the 1940s.[7]

Years after this publication, biologists are starting to face the limitations of the old school. Knowing all the parts of the machine is very useful, but it still does not tell us how the machine manages to organize itself. This is a problem currently being raised by physicist, Paul Davies, who discusses the issue of 'stupid atoms.'[8]

In the previous chapter, we discussed how some quantum theorists are suggesting that consciousness is fundamental to the universe, and that matter comes from consciousness, not the other way round. If we apply this principle to living systems, this may finally explain the behavior of seemingly dumb molecules.

From this new perspective, consciousness is not just an emergent phenomenon of the human brain, but is inherent in everything. We know that molecules are made up of atoms. Atoms, as we have seen, are really maps of information that tell us where something might exist. These maps are linked to our own observations, a fact that has moved some physicists to say that intelligent information, or consciousness, is fundamental to matter.

Could this inherent information hold the key to the complex dance of cellular molecules? If atoms and, therefore molecules, are capable of holding information deep within them, could they already know what part of the body they are to become and how they are going to behave? Do chromosomes and centromeres dance in a particular way, because they are deeply intelligent? If we apply the conclusions of quantum physicists, that consciousness is fundamental to the universe in biological situations, we can logically conclude that this is true. Intelligence is written into the fundamental fabric of the molecule.

The light within

The complex mechanisms behind every living system begin to make more sense if every component contains information inherent within it. This information may turn out to be the mysterious hidden conductor that orchestrates the ordered movements of molecules. Although this can be understood as a logical conclusion from quantum physics, we do have some experimental evidence of the existence of this information blueprint and how it is present around an organism before it even exists.

Harold Saxton Burr, a professor at Yale University in the 1950s and Robert Becker, an orthopedic surgeon, were prominent researchers into the electromagnetic fields associated with life. They both measured electromagnetic fields around animals. It was found that a disturbance in the field around the animal created a difference in the way the animal developed.[9, 10]

Furthermore, Burr found that an electromagnetic field in the shape of a salamander could be detected around a salamander egg even before it is fertilized. This suggests that the information of an organism transcends the actual molecule. This can only make sense if we take the view that information, or consciousness, gives rise to matter as described by Goswami and other physicists. This could explain why the information of the shape of a limb seems to be present right from the start of the formation of the limb.

More recently, the work of Fritz Albert Popp in Germany has shown us that light is emitted from dividing cells.[11] A particle of light is called a photon so Popp has named this biological light, *biphoton emissions*. The biphoton emission pattern of a cell whilst it is dividing is identical to the type of pattern that the chromosomes form. Do these patterns of light direct molecules? Have we found out how the molecules receive their instructions?

It would suggest that there is an informational system in these measurable fields that enables an organism to take shape. Although some would balk at this concept, science is based on making conclusions from observation and experiment. The above is a logical conclusion that may be made from the research done over the years by those such as Becker, Burr and Popp.

Reductionist biology from the old school has been very useful but still leaves us with some fundamental conundrums about life. If we start applying the conclusions of quantum physics to biology, that intelligent information or consciousness is the fundamental inherent property of the universe, we can open up new avenues in biology and, therefore, in health. Is there a way to tap into this blueprint and the way in which it shapes us? Is disease a reflection of a disturbance of the blueprint? If so, can we fix the blueprint and therefore heal the illness?

Having discovered how the activities of cells and the formation of an organism makes more sense if consciousness is fundamental to reality, a principle gained from quantum physics, we can apply this idea to other aspects of biology. Can it help us to understand the origin of life itself? Is there more to life?

References for Chapter 3

1. Krips H. Measurement in Quantum Theory. *The Stanford Encyclopedia of Philosophy.* Winter 1999 Edition. http://plato.stanford.edu/archives/win1999/entries/qt-measurement. [cited January 2006].

2. Goswami A. *The Self-Aware Universe.* (Tarcher/Putnam)1995.

3. Fox D. Do Fruit Flies dream of electric bananas? *New Scientist.* 14 February 2004; 32-35.

4. Else L. Trait Spotting. *New Scientist.* 12 June 2004; 50-51.

5. Gibbs WW. Cybernetic Cells. *Scientific American.* August 2001; 43-47.

6. Martindale D. Out on a limb. *New Scientist.* 29 March 2003; 32-35.

7. Shrödinger E. *What is Life?* (Cambridge University Press) 1967 (First published in 1944).

8. Davies P. The Ascent of life. *New Scientist.* 11 December 2004;

28-32.

9. Burr HS. *The Fields of life*. (Ballantine books)1972.

10. Becker RO, Selden G. *The Body Electric: Electromagnetism and the foundation of life*. (William Morrow) 1985.

11. Popp FA, Yan Y. Delayed Luminescence of Biological Systems in Terms of Coherent States. *Physics Letters A*. 2002; 293: 1-2: 93-97. http://www.lifescientists.de/publication/pub2001-07.htm

Chapter 4

There Must be More to Life

In an era when science is able to clone sheep and genetically modify our food, it would seem that we have a firm command of the principles of life. The public may have the impression that science has gained control over Nature and understands the secrets of life. This is actually far from the truth; there are many fundamental aspects of life that we still cannot explain. Not only do reductionist biologists have difficulty explaining the self-organizing nature of the cell, they have also failed to find satisfactory answers to how life first began.[1] This fact is not apparent from the public image of science, which gives the impression that we know how life began and can continue with cloning sheep. Cloning and genetic modification are controversial issues: is it right that we carry on with these practices when we don't even know how life has arisen in the first place?

What's the story?

Effectively the mechanism for the origin of life has been attributed to a story that has never been satisfactorily proved. Because the story has arisen over many years, people have added to it and its basic assumptions have become part of the furniture, allowing us to think that the issue has all been sorted. However, the story does not stand up to modern scrutiny and this is posing a problem for scientists today.

What is generally assumed by both the public and by many scientists alike, is that life developed billions of years ago in a pool of water on Earth. The basic building blocks of life gained the energy to form more complex molecules from a source such as lightning or other intense climatic conditions. These molecules organized themselves into the first single-celled organism, which is thought to have been a primitive version of the ones we see today. These single-celled creatures became organized into more complex organisms. After a period of a few million years, an amphibian-like creature crawled out of this primordial soup and became a lizard. Eventually birds and mammals emerged, including the first humans.

Although this has been the working hypothesis of biologists for some years, it does not actually stand up to scrutiny as a complete explanation for why life exists on Earth. There are several main areas of discrepancy behind the above story that are serious enough to mean that the origin of life on Earth is still a mystery. These issues also highlight the fact that reductionist biology has not been able to find answers to some of our fundamental questions.

Life from non-life

There are many biologists who remain convinced that if you have the right combination of organic molecules, certain energetic conditions and a bit of luck, the random movements of simple molecules will organize themselves into complex cells. They believe that these conditions were met billions of years ago on Earth and this rare, but fluke occurrence gave rise to life where there was none. This primordial seed was able to give rise to more complex creatures. An original spark created life from non-life and all life then emerged from this.

Experiments done in the early 20th century have helped fuel this belief. In the 1920s the work of JBS Haldane and Alexander Oparin gave rise to the phrase *primordial soup.*[2] They noticed how oil spontaneously forms droplets in water and postulated that this was how cells began. All cells have a cell membrane, which is mostly made out of a fatty substance. Haldane and Oparin realized that that these droplets could allow chemical reactions to take place inside them and assumed that cells began in this way.

At the time, the enormity of the complex workings of cells was not known and it was not unreasonable to assume that a few simple chemical reactions taking place in an oil droplet could have been the origin of life. The advantage of this idea is that we can see oil droplets being created quite naturally all the time, even when we do the dishes! It was assumed at the time that such spontaneous phenomena could give rise to life without any outside influences or weird life force.

Since then of course, we have much better knowledge about the way cells work. We know about the organs of cells, the organelles, and about the highly organized structure of DNA. Due to the complex nature of these structures, Haldane and Oparin's idea of a fatty bag containing a few chemical reactions seems unlikely in modern eyes. However, the idea that life arose spontaneously in the primordial soup has stuck and contributes to the belief that we know how life began.

In the 1950s a scientist called Harold Urey tried to recreate this soup in the laboratory.[3] He guessed that the constituents of the gases present on the surface of the Earth at the time were methane and hydrogen. Urey and his assistant, Miller, mixed the gases with water, added some sparks of electricity and watched as organic chemicals called amino acids emerged from the soup. Amino acids are the building blocks of molecules called proteins, which are essential for life.

The success of the experiment led to the extrapolation that, over time, more molecules can emerge this way including ones that are more complex. The origin of life appeared to have been solved.

Both these events have had huge significance, because at the time, they appeared to be the triumph of biology over religious ideas of creation. Biology seemed to have proved that life occurred spontaneously by the chance combination of inorganic chemicals to form organic ones. Chemicals in a solution naturally display random movement and will sometimes bump into one another. Some of these collisions will lead to chemical reactions. These spontaneous reactions were thought to be the type of event that led to the origin of life, perhaps by the formation of organic chemicals in a similar fashion to Urey and Miller's experiment. It was important for biologists to eradicate any hint of order, as order implies intelligence.

Intelligence implies a god-like creator and it was this idea that biology wished to eradicate.

Between Urey, Haldane and others, biology seemed to have proved that life is nothing but a random accident and science triumphed over religion. The idea that we know how life began has remained with us, but the experiments that gave us that idea are way past their sell-by date. In the case of Urey, we no longer think that the Earth was covered in the gases that he chose for his laboratory recreation.[4] Furthermore, we have since found that amino acids are created spontaneously all the time and it is not difficult to make them.

Even if amino acids are created easily and spontaneously, this does not mean that life automatically follows. Amino acids form the building blocks of proteins. There are just over twenty amino acids and the different combinations of amino acids create a sequence, which creates the different proteins. It is the precision of the order of amino acids in a chain that gives proteins their special properties. Changing the sequence of amino acids can even cause disease because it can change the shape and function of a protein.

The spontaneous assembly of a few amino acids in solution is one thing; it is a different prospect when discussing the spontaneous assembly of the precise sequence of amino acids that form proteins. As Paul Davies says in *The Fifth Miracle*, "Just as the discovery of a pile of bricks is no guarantee that a house lies around the corner, so a collection of amino acids is a long, long way from the large, specialized molecules such as proteins that life requires."[5]

We now know that the genetic code we carry in our cells, our DNA, also has a precise sequence of 'letters' which get translated into the amino acid sequence. Our DNA is a hugely complex and precise molecule. Exactly how did all this order come into place from the random movements of a few chemicals? The increasing knowledge of molecular biology has brought with it increasing awe at life's complexity. The idea that this complexity occurred spontaneously is looking less and less feasible, but many still cling to this idea.

There is a current trend to say that life on Earth actually originated from other planets and was seeded here via meteorites.[6] This is backed up by the fact that meteorites have been found on Earth that contain bacteria. Bacteria have been found on Earth in the most hostile of environments, suggesting the possibility of their survival on hostile planets. If life did originate on other planets, travel to Earth on a meteorite and seed life on this planet, it still leaves the question: how did life begin on that other planet? How did life appear from non-life, if it is here or on Mars?

What came first: RNA or proteins?

We have discussed the fact that many people are under the impression that life crawled out of a primordial soup and this idea arose because of some experiments that now seem incomplete and outdated. One of the reasons that they are seen as outdated is that we know so much more about the way the cell works.

In the years since James Watson and Francis Crick discovered the structure of DNA, the genetic code has been unraveled to the point that even the human genome has been mapped. We now know that DNA provides the information for the creation of proteins.

DNA is a type of molecule called a nucleic acid. In cells such as ours, DNA is found in the center of the cell: the nucleus. In some types of cells, a slightly different form of nucleic acid is found, ribonucleic acid (RNA). We also use RNA in an intermediary step between DNA to protein. DNA and RNA use almost identical 'alphabets' to translate information into proteins.

DNA and RNA are essential for cells to create proteins. They contain the information for the complex precise structure of proteins to be made. Yet they are complex structures in themselves. They are manufactured in cells with the help of enzymes. Enzymes are proteins that assist chemical reactions. Without them, chemical reactions are unlikely to occur. Left to their own devices, chemicals react occasionally due to random movements. With the help of a biological enzyme, the speed of reactions is increased many-fold.

We know how essential enzymes are in making the reactions of life possible and the creation of RNA and DNA is no exception. Yet enzymes function because of their precise shape, determined by the ordered way the constituent amino acids are laid out. Enzymes are proteins and gain their function due to their precise structure. The information of this structure is contained within cellular DNA and is translated into a protein via RNA. Nucleic acids, DNA and RNA, need protein enzymes in order to be created. So which came first: DNA and RNA or proteins?

And here we have a paradox that has not been solved by biologists, although they are working on ways to get round this. The current thinking is that RNA is the key to the evolution of life and that RNA itself acted as an enzyme for life's processes before proteins existed.[7] It is thought that the RNA molecule created longer chains of amino acids, called polypeptides. These mini-proteins then acted back onto the RNA to make copies of it, which then made more polypeptides and so on until proteins emerged.

So how did RNA come into being? How did diffuse organic molecules come together to spontaneously form such an ordered complex structure? Logically, something as complex as an RNA molecule would have taken a few attempts, but we have no prototype life forms. There is no evidence to say that life experimented with complexity before finally getting it right. Life seems to have appeared in all its complexity from the start and even the simplest cell contains the same type of nucleic acid that is present in all cells. The RNA/DNA/ protein paradox is just another example of how far we are from knowing about the precise origins of life.

Pushing against the tide

One of the basic laws of science says that a closed system moves from order to disorder. It takes less energy to maintain the disordered state then it does the ordered state. A good analogy is the teenage bedroom; if no effort is put into keeping it tidy, it rapidly disintegrates into disorder. Effort and energy needs to be expended to keep the room ordered and tidy.

This is the way of natural systems: they tend to move to the disordered state, as this requires less energy to maintain. This is known as the second law of thermodynamics and we observe this happening in non-living systems. Yet living systems break this law, they tend to remain ordered. In fact the whole movement of evolution is one of increasing order. Life is able to break the laws of entropy. What is so different about life that makes this possible?

Even as you are reading this book, you are expending large

amounts of energy to keep your systems in order without even having to think about it. Order is maintained in both complex creatures with brains and simple bacterial cells. Every single cell is complex and organized and remains that way, seemingly spontaneously.

There is a time when this is not the case. This is when an organism dies. It is then that the chemicals of the body, held in place so perfectly during life, start to fall apart and decay. They start to follow the laws of thermodynamics and move from order to disorder. What is it about the quality of life that keeps these molecules in place and highly organized?

The previous discussion about amino acids also raises this issue. As previously stated, we now know that amino acids can be formed spontaneously. This occurs by those random reactions we see constantly in Nature that do not need to be helped by enzymes. The spontaneous self-assembly of these amino acids into complex proteins is a different matter and is not a situation that has been witnessed happening in Nature other than as part of a living system. Part of the reason for this, is the energy required for chemical reaction. Whether a reaction occurs or not depends on the balance of energy. Often reactions can go either way according to the surrounding factors and the energy required to keep stable.

In order for some inorganic chemicals to come together as a long chain of amino acids and form a peptide chain, a great influx of energy is needed to keep the chain stable. This influx of energy is going against the grain of Nature as the tendency is for chemicals to find the spot where they need the least energy to maintain their position. It is similar to how most people get home from work and lounge around on a sofa rather than sit upright on a chair. It takes less energy to maintain that position.

A protein has another important quality namely, specific organization. This opens up a new avenue of questioning. We know how important the amino acid sequence is to the functioning of a protein: if the sequence is changed slightly the protein may not function. It is like jumbling the words of a sentence, the sentence may not make sense.

The creation of a protein consisting of a particular sequence of amino acids is a very ordered process. Reductionist biology has not yet explained how such complex order can arise spontaneously. We are back to the question of how do dumb molecules know what to do?

If you were to find a beautiful sentence written in the middle of nowhere, it would imply that an ordered society lived somewhere near. Someone has used their intelligence in order to write the sentence. The order found in proteins also implies an intelligent process behind their creation. Biology is extremely keen to dismiss the idea that life is an intelligent process, as it could imply the presence of a creator. Unfortunately it has not been able to produce a satisfactory explanation as to how ordered life emerges from disordered non-life.

Instead, there is a heated debate amongst biologists and creationists. Creationists point out the deficiencies of biology as evidence that the literal interpretation of the Bible is correct, an argument called Intelligent Design. The debate includes questioning what the second law of thermodynamics actually means and pointing to examples of spontaneous order in Nature such as crystals and galaxies. Despite the disputes, there is still no satisfactory explanation in reductionist biology as to how something as complex as a cell could have appeared spontaneously. How random processes could create something even more complex, such as a human being is even more of a mystery.

When biologists are not busy defending themselves against creationists they puzzle these very issues amongst themselves. Francis Crick, Nobel Laureate and co-discoverer of the structure in DNA commented, "An honest man, armed with all the knowledge available to us now, could only state that in some sense, the origin of life appears at the moment to be almost a miracle, so many are the conditions which would have to have been satisfied to get it going."[8]

Time heals all

Time is an essential factor in the model of evolution. It is seen as the magic ingredient that transforms a few chemicals in a primordial soup into the variety of life that we see today. "Time itself performs the miracles," wrote Nobel laureate George Wald, professor of biology at Harvard University in the 1950s, in *Scientific American*.[9]

It is generally agreed that the age of the Earth is approximately 4 billion years. An underlying assumption of biology is that life emerged and evolved in this time by random processes. Bacteria have been found which date back to 3.8 billion years ago.[10] If life really has evolved by random events alone, the appearance of such forms of life when the Earth was just a few million years old invokes the most fantastical odds. Even a simple bacterial cell is an extremely complex affair, a fact not known by the likes of Darwin and Haldane when they put forward their ideas of the spontaneous, random emergence of life.

Before modern microscopy, cells were believed to be simple aqueous bags, surrounded by a lipid membrane, with a few chemical reactions occurring inside them. Now that we have more information about cells and know how complex they are, the idea that they just emerged spontaneously is less palatable. No wonder people are turning to the theory that life has been seeded from other planets; there was not enough time for it to have appeared on Earth.

The problem was publicly discussed by maverick British astrophysicist, Fred Hoyle, who famously said, "To believe natural processes assembled a living cell is like believing a tornado could pass through a junkyard containing the bits and pieces of a airplane, and leave a Boeing 747 in its wake, fully assembled and ready to fly!" This prominent scientist concluded that life must be an intelligent process in his book, *Intelligent Life*. This contains a calculation showing that the chances that life appeared by random processes alone is very low.[11]

If time is really the only factor involved in the spontaneous emergence of life from non-life, then it should be springing up everywhere. If the probability really is in favor of spontaneous life, then we should be able to find at least one other model of life on Earth or even on meteors. As it is, all forms of life that we have found, even viruses, are made out of the same types of molecules. From viruses to humans, the same genetic material is used. Life as we know it on Earth has a common ancestry which suggests that it has only arisen once.

Biologists are currently searching for the smallest possible genome that is required for life.[12] They are extracting genes from bacterial cells in order to find out when they stop functioning. They have found that the organism with the smallest genome has only 400 genes. (It is called *Mycoplasma genitalium*, which is almost like a bacterium, except it has no cell wall.)

So far, the largest genome that has been put together in the laboratory is one hundred times smaller. Biologists are currently daunted with the task of recreating the minimal genome due to its complexity and size. If producing the minimal genome for life is so difficult when someone is actively creating it in the laboratory, then how was this supposed to happen randomly in Nature?

There are certainly discrepancies when leaving time to perform such miracles. Nobel laureate, Christian de Duve, summed things up rather nicely, "If you equate the probability of the birth of a bacteria cell to chance assembly of its atoms, eternity will not suffice to produce one."[13]

When even members of the scientific establishment are questioning the supposed story of how life began, we have to start wondering if it is anything more than a fairy tale. If the spontaneous emergence of life with all its complexity is so implausible, what is driving the process? When the only alternative is the argument of creationists that the Bible should be taken literally, it is no wonder that biologists have closed ranks and rarely discuss their own discrepancies openly.

Is there another way? Can we stay within the realms of science and still explain the origins of life? What is driving our biology?

References for Chapter 4

1. Russell M. *et al*. Evolution: five big questions. *New Scientist*. 14

June 2000; 33-39.

2. Oparin AI. *The Origin of Life*. (Dover) 1952 (First published in 1938).

3. Miller S. A Production of Amino Acids under Possible Primitive Earth Conditions. *Science, New Series*. 15 May 1953; 17, No 3046.

4. Davis P. *The Fifth Miracle*. (Allen Lane, Penguin Press) 1998.

5. Ibid.

6. Hoyle F, Wickramasinghe C. *Life on Mars: Case for a Cosmic Heritage*
(Clinical press) 1997.

7. Orgel LE. The Origin of Life on Earth. *Scientific American*. October 1994; 77-83.

8. Crick F. *Life itself: Its origin and nature*. (Futura) 1981.

9. Wald G. The Origin of Life. *Scientific American*. August 1954; 46.

10. Schroeder GL. *The Hidden Face of God*. (The Free Press) 2001.

11. Hoyle F. *The Intelligent Universe*. (Michael Joseph Limited) 1983.

12. Ainsworth C. The Facts of Life. *New Scientist*. 31 May 2003; 28-31.

13. De Duve C. *A Guided Tour of the Living Cell*. (Scientific American Library) 1984.

Chapter 5

Intelligent Life

Biology is destiny?

What makes us human? How do we gain the characteristics that we have? Why do we seem similar to our parents? Humankind has been asking these questions for centuries. Through years of scientific observation, we have realized that discrete components are involved in the inheritance of our physical characteristics.

These observations included the experiments of a scientist and monk, Gregor Mendel, in the 1860s. Though largely ignored in his day, he is now seen as the father of genetics. Mendel's experiments involved breeding pea plants, crossing tall and short varieties. This resulted in either a short or a tall plant, but no plants of a medium height, indicating that there were discrete components inside the plant that could be inherited. If a plant inherited the component that caused tall growth, it would become tall, inheriting the short component would make it small. This was a revolutionary idea; before Mendel, people assumed that the characteristics of parents simply merged in their progeny. If the height of a plant was determined in this way, people started to wonder if we inherited all of our characteristics in a similar fashion.

In Mendel's time, nobody knew about DNA or genes. It was with the advent of microscopy that we could see inside cells and see structures such as chromosomes. Chromosomes are the distinct units formed by DNA when a cell is ready to divide. We inherit one half of a set of chromosomes from each parent to make a full set. The discrete nature of the chromosomes made them the obvious candidates for the discrete components that Mendel had predicted. The 20th century witnessed a race to find the structure of DNA: a prize that was eventually won by Cambridge scientists James Watson and Francis Crick in 1953.

DNA is a molecule that can be read like a code. The code gets translated into protein molecules by the cell's machinery. The past fifty years or more have been dominated by the idea that cracking the code will lead to an understanding of the secrets of life. The philosophy behind this is so ingrained that we don't even notice it. We believe that what makes us humans is written in our genes.

We hear about 'the gene for cancer' or 'the gene for Alzheimer's disease' and various other headlines. The implication is that everything there is to know about you is predetermined and written into the cells that you inherited from your parents; there is nothing you can do about it. It is the luck of the draw as to what genes you have and therefore how you will fare in life. For over fifty years science has told us that biology is destiny.

Biologists have now reached the other side of the epic journey known as the human genome project. Each part of human DNA was decoded and translated. For biologists, this was the ultimate prize: to know what makes us human. Unfortunately we were in for a shock.

Before we had finished mapping the human genome, the genes of several other animals had been mapped. It was discovered that the fruit fly, a favorite subject of genetic studies, has 15,000 genes.[1] From this type of data it was possible to guess how many genes humans should have to reflect our superiority over the fruit fly. Initially it was predicted that we should have about 120,000 or at least 100,000. If genes determine who we are, then the complex behavior of humans would suggest this sort of number.

The human genome project has been complete for a few years now. Once again, just as in the early days of quantum physics, science is facing a paradigm-busting discovery. Instead of the 100,000 genes we were hoping to find, the human genome only contains 34,000 or less. Even a simple roundworm has 18,000 genes: only a third less than we have.[2] Mice have roughly the same amount of genes.[3] In fact we share 95 per cent of our genome with mice. The main difference is that mice make more proteins related to their sense of smell.

Biologists now have to admit that it is not our genes that make us human.[4] This has huge implications for the 'biology is destiny' idea. For a long time, genes have been where the action is. It is not easy to let go of this much-cherished idea and, in fact, many still believe that genes hold the keys to life. However, scientifically speaking, genes are not responsible for making us human. So the question remains, what does?

Many areas of the genome of any species contain the instructions to make proteins. It will also contain sections that do not code for proteins at all. These contain regulatory sequences and there are differences in these from species to species. The emphasis has shifted to examining the differences in these regulatory sequences and away from the coding sequences.[5] We may all use the same types of proteins, but the way in which we use them differs. This is where biologists are now looking for the keys to life: the regulation of protein production.

So how do these regulatory sequences get switched on and off? If these are the keys to what makes us human: what regulates the regulatory genes? We are back to the question of how do dumb molecules know what to do?

Liptonite biology

Dr Bruce Lipton is a molecular biologist who discusses this very question: how is the cell really controlled? In recent years, biologists have shifted the focus of cellular control from the genes themselves to their regulation. Yet even this regulatory aspect of the genome still needs to receive instruction from somewhere. So what is regulating the regulatory sequences? Lipton realized that the center of cellular control does not necessarily lie within the DNA. In fact, he makes it clear that the control of a cell is not within the cell at all. It is at the boundary between the cell and the outside world: the cell membrane.[6]

The cell membrane is the part of the cell that connects it to its environment. The environment of the cell is dictated by the content of the fluids that surround the cell. These fluids in turn receive most of their content from the bloodstream. Molecules, such as hormones, contained within these fluids can interact with receptors in the cell membrane. It is via these membrane receptors that central messages get transmitted to the whole body. For example, if an organ such as the adrenal gland produces the hormone adrenaline in response to something frightening, adrenaline enters the bloodstream and gets transmitted to the cells of the body which can 'see' the hormone via these membrane receptors

Figure 3 – Cellular receptors in the cell membrane.

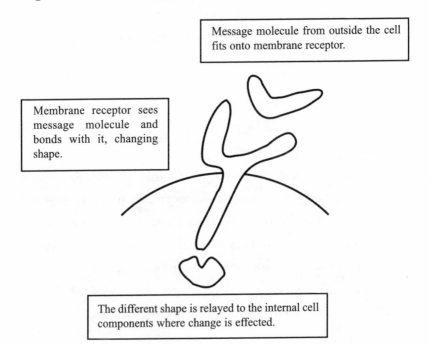

Message molecule from outside the cell fits onto membrane receptor.

Membrane receptor sees message molecule and bonds with it, changing shape.

The different shape is relayed to the internal cell components where change is effected.

The receptor is a protein of a particular shape, which becomes bonded for a moment with a particular message such as adrenaline. The bonding changes the shape of the receptor. As the receptor protein spans the membrane, contacting both the inside and the outside of the cell, the changes in shape are transmitted to the inside of the cell. The message gets transmitted to the DNA and the rest of the cell in a precise form of Chinese whispers. DNA expression may be altered accordingly. We now know that the regulatory sequences of DNA play a key role in this.

Most biologists would agree with this picture, although it was not always this way. We used to think that the genome was immune to outside influence. Back in the 1890s an experiment was done by August Weisman which appeared to prove this. He bred many successive generations of mice and then cut off the tails of some of the generations. The future generations of mice had tails; he therefore concluded that the environment cannot influence the genome.

Francis Crick, one of the discoverers of the structure of the DNA molecule, also propagated what is known as the 'central dogma' of DNA. This means that information flows out of DNA and not into it. So experience does not change the DNA sequence and the only way DNA changes is via unpredictable, random mutations in which the sequence changes by accident. It is now thought that although the sequence does not change, the environment feeds back in to the genome and changes the way in which it is expressed.[7]

The idea that information changes the way in which the genome is expressed is acceptable to most biologists. Now that we know that it is not our genes that make us different from other animals, we know that our genes are not in control of our cells. Some will accept

Lipton's idea that the real control of the cell comes from the cell membrane. Membrane receptors alter how the genome is expressed. If the signal that causes a change in genome expression comes from the cell membrane, which in turn takes its cue from outside the cell from the fluids surrounding it, how is *that* signal created. What causes the original signal?

The original signal is created in response to the external environment. Continuing with our above example, when someone is frightened by their environment, their brain tells their adrenal glands to produce adrenaline. This hormone then circulates in the body, and informs the cells via their cell membranes. This process may lead to an alteration in DNA expression and certain proteins being produced.

Interestingly, as Lipton points out, not everybody responds in the same way to a stimulus. Some people may perceive the situation as non-threatening. They would not make the same hormonal response to the stimulus and therefore would have a different cellular response. By this logic, it is the perception of reality that is in true control of the cell. The body responds according to how the environment is perceived, something Lipton calls the Biology of Belief.

Experimental data also shows that perception of the environment alters gene expression. Mothers who have a stressful environment in pregnancy have children with a 50 per cent higher risk of cranial malformation.[8] This is in response to the circulating hormones of the mother that are available to the developing fetus.

The hormones released in response to fear send a message to the embryo to get ready to run. So the hindbrain, which deals with muscle movement, develops more than the forebrain. This shows that the mother's perception of her environment has a direct correlation to cellular development.

If our perceptions control which parts of our genome are expressed then what affects our perceptions? Lipton argues that our belief system shapes our perceptions. Often we operate from belief systems that are unconscious and embedded from our childhood. If we become aware of our beliefs then we can learn to change them. As our beliefs input into the behavior of our cells then we can get into the driving seat of our biology. We used to think of ourselves as victims of our inherited genes and the luck of the draw. Now we are realizing that we can learn to manage our beliefs and perceptions and therefore our own biology.

This has huge implications for the way in which we view diseases such as cancer. A researcher who has done much work on this is a German doctor called Ryke Geerd Hamer.[9] He is medical oncologist by training and his own life experience led him to investigate the links between emotional shocks which we receive in life and the development of diseases such as cancer. He calls this *The New Medicine* and his work is backed by extensive patient data as well as radiological and histological evidence. This further substantiates the view that genes receive input from our perception of the environment. The findings of Psychoneuroimmunology, which rose to prominence in the 1980s and 90s, is also a large body of evidence linking emotions and beliefs to illness.[10]

The idea that our perceptions shape our cells has a direct correlation with the findings of quantum physics that consciousness shapes reality. We have learnt in physics that the heart of physical reality is not very physical at all but the fundamental quality of consciousness or information, from which physical matter arises. Now biology is undergoing a similar process in letting go of the much-cherished idea that our genes control our cells and our lives. Lipton, Hamer and others are showing us that the nebulous quality of perception controls gene expression.

The harder we look, the more obvious it becomes that genes do not control who we are, they simply contain the information for creating proteins. What is the ghost in the machine that does shape who we are? We shall now discuss how consciousness shapes biology and drives evolution.

Conscious evolution

One of the fundamental principles of established scientific thinking is that life appeared on Earth by accident. Randomness plays a key part in evolutionary theory. Not only has it been assumed that somehow life emerged from non-life by accident, but that each species emerged by random accidents too. The hypothesis that evolution occurred by random events is one that can never be tested scientifically, but despite this, it is treated as a fact.

It has been assumed that due to environmental pressure, those members of a species lucky enough to have a random mutation in their genome have a superior quality over the rest. A mutation occurs when part of the genome actually changes and is distinct from simply a change in the way the genome is expressed. It is like changing a word in a sentence to give a whole new meaning.

Various types of mutations can occur at any time. They may be due to mistakes during DNA copying or during cell division or something else. Some chemicals seem to result in a higher rate of mutation and that is why they can be dangerous. Some mutations result in a fetus dying soon after conception. Others can convey an advantage over other members of the species, for example people with the mutation that causes sickle cell anemia are less prone to malaria.

Hence, mutations may be detrimental, but they may allow survival in a hostile environment. Those with the mutation may dominate over the other members of the species who do not have this chance advantage. This is where we get our idea of 'survival of the fittest', a phrase that has spread from biology to other aspects of society.

At some point the two streams diverge and a new species develops. Thus, the development of new species is brought about by environmental pressure emphasizing the advantages of a random mutation to certain members of the old species. This is not believed to be an intelligent, ordered process.

There are problems encountered with this model. As previously mentioned, time has not been sufficient for the chances of even a single cell to have occurred by a series of accidents. Also, nobody has ever managed to make a new species through environmental stress and isolation in the expected time frames.[11] In fact new species appear side by side and do not need to have geographic isolation in order to emerge. Even stranger, there is evidence that mutations do not occur randomly at all. Hotspots have been identified in areas of DNA where mutations are particularly prone to occur. This suggests that the process of mutation is not random but occurs in specific areas.[12]

Some evidence suggests that when a mutation does occur it is a very specific reaction to the environment and even bacteria use an intelligent process to mutate their own genome.

We've got a fuzzbox and we're going to use it

A respected researcher, John Cairns, published a paper in *Nature* in 1988 which challenged received wisdom of the random nature of genetic mutation.[13] Cairns studied a type of bacteria called *Escherichia coli*. This type of *E.Coli* did not have the genes to produce the enzyme lactase that is needed to break down the sugar, lactose. He put the bacteria in a medium in which the only food source was lactose.

If mutations are truly random then the rate of mutations should have been the same in these bacteria than in a control group. Surprisingly, it was found that the bacteria started to mutate in order to be able to utilize the lactose as food. The mutations occurred far more frequently than in the control group. It seems that the bacteria were able to mutate to adapt to the environment, results which question the random nature of mutations.

At first glance this may seem like the environmental pressure effect discussed earlier. But environmental pressure should not influence the rate of random, chance happenings; they merely emphasize the advantages that they may give. Cairns was seeing that the bacteria were consistently, specifically and quickly changing their genes to cope with the environment; they knew what to mutate and they knew how to do it. Somehow the bacteria could sense and perceive their environment and mutate their own genome specially to cope with this.

Cairns' experiments have been wholly reproducible by other researchers. Adaptive mutations in a variety of bacteria have been detected. The results throw new light on the issue of evolution, suggesting it could be a directed process. It also raises the question how do bacteria have the intelligence to perform such a feat? Do bacteria have intelligence when they do not even have a nervous system? We have only just started to concede that other mammals have consciousness; it is a big leap to say that bacteria do too.

So what is the mechanism: how do bacteria know that they are surrounded by lactose and then how does this information translate into a mutation? How do they see their environment when they have no sensory organs? Reductionist biology sees the cell as a biological machine full of organized molecules. Cairns' results suggest that the molecules of this single-celled bacterium can sense their environment and make a specific change to its own genome. How do these dumb molecules know what to do?

Consciousness, or some sort of informational processing system, seems to be inherent even to the process of evolution. Could evolution be a conscious process? Could consciousness be inherent in the universe from the start, setting up the situation for life even before life existed? Could it be the force that organizes dumb molecules into cells and drives evolution?

Conclusions to Part II: are we close to a unified science of life?

We have discussed in previous chapters how some physicists have reached the logical conclusion that consciousness is the fundamental to reality and that matter arises from it. The idea that consciousness is an inherent part of everything would be a way to solve some of the deep conundrums in biology, discussed in Part II. Although many prominent scientists have spoken of the difficulties and limitations of current biology, the only alternative seems to be creationism.

Creationists have gleefully snapped up these inconsistencies as proof that an external god-like character created everything. By doing this, the debate moves out of the realm of science. Is there any way to be scientifically consistent and to solve some of the problems of biology?

With the arrival of the physics of consciousness, we have a new avenue to pursue which remains wholly in the realm of science. By placing consciousness, or intelligent, ordered information as fundamental to matter, we have an answer to how the dumb molecules know what to do and why they remain ordered.

Every atom, molecule, bacteria and cell is inherently intelligent. The information deep within every subatomic particle shapes life: from embryos to evolution. It is consciousness itself that undergoes evolution and this is reflected in the increasing complexity of species. The information of the form already exists and what we call physical matter follows suit.

This radical, but scientifically consistent solution is a new way to make sense of the puzzles of biology: how cells are ordered, how embryos form and how evolution occurs. By placing consciousness as the fundamental of reality and unifying biology with physics, we can at last find solutions to the conundrum of life itself.

During our discussion later on the Black Hole Principle, we shall return to look at the mechanisms behind evolution. But first, in Part III, we shall break down the doors of perception.

References for Chapter 5

1. Myers, EW. *et al.* A whole-genome assembly of *Drosophila*. *Science.* 24, March 2000; 287: 2196-2204.

2. The *C. elegans* Sequencing Consortium. Genome sequence of the nematode *C. elegans*: A Platform for Investigating Biology. *Science.* 11 December 1998; 282: 2012-2018.

3. Waterston RH *et al.* Initial sequencing and comparative analysis of the mouse genome. *Nature.* 5 December 2002; 420: 520-562.

4. Orwant R. What makes us human? *New Scientist.* 21 February 2004; 36-39.

5. Ibid.

6. Lipton BH. Insights into Cellular Consciousness. *Bridges* 2001; 12(1): 5. http://www.brucelipton.com/biology.php.

7. Ridley M. Genes are so liberating. *New Scientist.* 17 May 2003; 38-39.

8. Hansen D. *et al.* Severe Emotional Stress in First Trimester Linked with Congenital Malformations. *Lancet.* 2000; 356:875-880.

9. Hamer RG. *Excerpts from Summary of the New Medicine.* http://www.newmedicine.ca/excerpt.php 2001 [cited January 2006].

10. Martin P. *The Sickening Mind: Brain, Behavior, Immunity and Disease.* (HarperCollins)1997.

11. Turner G. How New Species are formed. *New Scientist.* 14 June 2003; 36.

12. Gilbert T. Death and Destruction. *New Scientist.* 31 May 2003; 32-35.

13. Cairns J. The Origin of Mutants. *Nature.* 1988; 9:335:142-145.

Part III

Breaking Down the Doors
of Perception

Chapter 6

There Goes the Neighborhood

Section One – the End of Locality

A unified world

Have a look around you. What do you see? Chances are you are reading this in a room, perhaps in an office. What is around you? Take a moment to list the objects in your mind. Maybe there are people around you. Where are you in this scene?

By now you should have a list of objects in your mind. You have also just signed up to a particular way of thinking - *that all these objects and people are separate from you and from each other*. Making a list of objects implies that there are separate objects to list. You may not have been aware of it, but you have been working within a certain scientific viewpoint that says that the world is made up of separate constituent parts. Astonishingly, this viewpoint is being superseded by a new scientific paradigm: one that says that the universe is deeply connected and not separate at all.

Have a look again at the objects around you. It seems obvious that they are separate from each other and yourself. At the level of our everyday reality, this is what we experience - there is no reason to think any differently.

It is easy to understand how this reasoning has been part of the scientific method for hundreds of years. In our everyday life we see a world made up of separate units and objects. When scientists began to consider what type of structure lay at the heart of these objects, they had no reason to doubt that the same rules applied at smaller levels too. Hence the atomic theory of the ancient Greeks who believed that 'stuff' was made of tiny solid particles.

In a world made up of discrete objects, the only way in which connection can occur is through physical touch or by exerting a local force, as is the case with electromagnetism. We see this is the case with even the most powerful magnets; the objects that are attracted to large magnets have to be within a certain distance - the further away, the more the attraction of the magnet tails off.

The only exception to this rule in this classical world was the force of gravity. According to Newton, gravity works instantaneously, no matter the distance between objects, something that has perplexed physicists for some time.[1] We shall be discussing gravity in more detail later in this book. For the moment, we shall simply say that gravity was the exception to the rule in the classical world of local forces.

Aside from the anomaly of gravity, the idea that objects could be connected at a distance was not even considered under the classical paradigm. Separate objects were seen as separate objects. What has changed to make this not so? Our everyday experiences make it seem obvious that we live in a world of separate objects and it is hard to imagine anything different.

There goes the neighborhood

The change began with the era of quantum physics. Until then, local effects ruled. In our previous discussion on quantum physics we have mentioned the fact that a particle can be seen either as a wave or a particle. This type of uncertainty applies to other qualities as well, namely position and momentum (which is to do with the movement of a particle). The idea that we can never know both qualities of a particle with absolute accuracy is known as Heisenberg's Uncertainty Principle. [2]

If we try to measure one of these qualities, then this changes the accuracy of our measurement of the other quality. So the more we know about the position of the particle the less we know about its momentum. If we try to measure the momentum more accurately then we lose the accuracy of the measurement of the position.

The method by which we measure a particle affects the information we can gain from it. This leads to a strange situation that we do not see in our everyday life – we can only estimate where something is likely to be. At the quantum level we can only say the *probability* of where a particle is. The accuracy of this measurement is dependent on the method used. This has led to the weird quantum world where we could say with 70 per cent accuracy that a particle exists on the palm of your hand but it also could exist anywhere: on the top of the Eiffel tower for example. At the quantum level, the concept of position is not one of absolutes, but of possibilities.

This is not how we experience our lives. We see an object where we see an object. We don't perceive it as 70 per cent probably there, with a chance it is also on top of the Eiffel tower. The quantum world seems far removed from our daily experience, but oddly enough, our everyday objects are made up of this very world! Why we don't see the coffee table popping in and out of existence is still a matter of debate, along with the entire meaning behind quantum physics.

Despite the weird implications, the principles of quantum physics are widely used in our modern technological appliances. What these principles actually mean for our reality is not so widely discussed. In fact, many find this type of questioning irrelevant, saying that the quantum reality only occurs at a very small level and has no bearing on our everyday lives. Yet these small quantum objects make up the very objects that we see around us. At a fundamental level, the coffee table is made up of particles displaying quantum behavior. What does that mean for how we view reality?

Spooky!

We have just looked at how, in the quantum world, we can never be 100 per cent certain of the position of a particle; we can simply talk about the likelihood of it being at a certain place. We have also discussed how the qualities of the particle can be affected by the method with which we look at it. So the qualities of the particle and the measurement of it are intertwined.

Before we actually measure the particle we cannot be sure what state it is in. Until then, it is as if the particle can exist in many states at once, something physicists call *superposition*. This is not how we experience objects: we do not see them as being many states at once. Some of the early quantum physicists did not like this idea either. Erwin Schrödinger even put forward a famous thought experiment in which a cat is placed in a box that contained a substance that could kill it. Whether or not the substance is actually released is subject to a random process, such as radioactive decay. If the decay occurs then the cat dies; if it does not, then the cat remains alive.

Because the cat is placed in a sealed box away from the outside world, until the box is opened nobody can know if the poison has killed the cat. Schrödinger said that before the box is opened, the cat is in a state of both being alive and dead at the same time. It is the act of observing the cat that makes it into either. It must be stated that Schrödinger did not really do this experiment and was merely pointing out the seemingly absurd nature of quantum behavior by using the analogy of a cat being both alive and dead at the same time.[3]

But this is how Nature works at a deep level: particles can exist in a state of superposition until we look at them. It is this extraordinary state of affairs which led physicists to realize that our world may not be so separate after all. Part of this journey began with Einstein who was not happy with what quantum physicists were saying about our world. He famously said "God does not play dice," referring to the uncertainty involved in measuring the properties of particles.[4] With his colleagues, Boris Podolsky and Nathan Rosen, he set up an experiment aimed to try and disprove the quantum effects, but in doing so uncovered something rather spooky.[5]

We have said that a particle can be in a state of superposition, which means it is in many states at once, until the process of measurement determines its state. It is possible to link two particles in an experiment so that they become related to each other. (I shall not complicate this text by explaining the technicalities of how this is done.) This is called *entanglement*. The particles end up having equal and opposite spin. One is spinning one way – let's say it is spinning up, and the other is spinning the other - let's say it is down. The two particles have been through the entanglement process and will forever be linked. They must henceforth always have equal and opposite spin.

Figure 4 – Pair of entangled particles

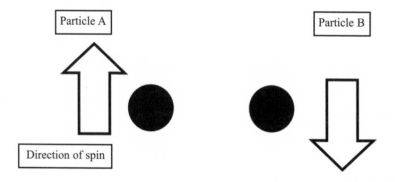

What is strange is that you don't know what state either particle is in until you actually measure them. Until then, both the particles are in a state of superposition. What Einstein realized was that if you have a look at the first particle, it collapses into a definite state of up or down. However, because the two particles have undergone the entanglement process and are linked, something rather odd occurs.

Even though the second particle has not been measured, the act of measuring the first particle determines the spin of the second, as their spins will always be opposite. It is as if the first particle somehow managed to communicate its state of spin to the other. Even weirder, the particles do not have to be anywhere near each other, yet still have this instantaneous connection; they could even have moved so far apart as to be on other sides of the universe, the effect would be the same.

Einstein did not like this at all: he called it "spooky action at a distance." One of the reasons for his objection was that if particles can communicate and send signals to each other instantaneously, regardless of distance, then they would be communicating faster than the speed of light, which would be violating his theory of relativity. He saw this as a problem and it is one that has been named after Einstein and his colleagues: the EPR paradox.

It was John Bell, an Irish physicist, who proposed a way to test the EPR paradox in the 1960s; it remained theoretical until being tested by experiment. His proposal is sometimes known as Bell's theorem. The experiment was actually performed by Alain Aspect and team in the 1980s.[7] They showed that entangled particles do display these spooky non-local connections.

Einstein seems to have been proved wrong, the universe seems to be spookier than he had envisaged it. Since Aspect and team performed these experiments, the idea of non-local connections is becoming more commonplace. There is even a strong trend in physics to utilize faster-than-light communication in a new, faster type of internet.[8] The idea of non-local connection is not only here to stay, but could become a vital part of our everyday technology.

Can you say Om?

Having established that distant parts of the universe can be connected instantaneously no matter how far apart, most physicists just got on with figuring out how to utilize this effect. However, the quantum world yet again leads us to a new philosophical horizon; how do distant parts of the universe know what each other are doing?

The physics of non-locality has been firmly embraced by mystics who cite this as scientific proof of the ancient spiritual idea that the universe is one entity. This idea of oneness means that the separation between objects is an illusion and that everything in the universe is actually from one source. It is as if the objects we see around us and also ourselves emerge from this one source, seemingly separate, but remaining connected. Although members of the scientific community, including the late physicist Richard Feynman, often dismiss this line of reasoning, some physicists actually embrace this idea. [9]

The non-local connections do seem to point to a deep unified quality of the universe. If parts of the universe know what other parts of it are doing, could it be that the universe is actually one? If quantum physics tells us that the universe is all about how we interpret it, then a connected universe is one way of interpreting the non-local behavior of quantum particles.

Whilst most physicists tend to ignore the more philosophical implications that non-locality has on their universe, a British physicist named David Bohm took a great interest in it. Bohm himself was interested in Eastern mysticism and even engaged in dialogue with the Indian mystic, Krishnamurthi.[10] He believed that the world we see around us, that appears disconnected, is actually a reflection of a much deeper reality. In this deeper reality which he called *the implicate order*, everything is one unified whole.[11] It is the starting point for everything in the universe and actually, it still unites everything. It is only our perspective that sees everything as separate.

Figure 5 – People are all outgrowths of the one underlying reality.

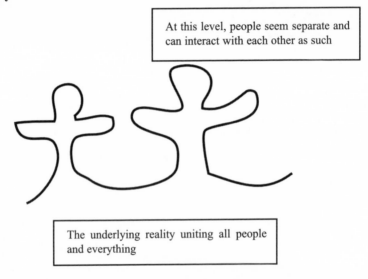

At this level, people seem separate and can interact with each other as such

The underlying reality uniting all people and everything

Figure 5 is a simple version of this idea. People are all outgrowths of the deeper reality. They view themselves as separate and can interact with each other as separate beings when in fact they are emergent from a united ground substance. Depending on your perspective you can see them as separate or, if you look a little deeper, you can see them as remaining part of the whole. They are united and separate at the same time. Bohm called this separateness, *the explicate order*. It is an idea that is very hard to put into words, because we are so used to things being one thing or another and not both things at once depending on perspective.

Bohm's way of viewing non-locality also solves Einstein's paradox of information traveling faster than light speed between two distant paired particles. According to Bohm's view, the particles, although seemingly separate, have always been and remain part of the unified whole. It is simply our perspective that sees them as separate, but if we were to travel deeper into reality we find that they are connected. So at some level the particles never separated. They remain part of the one ground substance. The reason why the information can pass between them instantaneously is that the information does not have anywhere to go!

This all sounds very esoteric and it is no wonder that many books linking physics to ancient mysticism have become popular in recent years. Science has always been about the search for knowledge in order to understand our universe. These types of interpretations of physics are arising from physicists themselves. Although many may balk at the apparent mysticism of this type of work, it is simply not good science to ignore this completely. We have entered an era when the concept of a unified world exists not only in mysticism, but also in science.

Non-local consciousness

Having established the idea of non-local interactions in science and that information can travel across the universe instantaneously, we can now combine this with the earlier idea in this book that consciousness is fundamental. As we remember, physicists such as Amit Goswami say that consciousness is more fundamental than matter and that matter arises from consciousness.[12] We also saw how this view made sense of a lot of the conundrums in biology: how dumb molecules know what to do.

If consciousness imbues everything and non-local connections are possible, then non-local connection of consciousness is possible. In effect this means that awareness is not limited to the immediate surroundings; awareness and influence are possible over a vast distance. So a thought that someone has in Antarctica for example, could instantaneously affect someone in Africa. This would all remain speculative had it not been for some pioneering research into varying aspects of non-local communication.

Indeed, the evidence is so compelling and plentiful that we should all be speaking with telepathy! Despite this, the scientific establishment has rejected a lot of this type of research. Some of the reasons for this shall be explored later in the section of this chapter dedicated to the subject of skepticism. As we shall see, the common complaint that there is no evidence for the effects of non-local consciousness is simply not true. The real problem may be the apparent lack of a scientific mechanism for these effects.

Yet we have already derived a mechanism for non-local consciousness using only principles that appear within the realm of science. So what happens when we have both evidence and explanation? What does it mean for the human race if we can no longer deny that the influence of our minds extends beyond local constraints of time and space? We shall examine some of the area of scientific study that has accumulated which points to a world of non-local consciousness.

Section Two
The Evidence

Prayer studies

Never having been of the Christian faith, I was amused to find that one of my papers was being circulated in local churches! [13] The reason for this was that the paper discussed the scientific study of prayer. One wonders what Galileo would think if he witnessed this 21st century boost to religion in the form of science.

Prayer has been the focus of numerous scientific trials. It has been subjected to the sort of rigorous scrutiny that is normally given to the testing of a new drug (namely double blind randomized studies). To the surprise of many, prayer actually seems to work! Just as in the trials of any clinical agent, some results are better than others. Similarly, if the initial trials show promise, further investigation would be needed to confirm this.

One of the most famous studies involved the patients of a coronary care unit and was published in a prestigious medical journal.[14] Patients admitted to the unit were randomly assigned to different groups; staff who were caring for them did not know which one. People of religious denominations prayed for the patients in one group and did not pray for the other group of patients. This trial showed that those patients who were prayed for ended up having fewer complications than those in the other group. Another study appeared to show that prayer almost doubled the rate of successful pregnancy during In Vitro Fertilization (IVF) treatment.[15]

So what is prayer? A simple explanation is that it is a focused intention, usually with religious connotations. If we view it in this way, then we are able to transcend the boundaries of religion and it becomes a universal human function. We can all learn to focus our intent on something or someone. People most often do this when they really need some help in life, regardless of their spiritual leanings.

What is intent? Intent is a focus of consciousness: when someone really turns their attention and will to something as opposed to just allowing their usual flow of thoughts. When the people praying in these studies pray for the patients, they will take a deliberate 'time-out' to focus their consciousness on that person getting better.

We could see intent as a type of 'movement' of consciousness. If a person is made up of atoms, and atoms are fundamentally consciousness, then we can say that people are also fundamentally consciousness. When people focus their attention, it is as if they are 'moving' their very deepest fabric in order to become focused. The attention on the subject in this way affects the subject and the effects of prayer are seen. This can only be explained if we see consciousness as fundamental and we understand non-local effects. We are now moving towards a scientific understanding of the mechanism of prayer and non-local intent.

There is an urgent need for this explanation, not only because it may be beneficial for patients, but also for the researchers. Tragically, this area of study is so controversial that the backlash contributed to the suicides of some of the foremost researchers in a project called Spindrift. Prayer researchers, Bruce and John Klingbeil were a father and son team who spent many years studying the effects of prayer under controlled conditions in the laboratory. Unfortunately, the very church establishment they hoped to verify rejected their work. They were banished from their church community and the emotional impact of this led to their suicides. Bill Sweet has written an account of their story.[16]

Other researchers who are being scrutinized are those who were involved with the study into prayer and IVF, mentioned above, which is now being reported by some as being fraudulent, despite its appearance in a respected medical journal and being co-authored by researchers at renowned medical institutions. Some of the violent reactions to prayer studies occur because people cannot provide a scientific explanation for them. There is a drive to try and discredit the results of the studies, because the lack of explanation suggests that positive results cannot be true. Yet as we have seen in the above derivation, it is possible to explain prayer in terms of non-local consciousness: wholly within the realms of science.

How to make friends and influence people – at a distance

Moving away from the religious aspects of intent, a lot of researchers simply study the effects of intent. These studies do not involve people from specific religious groups, giving a different angle to their research.

Dr William Tiller deserves a special mention in this area of scientific study. Until recently, he was professor in the Department of Materials Science and Engineering at Stanford University: a post he had held from 1964. In the conventional scientific arena, Tiller has published over 250 scientific papers and been associate editor of two journals amongst other achievements. In short, he knows how to conduct an experiment in accordance with established scientific methodology. This background awards special credence to his work on distant intention.

In one type of experimental design, a group of four people place specific intentions into a black box: an electronic imprinting device. The particular type of study determines the type of intention. For example, if an outcome of increased pH of a solution is desired, this is the intention placed into the device. The imprinting device is then shielded from environmental influences, such as electromagnetic activity, to prevent contamination. It is then used to influence the outcome of an experiment by placing it in proximity to it.

It is important to note that although four people are involved to place their intentions at the beginning, after this process, the device does not have contact with these people and it is the device that is used in the laboratory to produce the intended outcome. It is placed in proximity with the test substance and compared to a control set up: another black box that has not undergone the intention imprinting process.

The types of experimental outcomes being tested are for example: changes in the pH of water as compared to a control and increases in the activity of enzymes such alkaline phosphatase. The use of an imprinted device makes the distant intention process more standardized. The experiment designs and detailed laboratory results are published in the book *Conscious acts of Creation – the Emergence of a New Physics,* which Tiller wrote with Dr Walter

Dibble and Dr Michael Kohane.[17]

Their results show consistent differences between experiments done with imprinted and non-imprinted devices suggesting that distant intention influences the experiment, even when the source of intention is coming through a black box. I suggest that the reader examines their work for themselves, in order to judge whether they succeeded.

Going PEAR shaped

Another US university, Princeton, is the location for another group of researchers who have been investigating distant intention under controlled laboratory conditions. It has been named Princeton Engineering Anomalies Research or PEAR. Some of this work has involved the use of a random event generator (REG).[18] This is the equivalent of a machine that flips a coin many times. As we all know, when a coin is flipped many times the results will be very close to 50 per cent heads and 50 per cent tails. The more flips you do, the more these results apply.

The PEAR experiments involve an assigned influencer intending for one particular outcome: more heads than tails for example. The influencer performs several trials intending for various outcomes, the equivalent of more heads, more tails or neutral.

Analyses and meta-analyses of these trials have shown significant results, demonstrating that remote influence has an effect on the REG.[19] This points to an often-untapped potential of human abilities. Health journalist, Lynne McTaggart in her book, *The Field*, places the results of the PEAR studies into perspective by pointing out that these results are more statistically significant than in many drug trials for common drugs such as propanolol and aspirin.[20]

Doggie style

Yet another approach has been taken by Dr Rupert Sheldrake, who originally trained in the biological sciences, but is now known throughout the world for his theories on *morphic resonance*, which effectively rely on the physics of non-local consciousness. Interestingly his work includes some studies on non-local intention and animals. For example, some dogs seem to know when their owners are coming home and will get ready to greet them.[21] This can actually occur more than ten minutes before the owner arrives. This may be a common household observation, but it had never been studied scientifically before.

Sheldrake devised a series of experiments in which the owner leaves home and travels away to a distance of over three miles where no scent or noise can be detected by the dog. In some experiments, both owner and dog are tracked all day by cameras that are also recording the timings of events so that they can be compared later.

A pager is given to the owner so that the signal can be given for them to return home. This signal is not at a pre-agreed time, but has been chosen by a remote experimenter at random. No other contact is made between the owner and experimenter, nor is contact made with any person who may be with the dog at home. This ensures that the anticipated time of arrival is not conveyed to the dog in verbal or non-verbal clues.

What is so interesting about this experiment is that the owner does not even have to make a move towards the car before their dog gets ready for their arrival: it is the moment of intent which is vital.

As soon as the conscious decision to go home is made, their dog is filmed getting ready for their arrival at the same time, before the owner had even got into the car! It seems that animals are able to tune in, quite naturally, to the fundamental consciousness that pervades our universe.

All these experiments show us that, when meticulously tested by scientific methods, the effects of distant intentions are becoming evident. Before the science of non-local consciousness we had no other explanation for these effects, but this situation is changing, which may lead to greater acceptance of our non-local abilities.

Section Three – Skeptics' Corner

Before I continue, I wish to address the concept of skepticism. Not everyone in the scientific community accepts the above interpretations of physics and the experiments presented. Some even go as far as saying that this is not even a scientific discussion.

It is important for each of us to be discerning when examining theories and experimental data. I have also seen countless misappropriations of scientific terms by people from the so-called 'New Age' sector, who have recognized the need for science, but have not being rigorous in their use of terms or examination of data. Although this practice is widespread and can be unhelpful, there are people trained in science, such as those listed above, who are not so easily dismissible by skeptics. It is the science of this caliber that I wish to discuss here, as certain arguments are put forward by skeptics that tend to obscure these theories and findings. The main arguments put forward by skeptics are as follows.

The experimenters are all mad/stupid, frauds or cranks

Some experimenters in non-local intention research have conventional credentials such as PhDs. They may have academic posts and some, such as Dr Russell Targ, have even worked with the Central Intelligence Agency (CIA).[22] If it is possible to discount all these credentials on the basis of the sort of research they are doing, then what value are any credentials? The devaluation of a person's credentials if they mention the science of non-local consciousness even extends to Nobel Prize winners!

A humorous incident illustrating this occurred when British Nobel Laureate for physics, Brian Josephson, was featured on some commemorative stamps by the Royal Mail.[23] It all started pretty innocuously; the Royal Mail wished to celebrate British Nobelists and feature them on collectable stamps which would be available to purchase as a boxed set.

Josephson, professor of physics at the University of Cambridge and Nobel Prizewinner in 1973, was asked to write a short piece for a booklet accompanying the stamps. It was this article that caused a furor and demonstrated that even a Nobelist is not immune to criticism. The article mentioned non-local connections and that quantum theory might lead to an explanation of processes still not understood within conventional science, such as telepathy.

The subsequent outcry was interesting. Many physicists and other scientists were outraged by the suggestion that telepathy is a subject worthy of scientific consideration. The sticky issue remained that Josephson is a Nobel Laureate and therefore the holder of one of the greatest accolades a person can receive. A Royal Mail spokesperson meekly tried to explain to the press that because he had received this prize, they assumed that he had some knowledge about physics. An unnamed scientist was even quoted discussing, "the trouble with Nobel prizes."[24]

Never mind the evidence

Not only are there attempts to discredit the researchers, the research itself is often criticized, sometimes by a denial that it even exists. Skeptics often claim that they would believe that non-local consciousness effects existed if they saw some evidence to prove it, leading to a strange situation; very good research with positive results exist, but by not actually looking at the results, skeptics can honestly claim that they have seen no such evidence.

Rupert Sheldrake noted this during a debate between himself and skeptic, Lewis Wolpert at the Royal Society of Arts. In the transcript, which is available online, Sheldrake notes that Wolpert did not even look at a film that he made about animal telepathy. [25]

"Well, I noticed that when the parrot film was showing, Lewis wasn't looking at it! That film was shown on television ... and in early stage of our investigations, he did the same then. They asked a skeptic to commentate. Lewis appeared on the screen and he said, 'Telepathy is just junk ... there is no evidence whatsoever for any person, animal or thing being telepathic.' The filmmakers were surprised that he hadn't actually asked to see the evidence before he commented on it, and I think, this is rather like the Cardinal Bellarmine, and people not wanting to look through Galileo's Telescope. I think we have a level here of just not wanting to know, which is not real science ..."

I won't believe it till I see it – and if I see it I won't believe it

A lot of scientists like to think that they are rational, logical and only deal with hard evidence. But this is simply not the case; evidence exists for non-local effects that would convince scientists if they saw the raw data alone. However, if it is known that the data is linked to non-local effects, it may be rejected even though those same statistics would be accepted if presented as part of another type of study. It seems that the reception of scientific evidence comes down to a matter of belief in the subject being studied.

New Scientist magazine has addressed this issue by comparing the data from two types of trials, some relating to Extra-Sensory Perception (ESP) and the others looking at the effectiveness of a drug called streptokinase, now widely used in the treatment of heart attacks.[26] The ESP trial data is by far the strongest yet many still insist there is no evidence for this phenomenon, whilst streptokinase is now embraced as being 'evidence-based', with enough proof to be used in critical medical care.

This discrepancy in the acceptance of the two sets of data leads to the comment, "by all the normal rules for assessing scientific evidence, the case for ESP has been made. And yet most scientists refuse to believe the findings, maintaining that ESP simply does not exist."

Even in the face of evidence of non-local effects, some people refuse to believe it exists. This is usually due to a firm adherence in that person's mind as to what is common sense. The common sense view of the universe is usually Newtonian: the view that the universe is local and disconnected. Science has since proved that this model is simply an approximation to reality. It is actually now more scientific to speak of non-local connections, leaving the outdated scientific paradigm as the one based on belief and not on existing evidence.

Damn the experiment

As stated before, a common tactic of skeptics is to say that experimenters exploring non-local consciousness are charlatans and frauds. It often follows that their experimental methods are dismissed as shoddy and involving trickery. This is a great discredit to the people working in this field; their positive results are often seen as due to experimental error, bad design or fraud.

With any area of research, some experimental designs are better than others. Experiments exploring non-local effects are often compared to a gold standard of trial design: to randomize subjects into two groups, to minimize influences other than the one being studied and to minimize experimenter impact.

An issue rarely raised is the philosophical basis for this type of trial design. For example, the issue of randomness: how can we test if something is truly random? Yet randomness is essential to many trials including medical trials where subjects are assigned to the group taking the test agent versus the placebo on a random basis.

But how do we know that something is random? Some suggest that the only reason we think something is random is that we are not aware that it is actually ordered. It has even been suggested that the whole concept of randomness is a human superstition.[27] So if we are even questioning the rationale of our standard trial model, than who can really say what is a scientific trial and what is not?

Can we really achieve the other vital ingredient of a good trial: the eradication of the experimenter effect? In this post-quantum world where we are not even certain that objectivity exists, how is it possible to have an objective trial?

An unlikely team is exploring the experimenter effect: a parapsychology researcher in the US, Marilyn Schiltz, and psychologist and skeptic Richard Wiseman, at the University of

Hertfordshire, UK. Schlitz has performed some experiments on staring that involve placing a test subject in an isolated room with a video camera pointed at them. In a separate room another subject looks at them through the video link at random moments. The person in the isolated room has to report when they feel that someone is watching them. It is another example of testing non-local consciousness.[28]

Schiltz has found consistently significant results that suggest that people can indeed tell when someone is watching them, even remotely. When Wiseman repeated the experiments, he was unable to replicate the results. Swapping teams and laboratories did not make a difference: Schlitz still gained significant positive results and Wiseman did not. It is being postulated that this is an example of the experimenter effect where the beliefs of the experimenter influences the outcome.

Robert Rosenthal and colleagues have done various studies of the experimenter effect.[29] Could the experimenter effect be a macroscopic demonstration of quantum effects? Does the outcome of the experiment depend on the type of observation? Is this an example of collapsing one reality from infinite possibilities depending on whose consciousness is interacting with it? Many say that quantum effects cannot be seen at this macroscopic level, but some physicists are starting to say that they are and can even be measured.[30]

In the end skepticism maybe a beautiful example of the very paradigm that its members wish to disprove; the universe differs according to your perspective. As physicist Lee Smolin says in his book, *Three Roads to Quantum Gravity,* "we must acknowledge that each observer can have only a limited amount of information about the world and that different observers will have access to different information."[31] This may be why skeptics really are unable to see the existence of non-local effects; they truly do not have access to that information. Non-local effects really do not exist in their reality!

Distasteful though it may be to our 'common sense', non-local effects are increasingly being recognized by science. Although some would not agree that phenomena such as distant intention are explainable by physics, or that they even exist, some physicists are making the link between these abilities and subatomic behavior.

More people are realizing that their influence extends beyond their immediate locality, whether they realize this in childhood or from attending a course in Reiki (or something similar). This results in more observers who hold the view that the universe is non-locally connected. As their numbers grow, this view is becoming common sense and the more Newtonian sensibilities are being gradually superseded. We are entering the age of the universal neighborhood!

References for Chapter 6

1. Saviour E. Instantaneous (non local) Action without violating Causality. *Blaze Labs* 2004 http://www.blazelabs.com/f-p-inst.asp [cited January 2006].
2. Heisenberg W. *Physical Principles of the Quantum Theory.* (Dover Publications) 2003.
3. Al-Khalili J. *Quantum: A Guide for the Perplexed.* (Weidenfeld & Nicolson) 2003.

4. Born M, Einstein A. *The Born-Einstein Letters*. (Macmillan) 1971.

5. Einstein A, Podolsky B, Rosen N. Can quantum-mechanical description of physical reality be considered complete? *Physical Review*. 15 May 1953; 41: 777.

6. Bell J. On the Einstein Podolsky Rosen paradox. *Physics*.1964; 3: 195.

7. Aspect A, Grangier P, Roger G. Experimental realization of Einstein-Podolsky-Rosen-Bohm gedanken experiment; a new violation of Bell's inequalities. *Physical Review Letters*. 12 July 1982; 49:2: 91.

8. Mullins J. Entangled Web. *New Scientist*. 20 May 2000; 26 – 29.

9. Sykes C. (ed). *No Ordinary Genius*. (Weidenfield & Nicolson) 1994.

10. Bohm D, Krishnamurti J. *Ending of Time*. (Harper Collins) 1985.

11. Bohm D. *Wholeness and the implicate order*. (Routledge classics) 2002.

12. Goswami A. *The Self-Aware Universe*. (Tarcher/Putnam) 1995.

13. Samanta-Laughton M. Prayer and IVF. *Holistic Health*. Spring 2002; 72.

14. Harris WS, *et al*. A randomized, controlled trial of the effects of remote, intercessory prayer on outcomes in patients admitted to the coronary care unit. *Arch Intern Med*. 25 October 1999; 159:2273-8.

15. Cha KY, Wirth DP, Lobio RA. Does Prayer Influence the Success of in Vitro Fertilization–Embryo Transfer? Report of a Masked, Randomized Trial. *J Reprod Med*. September 2001; 46: 781-787.

16. Sweet B. *A Journey Into Prayer*. (Xlibris Corporation) 2003.

17. Tiller WA, Dibble WE, Kohane MJ, *Conscious Acts of Creation*. (Pavior) 2001.

18. Jahn R. *Margins of Reality*. (Harcourt Brace) 1989.

19 Radin D. *The Conscious Universe*. (HarperSanFrancisco) 1997.

20. McTaggart L. *The Field*. (Harper Collins) 2001.

21. Sheldrake R. *Dogs that know when their owners are coming home*. (Arrow) 2000.

22. Puthoff H, Targ R. *Mind-reach*. (Hampton Roads) 2005.

23. *Royal Mail achieves philatelic world 'first' with unique Nobel stamps*. 2001 http://www.royalmailgroup.com/news/expandarticle.asp?id=264&brand=royal_mail [cited April 2005].

24. McKie R. Royal Mail's Nobel guru in Telepathy row. *The Observer*. Sunday September 30 2001. http://observer.guardian.co.uk/uk_news/story/0,6903,560604,00.html.

25. Sheldrake R. Wolpert L. *Telepathy debate – the full text*. 15 January 2004. http://www.sheldrake.org/controversies/RSA_text.html [cited January 2006].

26. Mathews R. Opposites Detract. *New Scientist*. 13 March 2004; 39-41.

27. Stewart I. In the Lap of the Gods. *New Scientist*. 25 September 2004; 29- 33.

28. Wiseman R, Schlitz M. Experimenter effects and the Remote Detection of Staring. *Journal Of Parapsychology*. 1998; 61: 197-208.

29. Rosenthal R, Fode K L The effect of experimenter bias on the

performance of the albino rat. *Behavioral Science.* 1963; 8:183–189. http://www.journals.apa.org/prevention/volume5/pre0050038c.html

30. Goswami A. *The Visionary Window.* (Quest books) 2000.

31. Smolin L. *Three Roads to Quantum Gravity.* (Phoenix) 2001.

Chapter 7

Pretty Vacant

Nothing exists in a vacuum; everyone knows that. A vacuum is supposed to be empty, that's the whole point. So what if you were to find out it is not vacant, but a teeming mass of activity? Stranger still, 'empty' space could turn out to be a universal information source, hold the secret to psychic mediumship and even provide the solution to the world's energy problems. Enter the world of the pretty vacant.

Virtual reality

In the previous chapter, we discussed how quantum physics introduced the idea that we can never be absolutely sure of the exact whereabouts of a particle: we can only say how likely it is to be in a certain position. This leads to the odd situation in which we can say that a particle is probably in a particular place, but there is a possibility that the particle could be anywhere in the universe.

Due to this consequence of Heisenberg's uncertainty principle, physicists began to view the whole of the universe as a sea of potential particles.[1] These particles have the potential to appear anywhere, including in a vacuum, giving this sea of potential the title of the Quantum Vacuum (QV). What we previously saw as empty space is now thought to contain particles popping in and out of existence. They are sometimes known as virtual particles, as they only exist for a fleeting moment before disappearing again.

The QV would have remained a theoretical idea had its existence not been verified by experiment. It is possible to turn these virtual particles into real particles. When they become 'real' we can actually measure them because they have an effect on experimental apparatus. These effects are called Casimir forces.[2] Inspired by the fact that even a vacuum is alive with activity, some people are trying to utilize this energy. If they succeed, this would be a source of unlimited power, as it would literally be creating something out of nothing.[3, 4]

The QV is sometimes called the zero point field. This is because at zero point temperature, which is –273 degrees centigrade or zero degrees Kelvin on the Kelvin scale, all activity should cease. It is so cold at the absolute zero point that normal particles do not have the energy to move. Yet, experiments show that the QV remains active; it is still a teeming mass of activity.[5]

Out at sea

What does it actually mean to say that particles pop in and out of existence? What is really happening in the field? The QV is a sea of light, full of particles called photons. The photons cycle through a creation and destruction process, and this is how they appear to exist and then disappear. A photon, which has no charge or mass, splits into two particles. These particles are equal and opposite to each other. One is a particle of matter, such as an electron, which has positive mass and negative charge. The other is a particle of antimatter, such as a positron, which has negative mass and positive charge. These particles can exist independently, but if they find each other they cancel out and become a photon of light again.[6]

Figure 6 – The antimatter-matter-photon cycle

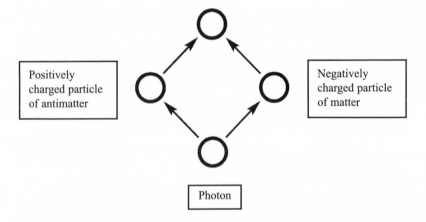

This process of cycling in and out of existence occurs in the QV. A British physicist named Paul Dirac first predicted the existence of antimatter particles. He gained this insight whilst examining the behavior of electrons inside an atom.[7] When an electron gains energy it can move to a higher energy level inside the atom. This movement effectively leaves a hole in the lower energy level where it has just come from. Dirac predicted that the hole left by the particle with positive mass – the electron, would be filled by a particle with negative mass – the positron.

Figure 7 – Electron ascending energy level leaves positron hole

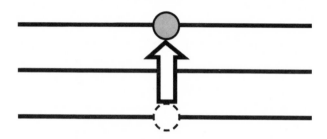

He also realized that the QV could be seen in a similar way: as the dance between antimatter, matter and light. Hence, the QV is sometimes known as the Dirac Sea. In the 1930s, the positrons Dirac had predicted were actually found by experimental physics. Today this principle of matter-antimatter annihilation is used in brain imaging: as part of Positron Emission Tomography (PET) scanning.

Dancing in the photon field

Whether it is known as the quantum vacuum, zero point field or the Dirac Sea, the concept of matter emerging from and interacting with a sea of photons has major implications for science.

For example, these interactions may explain why objects display inertia. Inertia is the difficulty of objects to change their motion: either to start moving or to change from one speed to another. For many years the exact cause of inertia has been a mystery, but recently physicists have explored the idea that it is caused by an interaction between matter and the QV.[8]

If objects interact with the QV, then so must living organisms, as we are made of the same 'stuff' as non-living matter. Scientist Ervin Laszlo has concluded that we are in constant dynamic with the QV: dancing between a real and virtual world.[9] We think that our bodies are solid, but our very particles flip in and out of this virtual sea.

The QV is also being seen as the mechanism behind the non-local connections we discussed in the previous chapter. It can be seen as a transmitter of information; a signal that is present in one part of the QV can be picked up in another distant part, like a ripple flowing across a sea.[10]

Information waves

We have just mentioned that the QV can transmit information. How is it able to do that? To answer this question we need to revisit what we have learnt about quantum physics. So far, we have discussed the QV as consisting of particles of light, popping in and out of existence. However, as mentioned in previous chapters, particles are not only definite points, they behave as particles or waves depending on how we look at them. They exist as neither one nor the other, but both at the same time.

The QV can be described in another way: as a vast inter-connecting network of light waves.[11] It is in this form that we can best envisage how light can hold information. It is well known that when two waves meet they can intersect or overlap. The point where they overlap is called an interference point. It is these interference points that can hold vast amounts of information.[12]

We see this happening in waves of water. Itzhak Bentov gives an example of an experiment to demonstrate this. Imagine a shallow pan of water. Now imagine dropping a pebble and then another one into the pan. The action of dropping the pebbles into the water would create waves radiating out from the pebbles. These waves would form interference patterns when they bumped into each other.

If we were to instantly freeze the pan of water, lift out the surface sheet of ice and shine the correct type of light through it, we would be able to see the image of the pebbles projected beyond the sheet of ice. (The correct type of light is a laser – more on this later.)

The interference patterns of the water have stored information about the pebbles! If we had never seen the pebbles in the first place and had only seen the sheet of ice, we would be able to tell where those pebbles had been in the tray. Information about the pebbles has been stored in the wave interference patterns.

Figure 8 – The information about the location of pebbles has been stored in the ice. (After Stalking the Wild Pendulum by Itzhak Bentov)

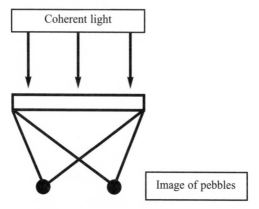

In fact, the interference patterns of waves are known as one of the most efficient information storage facilities we have; a small space can hold a vast amount of data.

Just imagine the capacity for storage available to us in this dynamic field of information that surrounds us. If we are in constant interaction with this field all the time, what does this mean for the way in which we understand our lives? To explore this further we need to discuss a particular aspect of light: the laser.

The Laser Age

We are living in the age of the laser: our CD players and credit cards are daily evidence of this. CD players utilize lasers to read discs and the shiny picture on your credit card is a common example of something called a hologram, which has been created using laser technology. Many scientists are comparing the principles behind holograms with the way our entire universe operates.

Holograms, such as the picture on your credit card or the image of Princess Leia in the film *Star Wars*, are images that can appear three-dimensional or many-layered even though they are created with something flat. The image on your credit card can give the appearance of depth although you know that it is a flat strip. These images are made with lasers, which were discovered as a consequence of the findings of quantum physics and of Albert Einstein.

This Light Amplification by Stimulated Emission of Radiation, or LASER, is different from normal light because all the light beams are traveling in an orderly fashion; they are all in phase with each other. Normal light, such as in an ordinary household torch, diffuses out in different directions because the light beams are not in phase and not orderly.

Figure 9 – Light from a laser versus light from a torch

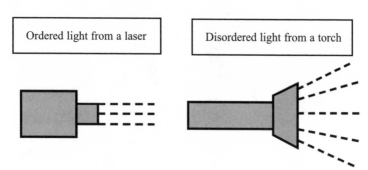

This orderliness makes lasers so useful in everything from CD players to surgical instruments. It is the use of lasers to create holograms that we shall go on to discuss, as this can help us to understand the QV.

In order to create a holographic three-dimensional image of an object, a laser beam is needed, which is split into two. The first beam is shone onto the object we wish to make an image of, let's say the object is an apple. Once the first beam has hit the object and bounced off it, the second beam then meets the first and they create an interference pattern. This interference pattern is captured on some photographic film.

The film itself does not look very interesting and consists of a swirling pattern. However, when another laser is shone through this film, a three-dimensional image appears of the original object: a virtual apple. The information about the apple has been stored in the interference patterns.

Furthermore, the whole film is not necessary to produce the image. If you were to take a pair of scissors and cut out a small piece of the film then shine a laser through it, the whole image would be

Figure 10 – The creation of a holographic film of an apple

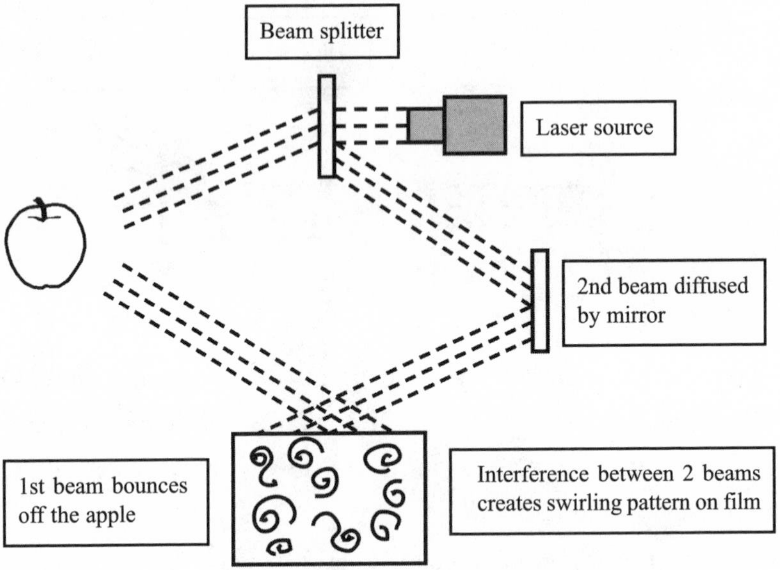

Beam splitter

Laser source

2nd beam diffused
by mirror

1st beam bounces
off the apple

Interference between 2 beams
creates swirling pattern on film

reproduced, not just a part. So an image of a whole apple can be produced from just a fragment of the film. This is because each part of
the film contains the information of the whole image.[13]

**Figure 11 – Producing a holographic image of an apple by
shining a laser through a holographic film**

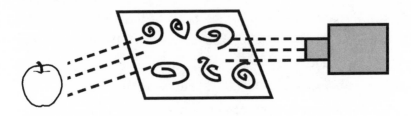

The Holographic Universe

So far we have discussed the QV and how it can be viewed as particles of light popping in and out of existence and also as interconnecting waves of light. These interference patterns can hold vast amounts of information, a fact seen in holograms. We have seen how a small piece of holographic film contains the information of the whole.

Now that we have understood these principles, we can explore how physicists are starting to view the entire universe as one big hologram. One of the pioneers of this holographic universe idea was David Bohm, whom we discussed in the last chapter.[14] He examined non-local connections and concluded that these are possible because everything in the universe arises from one source and just has the *appearance* of being separate.

Effectively, information does not travel anywhere, as seemingly separate parts of the universe are all part of the deeper whole. If the universe is not really separate, then we could also say that each part of the universe contains the information of the whole, just like a hologram. Bohm described the universe as *holomovement* to reflect its dynamic nature and the flow from light into matter and back again.

Bohm's concepts were pioneering at the time, but his concept of a holomovement of information does not sound dissimilar from ideas in modern mainstream physics. Physicists such as Lee Smolin and Leonard Susskind are currently working on a theory describing the universe that has some resemblance to Bohm's ideas, as seen in this quote from Smolin's book, *Three Roads to Quantum Gravity*. [15,16]

"It is not enough to say that the world is a hologram. The world must be a network of holograms, each of which contains coded within it information about the relationships between the others. In short, the holographic principle is the ultimate realization of the notion that the world is a network of relationships. Those relationships are revealed by this new principle to involve nothing but information. Any element in this network is nothing but a partial realization of the relationships between the other elements. In the end, perhaps, the history of a universe is nothing but the flow of information."

The hologram, the principle of relationship, and information flow are also key parts of the Bohmian view of reality. It seems that different people within physics are converging on the idea of the universe as a holographic web of information.

Mind, brain and hologram

If the universe is a holographic network of information, how do we relate to it? We have already discussed that we are in continuous dynamic relationship with the QV. Could it explain more about ourselves and who we are? Cutting-edge science links the QV with our own thought processes.

As we have previously discussed, neuroscience currently believes that our thoughts are a result of neuronal firings in the brain. How this neuronal activity becomes our inner thought processes is something of a mystery. Many believe that consciousness somehow emerges from the brain. Neuroscientists often insist that our inner thoughts and experiences are simply a result of the activity of our neurons, sharing signals and chemicals. How rich inner experiences arise from such relatively mechanistic processes is not fully explained and often put down to the magical process of emergence.[17]

One researcher who tackled this problem was Karl Pribram in the mid 20th century. Pribram endeavored to find the location of where memories are stored in the brain.[18] Neither he nor other researchers such as Karl Lashley or Paul Pietsch were able to locate the exact location of memories in various animal studies.[19] Instead they each found that when severe brain damage is inflicted upon the animals being tested, the animal is still able to perform tasks by remembering their previous training; it does not matter which part of the brain is damaged.[20]

Such research has helped to show that there is no particular area of the brain responsible for the function of memory storage. Modern brain research has indeed confirmed that the situation is more complex than having one specific area responsible for memory. Pribram was still left with the issue of how the inner experience is generated.

Pribram noted that neurons exhibit synchronous behavior. They can act in waves of activity that are not confined to the local region of the brain. This young neuroscientist, studying the wave-like behavior of neurons, came across some of the early pioneers in laser holography, the study of light waves. A sharing of ideas ensued.[21]

Discussing the principles of holography led Pribram to a radical new theory of brain functioning. He postulated that the brain utilizes waves in order to function and the interference patterns between the waves act as storage mechanisms for information.

The inner images we 'see' in our daily thoughts are a conversion of these wave interference patterns into an optical image! The brain uses the holographic principle. If the brain works in a similar way to a hologram, this would explain why the brain does not seem to forget tasks even if severe damage has been inflicted on it, as any one part of the brain contains the information of the whole.

Living in a mind field

Perhaps more radical than Pribram's ideas is the concept that the brain is not the storage mechanism for memories at all.[22] As we discussed earlier, extensive research has not pinpointed an exact storage area of memories in the brain. Cutting-edge science places memory storage in the QV. The brain then becomes the organ that receives memories and interprets them! When we see the different parts of the brain associated with different memory processes 'light up', it is reflective of the part of the brain that interprets the memories.

Much to the dismay of neuroscientists who wish to contain memories within the brain, nobody has ever found a brain structure that truly reflects the inner experience of remembering Auntie Flo's birthday. What we do find are genes being activated and cell membranes being strengthened: molecules mysteriously shifting around again.[23] How do dumb molecules know what to do whilst evoking such complex inner experiences?

Neuroscience has found processes within cells to do with memory, but they do not know what provides the instructions for this behavior.[24] Now we can suggest that memory storage occurs in the QV and switches on the various brain cells. It is a bit like looking at a set of Christmas lights and concluding that everything to power the lights is contained within the light itself, when actually the process driving the light is the elusive force of electricity that is surging through the wire.

This may seem like a radical shift, but it is one that can be reached logically from what we have discussed in this book so far. We have already looked at how quantum physicists are concluding that consciousness is fundamental to the universe and that everything arises from it. It follows that the QV also arises from consciousness and that it is imbued with the quality of sentience.

We can say that we live in and are connected to a vast interconnected ocean of consciousness: a web of thought. Having searched for the exact location of memory in the brain and not found it, does memory exist in the QV? Is this the way in which we interact with consciousness? It is around us and within us at the same time. We may not be the originators of our thoughts; they may all come from the interconnections in the QV and simply come *through* our brains, which are now seen as organs of interpretation of the QV.

The brain can relay messages from this information field to the rest of the body. Damage to the relay can often result in disability, both of motor and sensory modalities. Parts of the brain are still needed to interpret the signals from the QV. Yet the brain often regenerates and compensates and the signal can still be interpreted.

Professor Gary Schwartz of the University of Arizona makes the analogy that the brain is like a mobile phone.[25] The fact that many believe that thoughts originate in the brain is like saying that the voice you hear from the phone originates there. Damage to the phone would affect how well you could hear the voice; in fact you may not be able to hear it at all.

As it is with consciousness; because we witness the damage caused by strokes and other illnesses to do with the brain, we have wrongly assumed that consciousness exists in the brain. The QV gives us a mechanism by which consciousness can transcend the physical brain. Even Roger Penrose, prominent British mathematician, concedes that interactions between brain and the QV may be involved with what we experience as our inner consciousness.[26] At last, we don't have to make the leap from molecules and cells to our inner experience. The neurons do not generate them; they merely interpret them.

This also solves the rather embarrassing issue of people with brain lesions or little brain substance having normal or even above average intelligence.[27] If brain equals intelligence, then this does not make sense. There are even recorded cases of successful mathematicians having very little brain mass.[28]

By limiting consciousness to the brain, we have created some scientific enigmas. Studies with blind children in Russia show that some children can be trained to accurately report visual stimuli, even if it is physically impossible for them to see due to anatomical reasons.[25] This is possible to explain if information comes from the QV and not just through our senses per se.

This phenomenon of what is known as Blindsight also occurs in adults and baffles neuroscientists.[26] Subjects are able to 'see' in visual tests despite lesions in the optical pathways of the brain. All these cases are dismissed as unexplainable by the old brain-equals-consciousness paradigm, but we can start to see a scientific solution if we view the QV as the holder of information and the brain as the interpreter.

Genius

Where do flashes of inspiration come from? Moments of sudden insight have consistently played a role in human advancement. From Archimedes' famous Eureka moment to Einstein's musings on the behavior of light, big ideas seem to come out of nowhere. A recent example is the case of physicist Joao Magueijo, who recalls how an idea "fell out of the sky." [27]

Most people have had the experience of thinking hard about a problem, putting the problem aside for some time only to find the answer appears suddenly when the mind is focused elsewhere. It is at these moments of least effort that we seem to find the most inspiration and the solution appears. This could be when we are able to access the QV more effectively. All the information we need is present in the QV, yet we need to relax in order to access it more deeply.

Genius can be redefined as describing those people who are particularly skilled at taking information from the QV. Albert Einstein has become our iconic symbol of an original genius. A number of his quotes point to his own reliance on the power of imagination rather than knowledge alone. Could the great physicist himself be pointing to the secret of his own success as not the rumination of facts, but the stillness of mind and oneness with the QV? Although Einstein and Magueijo alike back up their inspiration with the perspiration of mathematics, it is their original leaps of consciousness that drive the whole process.

Physics is not the only area of genius however. Wolfgang Amadeus Mozart was a recognized musical genius. This may have reflected his own particular way of relating to the QV. In fact, I firmly believe that we each have our own particular genius: a personal skill that we excel at. This reflects how we relate to the QV in our own unique way, although many people never fully explore this aspect of themselves. The mechanism for our unique relationship to the QV will be explored in the next chapter.

Eternal mind

Just as the universe does not seem to care about locality of space when it comes to the transfer of information, nor does it seem to care about time. Startling research from the field of psychology shows us that we can actually respond to a stimulus even before the senses are exposed to it. Psychologist Dean Radin performed a series of studies in which random images were shown to study participants whilst their reactions were being recorded using electrodermal equipment.[28]

Some of the images were pleasant and some were shocking. The shocking images registered the largest response. However, the subject responded to the image *before* it was shown. This was a consistent result seeming to suggest that precognition is possible.

If we have the understanding that information is stored in the field and can be retrieved by the brain, is this an example of information being available beyond the constraints of time? The QV then becomes a source of information not only for events in the past or present, but also in the future.

Another recorded example of information being received beyond the constraints of space and time occurred at the Stanford Research Institute (SRI).[29] Physicists Hal Puthoff and Russell Targ were investigating remote viewing: a specific skill similar to clairvoyance whereby a person is able to 'see' a distant place without actually being there in person.

The possibility of using this skill in Cold War espionage attracted the US Central Intelligence Agency (CIA), who funded the program for many years, until hostilities towards the Soviet Union ceased and the work was no longer needed. Some of this research is still classified information.

The results that have been made available suggest a remarkable human ability to obtain information beyond the constraints of space and time. One type of study design consisted of placing a remote viewer in a closed room with no contact with the outside world. Outside the room, another person picks a location contained within a randomly chosen sealed envelope (the randomization is done by computer). This person goes to the location and acts as a focus for the viewer, although no contact is made between the traveler and the remote viewer after the location is known. The remote viewer then tries to gain information about the location. They can draw sketches of what they 'see' or describe certain aspects.

Under these controlled conditions, the remote viewers were shown to give accurate responses that were unlikely to have happened by chance alone. In one study, the traveler took a series of random turns in a car, which led them to arrive at a jetty. The remote viewer described the jetty scene complete with boats, a whole hour before the traveler arrived there and before the traveler himself knew that this was the destination. A researcher in the laboratory recorded the descriptions made by the remote viewer whilst another researcher recorded the journey with the traveler so that they could be correlated later. This is how we know that the remote viewer described the journey ahead of time; it has all been recorded using scientific methodology.

The remote viewers were able to pick up information about the future. This is evidence of precognition under scientifically controlled conditions. This suggests that information in the QV is not restricted to time or place. Each part of the field has the information of the whole, which means that it contains information about everything in the universe that has happened, is happening or will ever happen. The ancient Hindu mystics actually had a very similar idea: the concept of the *akashic* records. Traditionally, this stored all universal information: past, present and future.

Experiments like those of Radin and the SRI suggest that we are able to interact with the QV in order to gain information beyond our own time and place. If our brains are seen as conduits for information from the QV, then precognition is an example of a different type of access than the memory recall we discussed before. A key part of remote viewing is to relax; it does not seem to work if a person is trying too hard. Relaxing seems to help our minds to escape the constraints of space and time.

Before the era of relativity and quantum theory, there was no way that we could explain this scientifically. We did not have the science that acknowledged consciousness as fundamental, or the idea that the universe is a hologram, or that time is not a universal clock. We did not know that information could be contained in the QV and transcend space and time. The new scientific era is allowing us to explain ancient human talents. Because of the pioneering and scientifically conducted studies of subjects which have been previously labeled as paranormal, we not only have the evidence that information can be obtained outside of space and time, we also have the explanation of how.

The concept of consciousness existing beyond the boundaries of space and time can finally provide answers to an increasingly documented but perplexing phenomenon: the Near Death Experience (NDE).

Life after life

A surprisingly large percentage of people who have been close to death report having had an experience whilst their bodies were physically dead or almost dead. Few extensive epidemiological studies have been done on this subject, but some small surveys have found the number close to 50 per cent of those who have almost died.[30] Some can even report that they viewed the room in which they 'died' and even their own body. Sometimes conversations and actions of health professionals who are in attendance to that person are recalled, yet at the time that the events happened, the person was physically dead.

Despite the accumulation of data and reports, and increasing admittance of the existence of such cases by health professionals, this is a subject that is often seen as not worthy of scientific consideration. The concept of NDEs does not fit the orthodox view of the brain being the originator of consciousness.

According to reductionist neuroscience, if the brain isn't functioning, it is impossible for the person to experience anything. Reports of NDEs are often attributed to the abnormal and chaotic neuronal activity of the brain due to lack of oxygen.[31]

This does not easily explain why many reports of NDEs have

similar elements; many people report seeing a white light, meeting 'people' known to them, and some report incidents that happen in the room where they 'died', viewed from a perspective outside their body.

One of the most dramatic recorded cases is of a lady named Pam Reynolds.[32] This professional musician needed to undergo brain surgery to remove a large aneurysm in one of her brain's arteries. In order to safely do this, she needed to be taken to the edge of death. Her brain and heart were effectively stopped from activity during the surgery and both were monitored. Due to this monitoring, the evidence exists to show that her brain did not demonstrate electrical activity during the procedure.

Reynolds reports that she had a sentient experience during the time that her brain was not showing any electrical activity. She reports incidents in the room and even noted a surgical instrument which she had not seen before, but was able to describe when she recovered from surgery. She had detailed experiences at a time when all her vital signs showed that no experience could have been possible according to orthodox models of consciousness.

Is it possible for our consciousness to live on after our deaths? We have discussed during this book how some physicists are saying that consciousness is more fundamental than matter and how biology makes more sense if a sentient quality pervades every single cell and atom of our bodies.

Is consciousness the ghost in the molecular machine of the body that imbues us with the quality of life? If consciousness is more fundamental than the body, could it exist beyond physical death and out of space and time? Could it be that when we die, the part of us that we call our consciousness, returns to the sea of light from which it came?

Are we eternal beings who inhabit a physical body for a short moment in time? Is the information of each person, their fundamental consciousness, stored in the field for eternity?

If so, are the people who claim to speak to the dead telling the truth?

The science of mediumship

The art of mediumship has received a lot of attention recently. This is a skill that can be found in many cultures and essentially consists of a person acting as a medium between those who have died and their relatives left behind. Recently, this tradition has merged with modern entertainment creating some interesting social consequences.

Following the success of television shows such as *Crossing Over with John Edward,* a new entertainment genre has been born. In the UK, Living TV's *Most Haunted* also features psychic mediumship, whilst visiting sites that are reportedly haunted. During its live broadcasts, visitors to the website can reach almost 20 million; it is rare to attract this sort of attention in modern broadcasting. Speaking with the dead is now a cultural phenomenon.

Popular though these shows may be with the public, the issue of the scientific validity of mediumship is another matter. As with most topics considered paranormal, mediumship is often simply dismissed as fraud. Armed with the knowledge we now have of the QV, can we explain mediumship scientifically? Do we have any evidence that mediumship actually exists?

John Edward is perhaps the best-known celebrity medium. His

show is often a combination of group and personal readings for people he has never met before. He claims to be able to hear messages from people's family members who have died and these can bring comfort to a bereaved family.

The content of the messages often include mundane details from daily life which would be very hard to know if someone is not a family member because they are of little value outside the family and therefore not likely to be communicated. Sometimes he communicates messages regarding events that have occurred after the passing of that person. How does this occur? First let's look at the evidence that Edward is actually doing something at all.

In 1999, Edward was involved in research with Professor Gary Schwartz of the University of Arizona.[33] The study design consisted of five professional mediums asking questions of subjects directly or through another person. Questions were only allowed to be answered in a yes/no fashion. The mediums had no contact or prior knowledge of the subjects before the session. After the session, the subject would rate the information obtained in terms of accuracy on a scale of −3 to +3. Schwartz would only count a +3 as a hit.

Taking an average of the five mediums, an 83 per cent accuracy rate was obtained. This is compared with studies of the general public who are not mediums; their accuracy is 50 per cent at best.

This and further studies by Schwartz provide a scientific validity for the readings done by Edward and others. What we need now is an explanation for how mediumship works, which we can now piece together from the information in this chapter.

A talented individual such as Edward is able to tune into the QV where information transcends space and time. This is the particular genius of Edward, under our new definition of genius.

The fact that he obtains information pertaining to events after the death of the person suggests that consciousness does indeed transcend the physical body. Even after death, the fundamental aspect of a person retains a sentient presence. Consciousness is the aspect of ourselves that can neither be created nor destroyed. The QV may be the storage system of this aspect of us when our bodies no longer exist.

It is as if we are born from a sea of light and for a while we inhabit the world of mass and charge, held together by thought. And when we are done with the dance and no longer need to be weighed down with the burden of form, the essence of who we are returns once more to the light.

So if the spirit world exists, where is it? Why is it that some people claim to see spirits in the form of ghosts? Why are we not all John Edwards or Mozarts? Why do we all relate to the QV in a different way? If our thoughts are all in the field, how do we know which thoughts are ours? We shall go on to discuss these issues in the next chapter when we explore the world of vibration and of multidimensions.

Pretty vacant conclusions

The world of the pretty vacant is teeming with activity. It could also hold the answers to some of the secrets of the universe. From understanding our interaction with this sea of light, we can understand some of the greatest mysteries of our universe.

The new era of physics is starting to give us answers to age-old questions such as; can consciousness exist after death? In the old physics there was no room for consciousness and the answer was an unequivocal no. Yet as science has moved on, concepts such as consciousness and non-locality have entered the realm of physics and we can start to open up new ideas in how we view the world.

A brief note about time

A few times in this chapter we have discussed the concept of being out of space and time. This is compatible with what we know about the universe. Surprisingly, since the era of relativity, science has introduced the concept that time does not actually exist at all. The idea that the field holds information that transcends time is not out of the question. We shall discuss the nature of time in more detail later on in this book.

References for Chapter 7

1. Heisenberg W. *Physical Principles of the Quantum Theory*. (Dover Publications) 2003.

2. Bortman H. Energy Unlimited. *New Scientist*. 22 January 2000; 32- 34.

3. Walter R. *Scientists Claim to Tap the Free Energy of space*. 2001 http://www.mufor.org/nmachine.html. [cited January 2006].

4. Barrow JD. *The Book of Nothing*. (Vintage) 2001.

5. Bortman H. Energy Unlimited. *New Scientist*. 22 January 2000; 32- 34.

6. Hawking S. *A Brief History of Time*. (Bantam) 1995.

7. Pais A. *Paul Dirac: The Man and his work*. (Oxford University Press) 1998.

8. Davies P. Liquid Space. *New Scientist*. 3 November 2001; 30-34.

9. Laszlo E. *The Whispering Pond: a Personal Guide to the Emerging Vision of Science.* (Element) 1999.

10. McTaggart L. *The Field.* (Harper Collins) 2001.

11. Talbot M. *The Holographic Universe.* (Harper Collins) 1996.

12. Bentov I. *Stalking the Wild Pendulum: on the mechanics of consciousness.* (Inner traditions) 1988.

13. Talbot M. *The Holographic Universe.* (Harper Collins) 1996.

14. Bohm D. *Wholeness and the implicate order.* (Routledge classics) 2002.

15. Bekenstein J.D. Information in the Holographic Universe. *Scientific American.* August 2003; 48-55.

16. Smolin L. *Three Roads to Quantum Gravity.* (Phoenix) 2001.

17. Johnson S. *Emergence.* (Penguin) 2002.

18. Lashley K. In Search of the Engram. *Physiological Mechanisms in Animal Behavior.* (New York; academic press) 1950; 454-82.

19. Pietsch P. *Shufflebrain: the Quest for the Hologramic mind.* (Houghton Mifflin) 1981.

20. Pribram, KH. The Neurophysiology of Remembering. *Scientific American.* January 1969; 73-86.

21. McTaggart L. *The Field.* (Harper Collins) 2001.

22. Laszlo E. Life- a dance through the zero-field. *Caduceus.* Winter 1997; 38: 15-18.

23. Fields RD. Making Memories Stick. *Scientific American,* February 2005; 58-65.

24. Ibid.

25. Schwartz G. Presentation at the *Living the Field* conference, London April 5th 2003. www.livingthefield.com

26. Penrose R. *Shadows of the Mind: a search for the missing sci-*

ence of consciousness. (Vintage) 1995.

27. *Extraordinary people: the woman with no brain.* [Television documentary] Channel 5 Broadcasting 2002.

28. Bilimoria E. *Consciousness came first: Connecting non-locally with the whole.* Presentation at conference on Esoteric Perspectives on a science of consciousness. [PDF file] Scientific and Medical network. 31 May 2003, Rudolph Steiner House, London.

29. Korotkov K. *Human Energy Field: study with GDV bioelectrography.* (Backbone) 2002.

30. Holt J. *Blindsight and the Nature of Consciousness.* (Broadview Press) 2003.

31. Magueijo J. *Faster than the speed of light.* (Arrow) 2004.

32. Radin D. *The Conscious Universe.* (Harper Collins) 1997.

33. Puthoff H, Targ R. *Mind-reach.* (Hampton Roads) 2005.

34. Ring K. *Life at Death.* (New York: Coward, McCann & Geoghegan) 1980.

35. Blackmore S. *Dying to Live: Science and the near death experience.* (London, Grafton) 1993.

36. Sabom M. *Light and Death.* (Zondervan) 1998.

37. Schwartz G. *The Afterlife Experiments: Breakthrough Scientific Evidence of Life After Death.* (Simon and Schuster International) 2000.

Chapter 8

The New Wave

No more heroes

At the end of the 19th century, science was slowing down. The common feeling amongst scientists in Europe was one of completion. They believed that we had discovered all that it was possible to know about our universe and that the future of science lay in refining these ideas. It is easy to understand this attitude if we remember just how dramatic the century had been. The astounding achievements of Michael Faraday and James Clerk Maxwell had heralded the era of electromagnetism and laid the foundations for our modern world. With such successes so fresh in the collective memory, the scientific community felt there was nothing left to achieve.

It was into this scientific climate that the young Albert Einstein arrived, when he started his physics degree in Zurich. Lectures were obviously not to his taste, as he often skipped college to spend his days in cafes, pondering the universe.[1] This strategy seems to have worked rather well; Einstein's ponderings changed our understanding of the universe. It was not only the content of his work that was significant, but also his methods. Einstein's sense of perspective started a new era of unification.

If the kids are united

Since the days of Isaac Newton, the concept of a steadfast universal time remained unchallenged. Einstein's work showed that space and time are united and this is most apparent under certain circumstances, such as when traveling near the speed of light. He realized that the passage of time is not universal, but depends on where you are and how fast you are traveling. Furthermore, he unified mass and energy, elegantly demonstrating that one can be converted to the other.

The concept of unification was such a success that for the rest of his days, Einstein sought to find a *theory of everything*: one elegant concept that could describe the universe. However, Einstein was alone in his quest, as most of the physics community was preoccupied with quantum mechanics and viewed him as a bit of old relic.

Towards the end of the 20th century, Einstein's methods were revived and others took up the quest for unification. They developed Superstring Theory or String theory (ST), which may eventually emerge as the definitive theory of everything, uniting all known forces and particles with one elegant concept. ST is still being developed, but if it fulfils its promise, it would not only uncover the unity of the universe, but also describe its hidden realms, revealing the science behind ancient mysteries. This is the New Wave.

Problems

At the time of Einstein's death in the 1950s, physics was divided into two main areas: the theory of relativity, describing the world of large objects such as galaxies and quantum theory, describing the world of the very small, such as subatomic particles. This is largely the situation that still exists today. Both descriptions are successful, but simply do not agree with each other. This is a distressing situation for physicists, as it effectively means that the universe behaves differently according to what you are looking at. It would be more palatable to have one definitive description for both situations: a theory of everything. Instead, we have to make sense of a range of seemingly disparate aspects of the universe.

For example, nobody knows why so many particles exist in the universe and why they behave as they do. Huge particle colliders were built in the 20th century, such as the one at CERN in Geneva. In these massive underground tunnels, particles are accelerated to very high speeds and then smashed into each other. The analysis of the debris started to reveal exotic new particles such as muons and tau-neutrinos. Pretty soon physicists had a new hobby: documenting the characteristics of these new particles, like a cosmic stamp collection.

Although we can describe these particles, we cannot explain them. Why do all these particles exist and why do they have such precise characteristics? If the mass of an electron were to be slightly different, it would change the laws of the universe and the world would be a very different place. How did the electron get it right?

Not only did we discover new particles in the 20th century, we found new forces too. By probing into the atom, scientists discovered the nucleus and its associated strong and weak forces to add to the forces of gravity and electromagnetism that we already knew about.

Gravity is the force holding us to the surface of the Earth and in orbit around the sun. Contrary to what our intuition may lead us to believe, it is an incredibly weak force. This is something you can test for yourself by picking a pin off the floor with a household magnet, thus overcoming the gravitational force of the entire planet.

Electromagnetism is the force responsible for electricity and therefore for our household power and electrical storms. The strong nuclear force is responsible for holding all the positively charged protons together in the nucleus of the atom, as they would otherwise repel each other. The weak nuclear force is responsible for radioactive decay, as seen in elements such as uranium.

Relativity, quantum theory, particles and forces; how to bring all these together in one coherent whole, has been the persistent headache of physicists for almost a hundred years. Murray Gell-Mann, Steven Weinberg and colleagues made a valiant attempt at solving the problem by uniting three out of the four forces in something called the Standard Model. The Standard Model is also successful at classifying all those various particles into what has been described as a 'periodic table' of subatomic particles.

The predictions made by the Standard Model accurately match the experimental data. In fact, it has been so successful that some physicists have ceased to look for new theories.[2] However, aspects of the Standard Model are troubling. It is cumbersome; is Nature really that ugly? We witness so much beauty in Nature that physicists feel this should be reflected in the rules that underpin the universe.[3] It also has a glaring omission in that it does not incorporate the force of gravity. Like trying to squeeze an elephant into a Mini full of supermodels, all attempts to unite the forces of the large with the forces of the small have been thwarted.

For some years it did not seem to matter. The Standard Model was good enough for those concentrating on the world of small objects such as subatomic particles. Those dealing with relativity and large objects, such as galaxies, simply ignored the problem too. But a slow revolution was happening, one that gathered pace towards the end of the 20th century and would put the path of physics back onto the course of unification yet again.

Wiggle it, just a little bit

What does unification actually mean? How did Einstein unite space and time? Mathematically, it was as if he had climbed a cosmic ladder and viewed the universe from a higher perspective. From this vantage point he could see that space and time are not separate after all, they just appear to be.

Actually, the idea of gaining this mathematical higher perspective was not new. Maxwell had previously done this with electro-magnetism. The mathematician Georg Riemann had also previously developed this technique, but had not applied it to physics. In fact, when Einstein got stuck on a problem (and he did get stuck from time to time) he enlisted the help of a friend, who discovered that Riemann had actually solved the problem some 60 years before.[3]

Riemann's mathematics was crucial to Einstein. It provides

more 'wiggle room', which allows extra space for the forces to fit together. He was not the only one interested in Riemann's approach. In 1919 Einstein received a letter from Theodr Kaluza, proposing that we look at the universe from an even higher perspective.[4] When the universe is given this extra piece of wiggle room, both Einstein's and Maxwell's work emerges effortlessly. In 1926, an assistant professor, Oskar Klein published something similar, and this is now called Kaluza-Klein theory.

Despite the fact that this method was a success, this type of work was left dormant for a number of years until later in the century, when the work of John Schwarz, Leonard Susskind, Michael Green, Edward Witten and others would revive the Riemann and Kaluza-Klein approaches and give birth to Superstring Theory or String Theory (ST). This has become one of the strongest contenders for a theory of everything that we have today.

Triumph of the nerds

When those early pioneers started working on ST, most of their colleagues thought they were completely on the wrong track. Science writer Leonard Mlodinow recalls his own thoughts about Schwarz at the time and how he thought he was working on a 'crazy theory.'[5]

It is a common perception amongst many people that physicists are a bunch of nerds. Most physicists saw early string theorists as nerds: now that really is saying something!

Despite being deeply unfashionable, the early string theorists continued their work and started showing signs of success. Their 'crazy theory' has gained in popularity to become one of the leading contenders for the theory of everything. The number of string theorists has swelled from a handful to some hundreds.

One of its main successes has been to incorporate the force of gravity. However, ST has had its share of problems. At one point, five versions of the theory existed, a bit embarrassing when it is supposed to be the one definitive answer to everything. It is also a theory that cannot be tested in the laboratory or with cosmological data, leading to complaints that ST is not a science, but an abstract philosophy. [6]

Despite these issues, ST is currently entrenched in the world of 21st century physics. It attracts academic funding and pays people's wages. ST might be part of the establishment of mainstream science, but it introduces some radical concepts that seem more like science fiction. Furthermore, these concepts have the potential for explaining some of the ancient mysteries of our universe, from transcendental experiences to the symptoms of mental illness.

Universal twang

So what is so different about ST and how does it unite all those forces and particles? According to ST, there is something more fundamental than the forces and subatomic particles; the very heart of reality consists of tiny vibrations of energy or strings. These strings are so small that they are invisible to all our current methods of measurement.

They are smaller than subatomic particles such as quarks and electrons. In fact, according to ST, particles only appear like points because we are viewing them from a distance. If we could see them more closely, the particles would look like strings. A bit like the notes on a violin, the way a string vibrates determines which particular particle is created.

The fundamental forces of Nature also emerge from these vibrations. Much to the satisfaction of those early believers in ST, a lot of the major developments in physics such as Relativity and Maxwell's equations, pop out quite naturally from the mathematics of ST.

As Michael Green recalls in *The Elegant Universe*, "The moment you encounter string theory and realize that almost all of the major developments in physics over the last hundred years emerge – and emerge with such elegance – from such a simple starting point, you realize that this incredible compelling theory is in a class of its own."[4]

ST has had its share of successes as well as failures, but whether it proves to be the definitive description of the universe or not, it has introduced the idea that the universe consists of vibrations that give rise to all that is contained within it. But that is not all there is to ST. It has given us the music of hyperspace.

The music of hyperspace

As previously discussed, this concept of extra wiggle room is crucial to the principles of ST because it allows for the unification of the forces and particles of Nature. How is this wiggle room created? By adding extra dimensions to the universe, sometimes called hyperspace.

We normally think of ourselves living in three dimensions of space and one of time. We can move from side-to-side, up-and-down and back-and-forth in space. We utilize all of these spatial dimensions, along with the fourth dimension of time, whenever we arrange to meet someone.

If we tell our friend that we will meet them on the top of the Empire State building at 3pm on a particular day, we are using all of these dimensions. The street location would tell us where to meet in two dimensions: on Fifth Avenue, between 33rd and 34th Street and the floor number, 102, would give us the location in the third dimension of up and down. The fourth dimensional parameter is time, which is 3 o'clock. This is the type of information we need in order to precisely locate our friend within the universe.

What Riemann, Kaluza, Einstein and others did that was so radical was that they added fourth and fifth dimensions of space and time to the universe. String theorists later adopted this strategy of adding extra dimensions to the universe on their quest to find the theory of everything. Many found this idea preposterous at first; Mlodinow recalls that he overheard Richard Feynman shout down the corridor to John Schwarz, "Hey Schwarz, how many dimensions are you in today?"[7]

Part of the resistance to this idea is that we cannot visualize dimensions higher than our own. We are used to our world of three spatial dimensions and one of time. This is all we seem to be equipped to handle.

It is analogous to a person living in a flat land of two dimensions, attempting to visualize a world of three dimensions. A 'flatlander' would be accustomed to spatial dimensions of back-and-forth, side-to-side, but not up-and-down. That would be just weird to them! The classic Victorian novel by E A Abbott explores these themes and is still essential reading for physicists today. By using the analogy of a flatlander, Abbott demonstrates how hard it is to visualize a higher dimension.[8]

Nevertheless, when tiny vibrating strings are allowed to move in not just three, but eleven or even twenty-six dimensions, they are able to create the contents of the universe, prompting string theorist, Michio Kaku to proclaim that the mind of God is "music resonating through hyperspace."[9]

The cosmic symphony

Although the idea of a multidimensional universe seems strange at first, the idea has persisted and is proving to be an interesting concept to other physicists too. For example, cosmologists have been wondering if hyperspace holds the key to explaining some of their more troublesome findings. Recent data produced from observations of supernovae (exploding stars), has cast doubt on some cherished ideas in physics, namely the constants of Nature. It has long been believed that certain values, such as Planck's constant and the speed of light, never change, hence they are called constants. One of these is the fine structure constant, known as alpha, which relates to certain atomic characteristics.

A team at the University of New South Wales, Sydney, led by John Webb, has made some unexpected discoveries. When they interpreted their observations of supernovae, they found that the value of alpha appears to have changed over time, which means it is not constant after all.[10]

Because alpha is related to other constants in Nature, such as Planck's constant and the speed of light, those values could also be questioned. John D Barrow, of the University of Cambridge, suggests that we are mistaking certain values as constant, because we have a limited perspective of the universe. They may actually be three-dimensional shadows cast by hidden processes in higher dimensions. He writes, "any theory of everything that explains these constants can only exist if the world has many more dimensions than the three we see."[11]

Hyperspace may also harbor missing particles such as right-handed neutrinos. Neutrinos are strange, ghostly particles that travel at the speed of light. They are very hard to detect as they rarely interact with anything, but when one is found, it invariably has a left-handed spin. Do right-handed neutrinos exist but in higher dimensions? There are some who believe that this is the case.[12]

And this may not be all that is lurking in hyperspace. Professor Sean Carroll of the University of Chicago believes this is where the mysterious missing vacuum energy resides. All our calculations of a quantity known as vacuum energy produce a figure that is woefully off the mark. This is unlikely to be a simple miscalculation. Rather, we do not have all the information we need, because it is hidden in hyperspace.[13]

If the higher dimensions are so useful, where are they? Why can't we see them? For many years, physicists believed that other dimensions were too tiny to be seen, even though they existed all around us. They believed the dimensions were folded into small spaces, smaller than atoms. How can a dimension be folded up? It is hard to imagine, but the dimensions are folded up into geometric shapes like paper origami. This folding process hides the higher dimensions from our awareness, according to ST.

To visualize what this means, let's imagine a two-dimensional space existing in a three-dimensional space, such as a garden hose. Imagine you are an ant living on the surface of a garden hose. As far as you are concerned, the world is completely flat. There is a back and forth dimension, a side-to-side dimension, but no up-and-down dimension. You are effectively living in a world of two dimensions.

Now imagine that someone takes the hose and cuts a piece out. They then curl this up so it looks like a doughnut. To an ant on the surface of the hose, the world is still two-dimensional. But now the two dimensions have been folded up and exist in the three dimensional space of the doughnut. The ant is in a hyperspace universe of three dimensions but does not know it.[4]

We are in a similar situation; we are imbedded in hyperspace even though we are not aware that we are. Just as the ant cannot understand the concept of up and down, we cannot conceive of the geometry of higher dimensions.

Until recently, higher dimensions were thought to be tiny and this was partly why we couldn't see them. Opinion is changing, however and in a 2003 conference at Fermi Lab near Chicago, Professor Joseph Lykken remarked,

"We realized there are mechanisms of physics which can hide extra dimensions. Now we've realized that without invoking any exotic bizarre physics, but physics we already knew about, the extra dimensions could be just as large as the whole universe that we see and know. It could be that the world of extra dimensions could be just as interesting, just as rich and complicated, with its own topography, its own geology. It's a whole other universe beyond what we've already seen."[14]

The extra dimensions may not be so small after all, but exist just next to our world, hidden from us due to our inability to conceptualize their geometries.

Summary of the new wave

To conclude this chapter, let's recall what we have learnt. One of the strongest contenders for the theory of everything is called Superstring Theory (ST). ST states that subatomic particles and the four forces in Nature are made up of the vibrations of tiny strings of energy. The different frequencies of these vibrations create all that we see around us in the universe. These vibrations do not just exist in three spatial dimensions, but in many higher dimensions too. These higher dimensions could be complete worlds, existing just next to ours, yet we cannot access them as they are folded up in higher dimensional geometry that we cannot perceive. Or can we?

As we recall, some physicists have concluded from the findings of quantum physics that consciousness is fundamental to the universe. What if we were to take this concept and apply it to ST? What sorts of worlds could we encounter? Can we actually feel the vibe?

References for Chapter 8

1. Bodanis D. $E=MC^2$: A biography of the world's most famous equation. (Macmillan) 2000.
2. Kane G. The Dawn of Physics beyond the standard model. *Scientific American*. June 2003; 56-63.
3. Kaku M. *Hyperspace*. (Oxford Paperbacks) 1995.
4. Greene Brian. *The Elegant Universe*. (Random House) 2000.
5. Mlodinow L. *Euclid's Window*. (Penguin) 2003.

6. Chown M. It came from another dimension. *New Scientist.* 18 December 2004; 30- 33.

7. Mlodinow L. *Some time with Feynman.* (Penguin) 2004.

8. Abbott EA. *Flatland: a romance of many dimensions.* (Dover) 1992.

9. Kaku M. Essay: Unifying the Universe. *New Scientist.*16 April 2005; 48.

10. Webb J et al. Search for Time Variation of the Fine Structure Constant.
*Physical Review Letters.*1999; 82, 884–887.

11. Barrow JD. Enigma Variations. *New Scientist.* 7 September 2002; 30-33.

12. Close F. To catch a rising star. *New Scientist.* 7 December 2002; 33-37.

13. Carroll SM, Mersini L. Can We Live in a Self-Tuning Universe? *Phys. Rev. D* 2001; 64, 124008; hep-th/0105007.

14. Lykken J. *The Physics of Extra Dimensions.* Quick time video associated with lecture at Enrico Fermi institute.15 February 2003. http://hep.uchicago.edu/cdf/smaria/ms/aaas03.html [downloaded February 2003]

Chapter 9

Feeling the Vibe

Dumb and dumber

In the preceding chapter, we discussed how String Theory (ST) describes a universe consisting of tiny vibrating strings of energy. The different frequencies of the vibrations of these strings give rise to all the different particles and forces in Nature. In order to achieve this, these strings are given extra wiggle room, by providing the universe with extra dimensions.

So far so good, but even this poetic picture of a musical universe seems incomplete. Yet again, physics has produced a theory of everything that does not explain how we are able to think up such theories in the first place. In this respect, ST is similar to the Newtonian, mechanical vision of the universe; both fail to address the issue of consciousness.

In this book, we have already discussed how various physicists are concluding that consciousness is fundamental to reality. Harvard-educated physicist John Hagelin makes the explicit link between ST and consciousness, stating that this unified field *is* pure consciousness.[1] If consciousness is fundamental to matter, then even superstrings must be inherently intelligent.

Michio Kaku has said that the mind of God is "music resonating through hyperspace."[2] Is every note of that music imbued with an inherent sentience? What are the implications of a universe alive with vibrations of consciousness? Can we feel the vibe?

Body of evidence

We may not be able to measure superstrings directly, but can we measure them indirectly? The vibrations of superstrings are supposed to be responsible for all known forces, including the force of electromagnetism. It follows that changes in the electromagnetic force must be reflected in these fundamental vibrations. So if it can be demonstrated that electromagnetism is linked to consciousness, this infers that superstrings are too.

There is a growing body of evidence that suggests that this is the case. Most of this evidence has accrued in studies involving measurements of the electromagnetic fields around a person's body. This type of technique is extremely common in our society; every time someone takes an electrocardiogram (ECG), they are measuring the electrical activity from the heart. This is only possible because the heart creates a field around it that can be detected at some distance. (If you are curious about this, I recommend that you investigate the method used for performing a twelve lead ECG.)

The same type of principle is used in this research. Some of these studies have taken place in prominent universities. The results from these various centers do indeed suggest that a person's electro-magnetic fields reflect their inner thoughts, feelings and level of personal development. Because superstrings give rise to the force of electromagnetism, is this evidence that superstrings are linked to consciousness?

Valerie Hunt, a professor at the University of California, has been involved in this type of research.[3] She took measurements from subjects' bodies using the type of equipment that is normally used to monitor muscle activity: an electromyelogram (EMG). This involves applying electrodes to the skin, and measuring the electrical activity of the area. These results can be analyzed in terms of frequencies.

Hunt made some surprising discoveries and also raised a few eyebrows. She realized that the frequencies she had measured from various positions corresponded to the traditional sites of chakras, which are centers of the body described in esoteric Hindu traditions. Hence the position of the body corresponding to the red chakra has a lower frequency associated with it than the position of the blue chakra, and so on.

After further investigation, Hunt produced a scale of frequencies corresponding to state of mind and level of personal development. According to Hunt, people who are materialistically minded fall into the range of 250Hz and below. This range probably includes the majority of people. They are the ones who find it difficult to comprehend subjects such as non-local consciousness.

She also found that those with healing abilities exist between 400Hz and 800Hz. Those with psychic gifts have frequencies between 800Hz to 900Hz. Hunt also found that people with 'mystical personalities', Buddha or Christ-like people, have frequencies of 900Hz and above.

These results are similar to those of researcher Keith Wakelam, who used a different method to obtain readings.[4] He measured skin resistance, using a device similar to a lie detector test (a galvanometer). This type of equipment is best known for discerning whether someone is telling the truth. When a person lies, their autonomic nervous system becomes active and their skin resistance increases.

Wakelam used a more complex device that takes readings from both sides of the body and then measures the difference between them. The usual inaccuracies that are associated with lie detectors are eliminated, because the difference between the two sides of the body is considered, not the reading itself. He then used a method of interpreting the frequencies from the readings obtained.

He too, found a scale of personal development with frequencies ranging from 250Hz to over 1500Hz. He also discovered that readings alter as people undergo emotional changes; their frequencies differ as their attention changes, even whilst they are still attached to the equipment. Could this research be an indication of how changes in consciousness manifest as changes in our underlying frequencies?

Going underground

It seems that these changes are not only detectable in life. Konstantin Korotkov, a professor at St Petersburg State Technical University, has researched the changes that occur in the electromagnetic fields of the body after a person has died. He used yet another method of investigation: the Gas Discharge Visualization technique (GDV).[5]

This translates electromagnetic measurements from the body into detailed, color pictures, making it easy to spot any patterns.

He found that an electromagnetic field persists around the body for some days after a person's death. Interestingly, the type of pattern reflects the mode of death. A sudden and traumatic death such as a suicide or road traffic accident produces a different type of field to when the death was expected and natural. The emotional nature of the death seems to register in the electromagnetic activity of the body.

As we have discussed, according to ST, the force of electromagnetism is actually a tiny vibration of energy. Any change in the electromagnetic field must be related to this inherent vibration. If we find that there is a correlation between the behavior of the electromagnetic field and a person's thoughts and feelings, is this proof that our inherent vibrations, our superstrings, are related to consciousness?

When two hearts beat as one

William Tiller, formerly a professor at Stanford University, believes there is indeed a link between the frequencies of the electromagnetic field in a system and its inherent consciousness.[6] Tiller has done research with the Heart Math Institute, whose researchers and practitioners examine the electromagnetic radiation of the heart and teach techniques to gain control of one's inner state by decreasing the beat-to-beat variability of the heart rate.

Tiller and his team found that various training techniques, such as qigong, yoga and the Heart Math Institute's own system, are useful in achieving this inner control. They studied the effects of these techniques on the heart, using equipment similar to a regular ECG.[7] He also found that this type of training results in an increase in the range, or *bandwidth* of frequencies exhibited by the heart. Those people who develop this greater bandwidth are more likely to have more meaningful interactions with other people. Furthermore, when two people experience an empathic exchange, their heart rhythms synchronise.[8] Such positive interactions increases the bandwidth of each person even further and they are more likely to go on to have meaningful interactions with others, increasing their bandwidths even further.

An increase in bandwidth also increases the informational processing capability of a system.[9] (In this case, the system is a person or couple of people.) Tiller describes such a system as one of expanded consciousness: another link between measurable electromagnetic frequencies and consciousness.

The data collected by Tiller, Hunt and others, seem to hint at a process whereby our thoughts manifest as measurable frequencies. As a person makes progress with their inner development, this is reflected in their inherent frequencies. We exist as frequencies of consciousness that change as we change our minds.

Group therapy

A collective expansion of consciousness may be causing the change in people's interests at the moment. Some of the signs include the popularity of esoteric knowledge and complementary therapies. Tiller likens this change to applying heat to a container of gas.[10] Some of the molecules within it will start to vibrate at a higher rate. Other molecules will also increase in energy, but not as much as these 'molecular leaders'. The *average* temperature of the molecules in the container will increase, so all the molecules are affected, although some will be more energetic than others.

A similar process is occurring in our society at the moment, except it is the average frequency of consciousness, rather than the temperature that is increasing. As a result, a larger number of people have expanded frequencies of consciousness compared to previous years. These are the mystical personalities described by Hunt. It has always been possible for such people to be present, but now it is more statistically likely.

We have discussed how an increase in personal frequency reflects an increase in inner harmony, with better information processing ability and a greater capacity for meaningful interactions with others. As people move along the frequency scale and increase their bandwidth, they not only tend to become warmer people, but also more mystical.

Throughout the ages there have always been people who are known as mystics. Sometimes they are the village shamans, sages, saints, monks or even television mediums such as John Edward. They appear to have perceptual abilities that are outside the normal range. They claim to be able to see other worlds and have contact with beings other than humans, such as angels.

Until recently, science viewed such people as charlatans and questioned their sanity. Yet more people are displaying these perceptual abilities. They may live otherwise normal lives; these gifts are not synonymous with mental illness. Nor do they necessarily form the basis for the person's career, so the label of charlatan cannot be applied.

We need a more satisfactory explanation for these abilities, instead of dismissing them as products of the imagination or even madness. In this chapter, we have discussed the science of feeling the vibe, which goes some way to explaining these processes. To go further, we need to examine a set of principles known as sympathetic vibratory physics.

Singing the same song

As previously discussed, the Heart Math Institute found that when two people experience a meaningful exchange, their heart rates tend to synchronise.[8] Tiller explains that this process occurs through sympathetic vibratory physics (SVP).[12]

Simply put, vibrations that are similar tend to resonate in harmony and combine to have an additive effect. They also tend to attract each other. Conversely, when two vibrations are in discord, they repel and negate each other.[13] There are many instances in our daily lives where we can see this principle in effect, such as when a radio receiver picks up the signal.[14] Radio waves are electromagnetic vibrations that can resonate with a radio antenna and be transformed into sound.

When two people experience a meaningful exchange, their heart rates synchronize, leading to sympathetic resonance. According to Tiller, this has an expansive effect on the system (i.e. the two people involved in the exchange) and it experiences an enhanced informational processing capacity. Many people have probably experienced this when they are in a successful creative partnership. The partnership achieves better results in comparison to individual efforts. Most people have also experienced the opposite situation, when people are not empathic they are not in harmony and are therefore less creative.

Using the principle of SVP, we can now answer the question posed in Chapter 4; why do people have particular talents? Just to recap, we discussed the new definition of a genius as a person who is particularly gifted at obtaining a type of information from the quantum vacuum (QV). Why do people receive a particular type of information and not another? Why is the genius of John Edward different from that of Albert Einstein?

We can describe the QV as a holographic store of information in the form of light waves. Waves, which are a type of vibration or oscillation, have particular characteristics such as frequency. According to SVP, vibrations that are similar attract: they resonate with each other. From this, it follows that if we each have our own inherent frequency, the information we draw from the field is reflective of our own selves. Hence, we all have our own life purpose and creative genius, because we each have our own unique vibration.

What you vibrate: you create

This principle of SVP can be applied to other life situations. Have you ever noticed how some people repeatedly attract the same 'bad luck' into their lives? Maybe they have relationships with similar people. They may start to believe that their life has to be this way: that these events are external to them.

However, the patterns that exist in our lives are a reflection of our own consciousness. We each have our own signature vibration of consciousness, as does every person and even every object! So we attract towards us those people, objects and situations that resonate with us and reflect who we are, even those aspects of ourselves which we deem to be negative traits.

For example, if a woman holds a deep belief that she is unworthy of a kind partner, she will often attract the type of man (or woman) who will reinforce that belief. The behavior of the partner may not be apparent at first. This reiterates the fact that this is not a conscious decision, but an attraction based on resonance.

The idea that life's circumstances are connected to our inner processes forms the basis for many disciplines of personal development. These encourage us to change our thoughts and change our lives. However, even veterans of such practices are vulnerable to events that appear out of their control. This is because we attract reflections of both our conscious and subconscious beliefs. The subconscious beliefs also have signature vibrations that can give rise to situations in life that may not be pleasant.

The basis of good therapy is to help people identify and become aware of these hidden beliefs, so that they can change them. The moment a subconscious belief is recognized, the person undergoes a shift in consciousness. This alters their inherent vibrations, which then resonate in a different way and attract different situations in their life. This is a part of the process of personal growth. (We shall further explore the mechanism behind this, later in this book.)

The experimental data suggests that as people increase in awareness, their inherent frequencies increase. With more people becoming interested in personal development, it is likely that the average bandwidth of the human population is increasing.

As this process occurs, more people are reporting experiences that are out of the ordinary, such as angelic encounters. Is the increase in bandwidth allowing them to come in contact with higher frequencies via sympathetic resonance? In a universe that exists as vibrations of consciousness in many dimensions, can we actually explore hyperspace?

Exploring hyperspace

In the book, *Hyperspace*, physicist Michio Kaku describes his childhood visits to the Japanese Tea garden in San Francisco and his fascination with the carp in the pond there.[15] As a child, he pondered on how the carp probably do not realize that they are surrounded by water. He also wondered if they are aware of the world outside the surface of the pond.

Kaku imagined taking a carp out of the water and throwing it back in; to the other carp it would seem as if their friend had disappeared. The young Kaku imagined that the fish would give the following report on returning to the pond.

"I was somehow lifted out of the universe (the pond) and hurled into a mysterious nether world, with blinding lights and strangely shaped objects that I had never seen before. The strangest of all was the creature who held me prisoner, who did not resemble a fish in the slightest. I was shocked to see that it had no fins whatsoever, but nevertheless could move without them. It struck me that the familiar laws of nature no longer applied in this netherworld. Then just as suddenly I found myself back into our universe."

Kaku realized that the other carp would dismiss their friend's claims as the ramblings of a mad carp; every carp knows that there is nothing beyond the pond universe.

Like carp in a pond, the human race are also limited in what we experience of the world. We are unaware of the dimensions that exist just next to us. Despite this, there are examples throughout history of people who claim to have glimpsed other realms. These people have traditionally been known as shamans and mystics. Modern Western culture tends not to accommodate these gifts, as we currently have no scientific explanation for them. Accordingly, if people claim to have experienced other worlds, they may be labeled as insane.

Some people will read the above description of the carp adventure and know exactly why I have included this analogy. These are the people who have had a mystical experience. Knowing what the reaction from others might be, people often keep these experiences to themselves.

However, on careful examination, the mystical experience is part of the fabric of societies around the world. From Joan of Arc to Socrates to Carl Jung, a variety of our cultural heroes claim to have had experiences that are unusual or otherworldly.

Socrates' famous allegory of the cave, which features in Plato's *Republic*, alludes to our reality consisting of mere shadows, cast by light from another source.[16] Could this higher source be hyperspace? In the allegory, the people in the cave are not aware of other realities and remain imprisoned. Was Socrates trying to explain his experiences of higher dimensions? He was often misunderstood: a common fate for mystics. Like the carp who told of his adventures beyond the pond, many people simply do not believe them.

Although there have been no official surveys of mystical experiences becoming more widespread in today's society, there are certain indicators that they are increasing. The success of the film *What the Bleep do We Know?* and the increase in books and workshops discussing such subjects, suggest that many people are questioning that the three-dimensional reality is the only one that exists.[17] As science starts to accept a world of many dimensions, is it possible that we are nearing a scientific explanation of mysticism?

Insane in the brane

As ST has evolved, it has become M-theory.[18] Nobody really knows what the 'M' stands for, but some say it is the Mother of all theories. In M theory, strings are seen from an even higher dimension where they are spread out into a brane. We can visualize a brane as a rippled surface. In our three-dimensional reality, it is as if we are stuck on our particular brane, unaware of higher dimensions around us.

But are we? Is the mystical experience a glimpse of those higher dimensions? From all we have discussed so far, we are now in a position to describe a mechanism by which this may be possible.

The dimensions of ST are defined by different frequencies of vibration: a higher dimension has a higher frequency. We have discussed in this book how these vibrations must be inherently sentient, making this a universe of many vibrations of consciousness.

As the bandwidth of the human population increases through personal development, could we be coming into contact with higher dimensions, through the principle of SVP? Are our vibrations beginning to resonate with those of higher dimensions?

Superstring Theorists believe that we may never travel to these higher dimensions or even conceive them. But although we may never be able to travel physically to these dimensions, does that stop the part of us that is pure consciousness from doing so? If, like the rest of the universe, consciousness is fundamental to our existence and transcends our physical properties, could our consciousness leap to other dimensions in order to experience them? Our consciousness may be the one aspect of ourselves that is not bound to the three-dimensional brane and is free to explore other realms, even higher dimensions. Just like the carp that glimpsed a world beyond the pond, could some of us experience worlds beyond the confines of our particular brane, simply by shifting our consciousness?

These experiences involve inner processes and as such are not easy to prove. The witness of higher dimensions is consciousness itself. Just as when you take apart the brain, you cannot find the memory of Auntie Flo's birthday party, this experience is not solid. It is elusive and beyond the material world.

For people who have not had such an experience, the idea seems outrageous. It would seem to them that a person making such a claim is either lying, a fantasist, or has lost their mind. However, ST itself currently has no proof of the existence of higher dimensions.[19] The higher dimensional experience is also impossible to prove physically because is not a *physical* entity.

We cannot take a higher dimension into a laboratory and examine it, as the old Newtonian scientific paradigm demands, in order to provide proof that something exists. We are moving beyond this approach, both in the way we do science, and in the way we relate to our world. Too many people are reporting higher dimensional experiences for us to ignore that this is happening. Nowhere is this more apparent then the growth of interest in angels and increased reports of angelic experiences.

Angelic upstarts

During Keith Wakelam's investigations with a galvonometer, he made a startling discovery.[20] Certain people displayed very high frequency spikes whilst meditating. Interestingly these people subjectively reported these moments as when they felt the presence of their spirit guides. When the studies were repeated, specifically to look for the spikes, they no longer appeared. Had Wakelam uncovered evidence of angels, albeit rather shy ones?

In the last decade, angels have become a popular subject with the public. There has been a growth in the number of books which explain topics such as how to make contact with your guardian angel. Cynics would dismiss this trend as part of the human need to replace orthodox religions, but is there any substance behind this 'New Age' craze? Are angels real and if so, are people really able to contact them?

Religious texts are littered with angelic experiences. The text of the *Koran* was supposed to have been dictated to the Prophet Mohammad by an angel and an angel was supposed to have appeared to Mary, mother of Jesus, before his birth. Our modern perspective makes it difficult to view these stories as more than just fairy tales or metaphors. Few would launch a scientific investigation into what these stories actually mean.

The idea that we are looked after by friendly, shining winged creatures is comforting to many, but the current explosion of interest in angels is also reflective of something else: increased reports of angelic contact. Two prominent authors, Doreen Virtue and Diana Cooper, claim that angelic encounters led to them write their books.[21, 22] Before their respective experiences, both women were not involved with this subject: Virtue was a clinical psychologist. Some might say she starting writing about angels because it is profitable and she had fabricated the stories of angelic encounters. However, is there a possibility that she is telling the truth?

Cooper and Virtue are not alone; many others claim to have had angelic experiences. Either they are all insane attention-seekers with vivid imaginations, or there is some truth to their claims. In the old world of Newtonian physics, angelic experiences would be impossible to explain. Unless one of these angels was fully examined in laboratory conditions, their existence could not be verified. The new scientific paradigm, with its quantum uncertainties and its brane-worlds of many dimensions, is starting to seem just as ethereal as esoteric wisdom. It might just be weird enough to explain angelic realms.

Just to be clear, this is not an argument to prove that angels exist. This is about demonstrating that, according to the principles we have described in this book, angels are scientifically possible. The key to this explanation is the idea that the universe exists as many dimensions of consciousness. This allows for the quality of consciousness to be present in areas other than three-dimensional reality. If it is possible for conscious beings to exist in the range of frequencies that make up our dimension, is it possible for them to exist in dimensions of higher frequencies? Is this where angels reside?

Wakelam may have captured a lower harmonic frequency of a being in a higher dimension. He may not have measured the actual 'angel' itself, but frequencies that were high enough to resonate with dimensions above. As people increase their consciousness bandwidth through meditation and other practices, this may allow contact with higher dimensions in this way. As the average bandwidth of a population increases, such experiences become more common. This may be the reason why angelic contact is increasing.

What are these higher beings like? As we are only really capable of interpreting the world of three-dimensional experience, we never truly conceptualize the worlds of higher dimensions. We are simply capable of interpreting an experience in higher dimensions in terms of three-dimensional reality.

If Archangel Michael really exists, why does he always seem to appear to people like a human being of European origin? Just as we interpret the information from the QV through our brains, the higher dimensional experience has to be interpreted as well. Our reporting of the appearance of divine beings is colored by our cultural heritage. There are at least some esoteric teachings that identify Archangel Michael with the Hindu God Vishnu, who has a different 'physical' appearance.

This might be an indication that these beings of consciousness do not have a physical form, but just a signature vibration. The vibration becomes interpreted and shaped according to the beliefs of the person who is witnessing it. Objective reality in higher dimensions may be impossible, as quantum physics suggests is the case in our dimension. Hence a particular vibration of consciousness appears European to someone from Europe and Indian to someone from India. It is all down to the interpretation.

Haunted by hyperspace

If it is possible for beings of other dimensions to exist, why stop at angels? Reported sightings of ghosts are found in every culture of the world and have always been a part of the human experience. Ghosts generally appear as physical representations of people who have died. Often a severe trauma occurred during the person's lifetime: a violent death for example. Sometimes, ghosts negotiate their surroundings as if they still existed in the same way as when the person was alive, for example, if the ground has eroded since the person's lifetime, the ghost appears to be floating.

In this chapter we have described the universe as consisting of many dimensions of consciousness, separated only by frequency. In a previous chapter we discussed how the consciousness of a person can exist outside the constraints of space and time and can persist even after death. It follows that we can describe ghosts as beings of consciousness in a different frequency dimension.

A common aspect of many ghostly apparitions is that the person was associated with a traumatic event during their lifetime. The resulting intense emotions are also aspects of consciousness. This suggests that consciousness plays a part in the mechanism of ghostly appearances. Perhaps the trauma results in producing a region of that person's consciousness that is of a lower frequency than normal: a negative expansion of bandwidth. This makes it easier for a part of their consciousness to appear to those who are living. This fits the traditional description of ghosts as being 'trapped on the Earth plane'; their frequencies of consciousness are held in lower regions due to unresolved traumatic emotions.

The traditional scientific view has been simple; ghosts do not exist and anyone who claims to have seen one is obviously delusional. It has never been a subject for serious discussion, despite the ubiquitous nature of such phenomena. Any scientific investigations of ghosts that do take place focus on finding physical evidence of their existence.

If ghosts are vibrations of consciousness in higher dimensions, they are unlikely to be measurable by three-dimensional instruments. It is even less likely that a ghost can be measured repeatedly: one of the hallmarks of reductionist science.

As we enter this new era of hyperspace physics with its universe of multidimensional consciousness, we can adjust our ideas of what is scientifically possible. We can examine ghostly apparitions in a new scientific light and at last start to understand this ancient mystery.

Aliens amongst us

Alien visitations are not discussed in polite scientific society. The idea that creatures from other planets have visited Earth is simply not entertained. Yet many people declare that they have seen alien craft or have even been abducted by aliens. For the abductees, this is often a harrowing experience, made worse by the fact that nobody believes them and most people think their story is ridiculous. The current scientific standpoint is that these experiences are strong fantasies. Quite an elaborate branch of psychology has even been created due to so-called abduction experiences.

John Mack was a professor of psychiatry at Harvard University until he died in a road traffic accident in 2004. He too, was initially skeptical about alien abductions, but his experiences with so-called abductees led him to undertake four years of research with such people.[23] He concluded that the alien beings in question are not from another planet, traveling to Earth in space ships, but entities that exist in other dimensions, parallel to ours.[24] It was a surprising announcement from someone in a position of such authority.

This conclusion fits all that we have discussed in this chapter. It may also go some way to explaining some of the peculiar features of alien abduction such as the strange bodily marks that abductees claim are a result of surgery performed by aliens. If these beings exist in a higher dimension to ours, can they see into our bodies in the way that we would be able to see into the bodies of flatlanders?

After sighting a UFO, people often describe its sudden disappearance. Is this the result of a sudden change in the frequency of the craft, making it invisible to our consciousness? We may now be able to answer the classic question; if aliens exist, why don't they land on the White House lawn? They may have been there all along, but we have been unable to perceive them, as they are in another dimension!

A common argument against the existence of aliens and UFOs is that abductions and flying saucer sightings have only occurred since the 20th century: in the era of science fiction. Therefore, these experiences are often dismissed as the effects of popular culture on the psyche. However, as we have previously discussed, the realms of higher dimensions are not really physical, they are vibrations of consciousness. They have to be interpreted through our three-dimensional selves, giving them a physical form. This process can indeed be influenced by the prevailing culture.

People may have encountered aliens throughout history, but the language they used to describe the experiences may have been different from ours. In fact, some authors, such as Erich Von

Daniken, have researched ancient scriptures and raise the possibility that they actually describe alien encounters, written in the language of the age.[25]

Scriptures such as the *Mahabharata* and the Bible, describe flying chariots, men who came from the sky and super human races of gods. The people of ancient times did not have access to science fiction literature, so would have described these experiences in the language of the times. Hence flying saucers are described as chariots or, as in Ancient Egyptian texts, 'reed boats in the sky'.[26] Cultural interpretation is an important aspect to an experience of higher dimensions.

The above section is not meant to be proof that aliens exist, but merely demonstrating how science can now provide a mechanism for their existence. If aliens do exist, in a dimension of consciousness parallel to ours, has anybody had meaningful contact with them? Surprisingly, it appears to happen quite often.

Is anybody in here?

Barbara Marciniak is an internationally best-selling author. Her books have sold over half a million copies and have been translated into several languages.[27] Strangely, she openly admits that she did not write them herself. A group of beings known as the Pleiadians wrote them through her; she claims that she channeled them.

Although channeling is now associated with the so-called New Age movement, it is not at all new. Careful consideration of old religions reveal many episodes of channeling: from the Angel Gabriel dictating the *Koran* to the Prophet Mohammad, to Moses being given the Ten Commandments by God, to the oracles of Delphi.

Channeling is a part of life for many societies; it is often the source of power of shamanism in traditional cultures. However, our modern technological society has become divorced from this process.

This cultural amnesia means that we no longer understand what it means to gain 'divine inspiration'. We have started to question who wrote the Bible and other scriptures, as the idea of them being written or dictated by God has no meaning in our culture. Because channeling has been lost from our society, the idea that God wrote them means some supernatural being had to literally reach down with a cosmic pen and write the scriptures: an extremely farfetched idea.

This questioning process may lead to the conclusion that ancient scriptures were written by ordinary people with all their faults and prejudices. This may be a sign of empowerment, but to debate the merits of this process is beyond the scope of this book. More to the point, people have lost touch with the art of contacting beings of higher dimensions, so the possible inspiration behind such texts is beyond the modern perspective. It is a situation comparable to when we look at Stonehenge or the pyramids at Giza. We cannot comprehend the motivation behind these colossal monuments, especially the fact that they have astronomical significance.

So how does channeling occur? Earlier in this book, we discussed the new model of brain functioning, which says that all thought involves taking information from the QV and interpreting it through the brain. The QV allows for a holographic storage of information so that information from the past, present and future is available to all parts of the universe.

If the universe truly acts as a hologram, with one part containing the information of the whole, why limit this information to that of our dimension? If the information from our own consciousness is present in the QV and available to psychics and mediums even after we die, why not the information of beings in other dimensions?

Just as with mediumship, some gifted individuals may be able to explore the QV to higher levels than most, in order to receive information from higher dimensions. What exactly they can tune into depends on the signature vibration of the receiver, as similar vibrations attract, according to the principles of SVP. So some people can contact angels, some the Pleiadians and some Princess Diana![28]

Of course, as with any higher dimensional experience, the information is colored by the personality of the receiver and their cultural influences. If you choose to believe or follow any channeled material, from the ancient to the modern, it is a good idea to follow what feels right to your own signature vibration and what you resonate with.

Again, the above section is not meant to act as proof of channeling or to say that all channeled material has been verified and should be followed. It is simply a description of the possible process of channeling using the science that has been used in this book. This ancient skill might now be explained in the new scientific paradigm. This paradigm may also shed light on yet another ancient mystery, mental illness.

Credit in the straight world

For a lot of people, there is no difference between a person having a spiritual angelic encounter and experiencing a hallucination. This is a prevalent attitude within our current medical profession. Carlos Warter, a psychiatrist, recalls an incident from his early medical training in *Recovery of the Sacred.* [29]

"I thought back to an 18 year old woman under another psychiatrist's care two weeks before. She was beautiful, blissful and the cause of great alarm in her family and in her doctor because she was in constant prayer and announced that she could talk to angels. To them, she was hallucinating; I wasn't sure. The peace and calmness she exhibited extended to a depth I had seen in few people on our planet."

Warter reports the fate of this woman "She was given electroshock treatments and in her disorientation, forgot all about angels. This wise, blissful young woman became tired, confused and, I thought, very unhappy."

This disturbing story illustrates how far we have come from the days when the scriptures of our world's religions were written and angelic contact seemed to be a sign of enlightenment, not insanity. If we were to look at characteristics of many figures throughout the ages, the modern lens would interpret their behaviors as that of mental illness.

Science itself proudly traces its past to the Ancient Greek philosophers. Yet, one of the forefathers of Western thought, Socrates, is recorded as stating that he had a spirit guide. During his trial, he refers to this guide as a 'sign' who talks to him.[30]

"A surprising thing has happened to me, judges… At all previous times my usual mantic sign frequently opposes me, even in small matters, when I was about to wrong... In other talks it often held me back in the middle of my speaking."

Socrates is viewed as one of the founders of modern civilization, yet he displayed some of the characteristics that many would see as insanity.

The famous French heroine, Joan of Arc, seems to have gained some of her conviction to charge into battle from hearing voices as a child.[31] She claimed that they were the voices of angels. Modern analysis would see these incidents as signs of a psychotic illness.

Perhaps the most startling example is Carl Jung. It is fascinating and ironic that one of the fathers of modern psychiatry appears to have obtained part of his information from his own spirit guide called Philemon.[32] Apparently, Jung waited until he was quite elderly before publishing his memoirs. This might have been because he too recognized the odd situation.

"It is of course, ironical that I, a psychiatrist, should at almost every step of my experiment have run into the same psychic material which is the stuff of psychosis and is found in the insane. This is the fund of unconscious images which fatally confuse the mental patient, but it is also the matrix of mythopoetic imagination which has vanished from our rational age."

Jung clearly describes the process of channeling, "Philemon represented a force which was not myself. In my fantasies I held conversations with him, and he said things which I had not consciously thought. For I observed clearly that it was he who spoke, not I."

His memoirs even contain a sketch of Philemon, who seems to

have wings: a guardian angel perhaps? From Jung's own accounts, these sessions that he calls 'fantasies' provided him with a source of information. And so modern psychiatry owes some of its content to channeled material!

Pretty on the inside

This chapter has contained some challenging material. It is extremely unusual to discuss topics like alien encounters and channeling in a scientific context. Some people believe that such experiences are a sign of insanity. It is true that people suffering with mental illness sometimes have thoughts and experiences that seem similar to multidimensional experiences. Without a scientific explanation of either, it is easy to see how they are placed into the same category.

But what exactly is mental illness, what is the scientific basis for the symptoms experienced by sufferers? It may come as a surprise that modern medicine is surprisingly sketchy on the exact mechanism for the generation of symptoms. Armed with the science of multidimensional consciousness, can the new scientific paradigm explain mental illness?

Despite all the successes of modern medicine, it cannot provide a full explanation for why mental illness occurs. In my own medical training, I was taught several theories about this, but no definitive answer. One of these is the biochemical model, in which the brain is a machine of broken molecular parts. This is the theory that is most favored, partly due to the success of modern pharmaceutical agents in controlling the symptoms of disease.

However, this still does not adequately explain why these types of symptoms occur. Why do people feel paranoid? Why do they hear voices telling them what to do? How do molecular imbalances in the brain lead to this spectrum of symptoms? One of the problems is that medicine is based on the reductionist approach. This almost ignores consciousness and views the body as a machine. A symptom such as thought insertion is pretty hard to explain within a paradigm that barely acknowledges the existence of thought in the first place.

A common public perception is that medicine has the answer to diseases such as schizophrenia, mania and depression. They are portrayed as molecular deficiencies of the brain that need to be corrected by drugs. In reality, we are far from a comprehensive explanation of mental illness. Certainly genetic, environmental and neurological factors contribute, but there is no overall satisfactory theory of why mental illness occurs.

How can the new scientific paradigm solve the problem? With the principles we have discussed in this chapter, mental illnesses can be redefined as pathological multidimensional experiences or abnormal forays into hyperspace. So people who are experiencing bizarre things, typical of illnesses such as schizophrenia, are having an actual experience: just not in this dimension of consciousness.

This could be why delusions are so firmly held by people: in a certain dimension of consciousness, these experiences are 'real'. In the new scientific paradigm, our concept of reality has changed. We now understand that nothing in our universe is solid, blurring the distinction between reality and non-reality. In fact it is difficult to say what reality is, the bizarre ideas held by some people might be just as real as those beliefs that we see as normal. (Delusions are unshakable beliefs that are not in keeping with that person's cultural background.)

Someone who understood the importance of this was Jung. Jung's methods were radical; he listened seriously to the bizarre stories his patients told him, instead of dismissing them. In his memoirs, he outlined a case of a young girl who had been severely traumatized by rape and incest until she was no longer able to speak and had become catatonic.[33]

Over a period of weeks, Jung managed to get his patient to speak, whereupon she told him of the elaborate world she had escaped to. Through the process of conversing with her doctor, she engaged with the world again. The girl made a full recovery.

Could this girl have been having a multidimensional experience? Was her consciousness stuck in different frequency range, whilst ignoring the three-dimensional, thus making her appear catatonic and distant?

The diagram Figure 12, shows what might be occurring in such cases. In a bid to escape from emotional trauma, the person becomes uncoupled from the lower frequencies of consciousness that are associated with three-dimensional reality. Their consciousness exists in a pathologically high bandwidth. The experiences are 'real' in the sense that they are being witnessed by their consciousness. By healing the trauma, the person may feel able to move back down to the lower frequencies, and rejoin our world.

This type of shift in the frequencies of a person's consciousness may also be responsible for some other symptoms found in mental illnesses. If we recall in the chapter on the QV, genius can be redefined as being particularly talented at interpreting information held in the QV. What if you are too good? What if information came through so quickly it was troubling you and you felt debilitated? Is this what we are witnessing in a manic episode, someone whose consciousness has gone too far into the field?

Figure 12 – The consciousness of a person escaping three-dimensional reality versus that of a grounded person

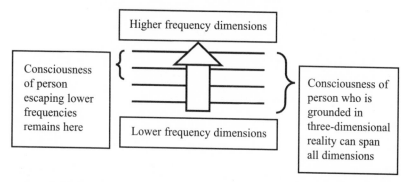

It is a known fact that many people who are considered creative geniuses suffer with episodes of hypomania or mania. Sometimes the illness is accompanied by periods of depression. Is this the swing back into lower frequencies, even lower than what could be considered normal? These swings of consciousness are reflected in the brain, but the brain does not generate them. Hence pharmaceutical agents can indeed help bring moods back to balance, but they are not acting on the cause itself, which lies beyond the molecule.

Other symptoms of mental illness are paranoia and grandiosity. Our model may also explain these. In Chapter six, we discussed the work of David Bohm and his views on non-locality. He said that the universe is connected at a deep level. We are outgrowths from the one fundamental source, but we appear separate. We are unified and separate at the same time.

Esoteric teachings often label this separation as ego and view it as something to lose as soon as possible. In fact, it is probably healthy to have a degree of separation from the unified whole, as symptoms such as paranoia may be a result of a person's consciousness falling too deeply into unity. At this deep level of the universe, there is less separation and more unity, so someone who can operate at this level might mistake information in the field as pertaining to them, when actually it has nothing to do with them.

The person has no sense of self and of boundaries in consciousness. All information in the field then becomes relevant. This can play out in various ways such as feelings of grandeur or self-importance, as if they have a special mission. They can literally feel the whole world, as they move too far in the realm of the collective field.

These sorts of processes also illustrate the fine line between spiritual practices and these types of symptoms. For example, it is very important for a person to be grounded when learning how to channel. This keeps a person in awareness of the three-dimensional frequencies of consciousness. Good teachers of such arts will incorporate some balancing principles into their instruction.

Lil' devil

Some of the strangest manifestations of mental illness are visual and auditory hallucinations. People can sometimes hear voices giving them instructions that they feel compelled to obey. How does this happen?

As stated before, the current theories of illnesses, such as schizophrenia, are based around biochemical imbalances of the brain. Researchers have also identified a gene linked to the illness. Again we are back to the question of how do dumb molecules know what to do? How do biochemical processes translate into an actual voice, sometimes with a full personality associated?

An extremely controversial answer is that these voices actually belong to someone! Just as higher entities may be channeled and the voice is experienced as other than the person's own, lower entities may also be heard, but their information is not so nice and may even be destructive.

There has been a long tradition of mental illness being caused by demonic possession. Although this idea has been relegated to the past, can we really say that we are any closer to a full scientific explanation of hallucinations? Yes we can examine the brain and the genome for molecular clues, but how do these translate to a full explanation of symptoms?

According to the principles discussed in this chapter, it is possible for beings of consciousness to exist in another dimension to ours, but in a different level to that of angels. These beings are traditionally called entities. Interestingly, Keith Wakelam reports an incident when a persistent reading of 300Hz was produced, which he speculated might be due to an entity, although this result is far from conclusive proof.[34]

If entities exist, they could become attracted to people with emotional difficulties through the principles of SVP. The consciousness frequencies caused by emotional trauma may somehow attract them. The influence of these entities may cause some of these mysterious symptoms present in schizophrenia, such as thought control and insertion. Because they are not 'physical' as such, they exert their influence through the modality of thought. Hence voices seem to come from outside the person, but appear 'all in the mind'.

One of the most distressing aspects of hallucinations is that they appear very real to that person, but nobody else can see or hear them. Medicine currently dismisses hallucinations as being totally unreal and the manifestations of abnormal brain activity. In this new explanation of mental illness, these hallucinations are real. They exist in a frequency dimension of consciousness that is being interpreted only by the person in question.

The Oscar-winning film, *A Beautiful Mind*, based on the book by Sylvia Nasar, told the story of the Nobel prizewinning mathematician John Nash and his struggle with schizophrenia.[35] His story demonstrates some of the principles we are discussing. Firstly, his achievements are classic examples of going deeply into the QV. He is able to see relationships from a higher dimensional perspective and effortlessly see patterns that nobody else can.

His ability to look into other dimensions also manifests as seeing people who nobody else can see and the feeling of having a very important mission. To Nash, these people and situations are real. He himself said, "The ideas I had about supernatural beings come to me the same way that my mathematical ideas did. So I took them seriously."

One of the breakthrough moments in his life occurred when Nash realized that one of the people he sees, a little girl, never grows up; she remains as child. He also never truly lost his ability to see her; he just chooses to ignore her.

If we apply our model of mania to Nash's illness, we could say that his consciousness fell too deeply into the sense of unity in the QV, so felt a huge burden of responsibility for the world. The people he sees, such as the girl, do exist, simply not in this dimension. The dimension exists out of normal space and time; hence the girl never grows up. He decides one day to ignore the hallucinations, thus shifting his own consciousness. It is this mechanism that is key to Nash's recovery.

Some people claim to have success at treating mental illnesses by actively removing entities surrounding a person. One such organization is the Hickman Academy. It is important to note that their therapists usually see the problem cases: the ones where conventional routes have already been taken without success. Occasionally, psychiatrists have also discovered the success of such therapies, such as Dr Alan Sanderson in the UK.[36]

This is simply a start in examining how psychiatry may be able to benefit from insights we are gaining from physics. This new scientific era may finally provide some answers to the mysteries of the human condition.

The above account is not meant to be a criticism of the medical profession, nor of pharmaceutical companies adopting the biochemical model of mental illness; both bodies are working within the scientific remit currently employed by our society. It is meant to be an exploration as to the scientific basis for symptoms found in mental illness, which have remained mysterious until now.

References for Chapter 9

1. Hagelin J. *Manual for a perfect government*. (Maharishi

University of Management Press) 1998.

2. Kaku M. Essay: Unifying the Universe. *New Scientist.* 16 April 2005; 48.

3. Hunt V. Electronic Evidence of Auras and Chakras in UCLA study. *Brain/Mind Bulletin.* 1978; 3:9.

4.Wakelam KB. *Biofeedback and the Human Energy Field.* (2000) www.trans4mind.com/psychotechnics. [E-book downloaded November 2003.]

5. Korotkov K. *Aura and Consciousness.* (Kultura) 1998.

6. Tiller WA. *Science and human transformation.* (Pavior) 1997.

7. McCraty R, Atkinson M, Tiller WA. New Electrophysiological Correlates Associated with Intentional Heart Focus. *Subtle energies and energy medicine journal.* 1993; 4:3: 251-262.

8. McCraty R. Atkinson M, Tomasino D, Tiller W.A. The Electricity of Touch: Detection and Measurement of Cardiac Energy Exchange Between People.

In: Karl H. Pribram, ed. *Brain and Values: Is a Biological Science of Values Possible.* (Mahwah, NJ: Lawrence Erlbaum Associates, Publishers) 1998; 359-379.

9. Tiller WA. *Science and human transformation.* (Pavior) 1997.

10. Ibid.

11. McCraty R. Atkinson M, Tomasino D, Tiller W.A. The Electricity of Touch: Detection and Measurement of Cardiac Energy Exchange Between People.

In: Karl H. Pribram, ed. *Brain and Values: Is a Biological Science of Values Possible.* (Mahwah, NJ: Lawrence Erlbaum Associates, Publishers) 1998; 359-379.

12. Pond D. ed. *Universal Laws Never Before Revealed.*

(Infotainment world Books) 1995.

13. Ibid.

14. Strogatz S. *Sync* (Penguin Allen Lane) 2003.

15. Kaku M. *Hyperspace.* (Oxford Paperbacks) 1995.

16. Plato, Waterfield R (Ed). *Republic.* (Oxford Paperbacks) 2004.

17. Vincente M, Arntz W, Chasse B. *What the Bleep do we know?* [DVD]. (Revolver Entertainment) 2005.

18. Randall L. *Warped Passages.* (Allen Lane) 2005..

19. Chown M. It came from another dimension. *New Scientist.* 18 December 2004; 30- 33.

20. Wakelam KB. *Biofeedback and the Human Energy Field.* (2000). www.trans4mind.com/psychotechnics. [E-book downloaded November 2003].

21. Virtue D. *Angel Visions.* (Hay House) 2000.

22. Cooper D. *Angel Inspiration.* (Hodder Mobius) 2001.

23. Mack JE. *Abduction.* (Ballantine Books) 1995.

24. Mack JE. *Passport to the cosmos.* (Crown) 1999.

25. Von Daniken E. *Chariots of the Gods.* (Souvenir Press) 1990.

26. Faulkner RO. *The Ancient Egyptian Pyramid Texts 1910.* (Kessinger) 2004; Line 458.

27. Marciniak B. *Bringers of the Dawn.* (Bear and Company) 1992.

28. Courtney H. *Divine Intervention.* (Cico books) 2005.

29. Warter C. *Recovery of the Sacred.* (Health communications Inc) 1994.

30. Plato, Tarrant H (Ed) *The Last Days of Socrates* (Penguin Classics) 2003.

31. Saint Joan, Trask R W. *Joan of Arc: in her own words.* (Turtlepoint press) 1996.

32. Jung CG. *Memories, Dreams, Reflections*. (Fontana Press)1995.

33. Ibid.

34. Wakelam KB. *Biofeedback and the Human Energy Field*. (2000) www.trans4mind.com/psychotechnics. [E-book downloaded November 2003].

35. Nasar S. *A Beautiful Mind*. (Faber & Faber) 1999.

36. Sanderson A. Spirit Releasement therapy in a case featuring depression and panic disorder. *European Journal of clinical hypnosis*. 1998; 4: 196-205.

Part IV

The Black Hole Principle

Chapter 10

The Beginner's Guide to
the Universe

So far in this book, we have discussed principles that already exist within the realm of science, albeit with novel applications: using Superstring Theory to explain the possible existence of angels, for example.

These last few chapters contain science that builds upon all the previous ideas in this book, but treads new ground. This culminates in a description of the universe, called the Black Hole Principle, which is simple, elegant and original, but also fits the observational evidence, makes testable predictions and has a mathematical counterpart.

Einstein is often quoted as having said that the problems of the world cannot be solved with the same thinking that created them. Every single scientific leap we have taken has required a novel way of thinking, a new consciousness.

This is the exact opposite of what is commonly found in science. Many tend to stay within the safe ground that has been trodden before. This also tends to be the safest way to secure research funding. The trouble is, this has led to a stagnation of science. As mentioned in the preface, people are already ringing the death knell for science, claiming that all there is to know about our universe has already been discovered.[1]

How have we entered into this situation? Is there something that we are missing? What was so special about those previous giant leaps of science? Or has everything really been discovered?

If we examine the methods behind these breakthroughs, we find that some were made without the help of big research funding. It seems that the power of thought alone has been responsible for some of the great leaps of science. Many have taken this to mean the power of the imagination. This assumption has led to modern physics being filled with a plethora of exotic ideas from M-theory to loop quantum gravity, as physicists imagine many possible scenarios for the workings of our universe.

How do we distinguish which is the true picture of our universe? Are breakthroughs in science found by these types of machinations, or are they the results of leaps in consciousness itself? The evidence from the past suggests the latter.

We always view history through the lens of the present. Today it is difficult for many to understand how the science of the past utilized the skill of personal, inner development as part of the process. A variety of evidence suggests that in the past, mysticism and science were one. People gained knowledge of the universe by direct conscious experience of it; a method that is currently ignored as a way of obtaining knowledge. In fact, this will seem ludicrous to many of today's scientific community.

We have spent some time in previous chapters describing the mechanics of these types of processes, of taking information from the holographic quantum vacuum and of transcendent experiences. It is through this direct knowledge and experience that humanity has made its major leaps in wisdom.

This is not the type of knowledge that can be gained from speculation or intellectual pursuits. It is the result of receiving information from the quantum vacuum that contains holographic information, as discussed in Chapter 7. Various practices, such as meditation, can improve a person's ability to be a receiver, but people who do not employ these methods can also gain spontaneous insights. This is the type of practice found in the ancient mystery schools and philosophical academies, whose records emphasize a type of inner knowledge.[2]

As initiates became more advanced in their training, their ability to obtain knowledge from the universe improved. Reading the accounts of such disciplines in this light, it becomes clear that inner knowledge was the goal. The consciousness of the initiate began to expand through such practices and they were able to perceive aspects of the universe that are normally hidden.

Nature reveals itself to those who are able to receive it! As modern science has evolved from these early sources, we can argue that this is how science has always moved forward: through direct insight and revelation. This can only be achieved by what is known as the mystical experience of direct knowledge of Nature. This is the method behind all of the great leaps of science: a shift in consciousness that allows direct perception of the universe.

This also seems to be the method used by one of the world's most celebrated figures, Leonardo Da Vinci. He discussed at length the difference between those who go directly to Nature for knowledge and those who simply act as intermediaries between those who do and the rest of the world. He was so scornful of the latter he compared them to cattle![3]

This method of direct insight of the universe does not negate the current methods of science. What we describe as the scientific method, which involves experimentation, is still essential, as only this can validate the insights gained. Hence Einstein did 'thought experiments' first and then proved his insights using mathematics later. Others would prove his thoughts by experiment. Both methods are essential to science, but only the method of direct insight allows us to make the great conceptual leaps.

Many will find it abhorrent to even contemplate that the big scientific leaps have occurred in this way. It is ironic that Isaac Newton, so long thought to be the originator of the mechanical worldview, was actually deeply spiritual and was known to be fluent in alchemical and esoteric principles. He probably also practiced methods of gaining direct insight into the universe.

The evidence obtained from his notebooks, which were discovered in 20th century, show that God was essential to Newton's view of the universe. This was not, however, the picture of God as a white-bearded man in the sky who tends to get angry. Newton's description of God in his landmark book, *Principia*, is as follows:

"He is utterly void of all body and bodily figure, and can

therefore neither be seen, nor heard, nor touched; nor ought he to be worshipped under the representation of any corporeal thing. We have ideas of his attributes, but what the real substance of anything is we know not."[4]

Newton's God is clearly the unknowable force that has been 'described' in mystical traditions old and new for thousands of years. Newton also clearly knew that this force could never be adequately described; it can only be experienced. People interpreting *Principia* have often been puzzled by this mysticism. Many have used the mathematical sections and disregarded the spiritual elements. Yet it is clear from the amount of writing he did on the subject that Newton's focus was on his spiritual or alchemical development. Without this, his science would not have emerged, which would have led to a very different modern world, as we use his science in our daily lives.

Another celebrated figure, Michael Faraday, succeeded in realizing the laws of electromagnetism because he wanted to understand Nature, not just presuming what Nature does and then making the math fit, which is what most people believe science is. In fact, he described how he could almost 'see' the curved lines of electromagnetic force. Was he describing the classical inner vision of the mystic, which is not with the eyes, but with consciousness itself? Of course, he went on to rigorously test his insights by experiment.[5]

Albert Einstein changed the world simply by thought. Was he really just 'thinking' or was he actually experiencing the universe by moving his consciousness to gain information? Neils Bohr supposedly saw the structure of the atom in a dream, a mode of revelation that also occurred to Kekule who saw the structure of the benzene ring whilst dreaming.[6,7]

We have so much evidence that scientific leaps are taken, not by intellectual ponderings, but by revelation, by listening to the universe and understanding its secrets. We discussed the mechanism behind this process in Chapter 8. This is so far removed from the way modern science is done. Yet here we are at the beginning of a new century and again we are facing a situation where people are commenting that science has come to an end, just as they did in the last century, before Einstein's publications of 1905. In fact, Lord Kelvin is quoted as saying at the time, "There is nothing new to be discovered in physics now. All that remains is more and more precise measurements."[8]

If we continue with our current scientific methods, allowing one 'theory of everything' to come into vogue, to simply be replaced by another, is there any guarantee that we will ever really find the answers to the big questions such as how did the universe originate? How can we find new answers by using the same methods?

People within its own establishment have not always solved the problems of science. I believe the same is happening now. We have gone as far as we can within the material paradigm. What we now call science is simply the examining of smaller and smaller aspects of Nature in order to obtain university funding or technology. Is anybody making those giant leaps of consciousness that have always taken us forward in science?

We need people who firmly understand that consciousness is fundamental to the universe: people who know that the universe is intelligent, because they experience it as such. Like Pythagoras,

Newton and Faraday, they have the skill of merging their consciousness with the universe in order to gain insights into its workings. Unlike the above, we now have the advantage of many more years of mechanistic science. We have come full circle; this is an era in which we are going to move forward with a combination of old and new.

There is a growing movement in science, which perhaps began with real fervor in the early 1970s. It started with physicists noticing the similarities between the ideas in the physics of the 20th century and ancient Eastern wisdom. It was aided by the hippy ideals and experimentation of the 1960s. The 1980s saw the appearance of several books describing these ideas. The recent popularity of the film, *What the Bleep do We Know?* shows that this movement grows apace.[9] This is the realm where science is not separate from spirit, where the two worlds are integrated. This is not merely the philosophy of ancient times; this is a new path, which fully incorporates the modern scientific era.

Several individuals are now taking this movement even further. Instead of simply combining modern physics with ancient wisdom, they are actually changing our scientific worldview, using the skills of both disciplines in a fully integrated fashion. This is a return to the old intuitive ways of science with the full advantage of modern observational and mathematical methods. The method of gaining information directly from the universe informs this process, but it is essential to then prove the insight for it to be truly in the realms of science and not just esoteric wisdom.

This is different from the science and spirituality movement of the last few decades, because it is revealing new knowledge altogether. People using this method include Nassim Haramein, who has been having visions since childhood which inspired him to be a physicist, Lynneclaire Dennis, whose near-death experience revealed so much information to her that she is now in collaboration with physicists and... myself.[10,11]

In the preface to this book, I described the personal experience that gave me the framework for a new vision of reality. This part of the book contains the result of my revelations. The summit of this experience was a powerful vision, which lasted a few moments, but was so complete that it contained many insights. I call this framework for reality the Black Hole Principle (BHP).

I wish to stress that my scientific training has been as a medical doctor and not in physics. This is not meant to be a true physics publication. Nor is it simply an account of channeled information from the quantum vacuum, but a true integrated mix of the two, following in the tradition of those like Einstein and Newton who saw the universal laws first and gained proof afterwards. I ask the reader to both forgive the very basic knowledge that I have of physics, but also to celebrate it, as I truly believe that if I had been fully trained in this subject I would not have had the freedom of mind to gain the insights in the first place.

In 2004, I was delighted to discover that a group of physicists, including Nassim Haramein and Elisabeth Rauscher, had made some very similar conclusions to my own. They have discovered and published a mathematical version of these concepts.[10] I have since found some more people, such as Chaim H Tejman.[12]

Whenever a big discovery is made in science, it is usually found simultaneously by several people, independently of each other. We can understand, from the principles discussed earlier in this book, that this is simply a reflection of the evolution of consciousness. As consciousness itself progresses, more can be revealed to us as a human race. This phenomenon is also a manifestation of the holographic principle; once information is brought into awareness in one part of the universe, it is also becomes available elsewhere.

After I had received the vision, I seemed to be led to many articles containing evidence that supported what I had been shown. These often were the observations of astrophysicists via telescopes orbiting the cosmos. It soon became clear to me that a lot of this data was perplexing to physicists because they have no framework for it. I gradually became convinced that my vision had indeed revealed how the universe works, as the data fitted perfectly. I began to make predictions about what should be observable in the future, if I was right. Gradually, I accumulated proofs of many of these predictions and will present these in later chapters.

Not only did I discover the scientific data that supported my theories, but I also discovered that this information was not actually new: this picture of the universe was already known in ancient times. Throughout these chapters, I will quote from some of the ancient scriptures of the Gnostics and the ancient Taoist philosophers, to demonstrate the similarity between their ideas, which have been gained by direct insight, and this new vision of the cosmos, which is supported by astronomical data. It seems that the universe behaves in a definite way and has certain rules. By intellectualizing on what they might be, one can gain many possible answers, but these may not be the truth of the universe. By directly experiencing the universe we can rediscover the knowledge that was known to the ancient people.

Although the ancients seem to have had such advanced knowledge, perhaps it has been useful that we have forgotten it, so we can we rediscover it through modern scientific methods. This makes it even more powerful, because we have found the same answers almost despite ourselves. The key to this new scientific vision is the basic idea in this book: that consciousness is fundamental to the universe. Once we accept this, then we discover how the data and observations fit simply and effortlessly into a new vision of the cosmos.

References for Chapter 10

1. Horgan J. *The End of Science*. (Broadway) 1997.

2. Plato, Lee D (introduction). *The Republic*. (Penguin Classics) 2003.

3. Da Vinci L, Sun HA. (Ed) *Leonardo's Notebooks*. (Black Dog and Leventhal) 2005.

4. Newton I, Mott A (translator). *Principia*. (Prometheus books) 1995.

5. Bodanis D. $E=MC^2$: *A biography of the world's most famous equation*. (Macmillan) 2000.

6. Black P. *Neils Bohr Dream leads to Nobel Prize*. (Bella Online) http://www.bellaonline.com/articles/art19116.asp [cited Dec 2005].

7. Roberts RM. *Serendipity – accidental discoveries in science*. (John Wiley and sons) 1989.

8. Weisstein EW. *Kelvin, Lord William Thompson*. 1996-2006. http://scienceworld.wolfram.com/biography/Kelvin.html [cited Dec 2005].

9. Vincente M, Arntz W, Chasse B. *What the Bleep do we know?* [DVD]. (Revolver Entertainment) 2005.

10. Haramein N, Rauscher EA. The origin of spin: a consideration of torque and coriolis forces in Einstein's field equations and grand unification theory. *Noetic Journa.l* June 2005; 6:1-4:143-162.

11. Dennis L. *The Pattern.* (Integral Publishing.) 1997.

12. Tejman CH. *United Nature theory: Wave theory.* 2001http://www.grandunifiedtheory.org.il/book1.htm [cited Dec 2005]

Chapter 11

Universal Nutshell

Fashion

At the start of the 21st century, we still have many unanswered questions about our universe. To make matters worse, the more we observe about the universe, the more confused we become. Our modern instruments are revealing data with unexpected anomalies, leading us back to the drawing board regarding how we think our world works.

Modern physics is rife with exotic and contrived theories that desperately strain to make our picture of the universe correspond with this new data. Despite physicists' best mathematical contortions, a definitive theory of everything evades them. Every generation feels sure that they are going to crack the big problem, producing successive theories that rise and fall in fashion. We seem unable to raise one above the rest and keep it there. Hence, Superstring Theory may give way to M-theory or to Loop Quantum gravity etc. Although the mathematics can be manipulated to fit, how do we know if any of these are the true description of our universe?

This part of the book will deal with the branch of physics called cosmology. Cosmology deals with models of the universe and, until recently, was not seen as a serious branch of physics because of the difficulties in testing theories that apply to the entire universe. Even so, cosmologists have enjoyed recent successes due to the appearance of observational data that seems to confirm their most cherished beliefs.

However, as we shall see, not everybody agrees that the universe is done and dusted. In this chapter, we shall be exploring the history of modern cosmology and its successes. We shall go onto explore some of its limitations before discussing the new vision of the cosmos known as the Black Hole Principle.

The universe in a nutshell?

Cosmology deals with the universe on a large scale. This can present some problems, as it is a little difficult to test a hypothesis when you are discussing the creation of the universe itself! Nevertheless, there are certain aspects of cosmology that can be tested. This has culminated in what is known as the 'standard model' of cosmology, in which all the known data has been put together to provide a picture of our universe: how it was created and how it evolved.

Included in this standard model is one of the big successes of modern cosmology: Big Bang theory. The idea that the universe began with a Big Bang is so embedded in modern culture that we tend to forget it is relatively recent. Before Big Bang theory emerged, there were many other hypotheses of how the universe began and evolved. In the early 20th century, physicists commonly believed that the universe exists as a steady state and is neither expanding nor contracting.

This all changed in 1929 when Edward Hubble observed that distant galaxies are moving away from us in all directions. He realized that the universe is expanding, a prediction made by Alexander Friedmann some years earlier. The discovery of the expanding universe led people to wonder where it was expanding from. It was the charismatic Ukrainian-born George Gamow who first proposed the modern Big Bang theory in 1948. Gamow said that the universe was originally very hot and dense, before expanding and cooling over billions of years.

During the 1960s, two US physicists, Bob Dicke and Jim Peebles, set out to prove Gamow right. According to his theory, we should be able to detect the signature of the early universe in the form of microwave radiation. (Microwaves are light waves with a wavelength of a centimeter.)

Unfortunately for them, two other physicists, Arno Penzias and Robert Wilson, beat them to it, bagging themselves the Nobel Prize. In the case of Penzias and Wilson, they discovered the signal completely by accident. They had originally mistaken the reading as being caused by bird droppings on their instruments! It was only when they happened to hear that Dicke and Peebles were looking for the cosmic microwave background that they realized they had found it.

Their discovery was proof that the early universe was indeed as hot and dense as Gamow had predicted – a Big Bang had occurred.

Because of this success, all other contenders for a model of the universe have faded away. Today, physicists speak with confidence about tracing the universe back to the very first few seconds of its existence. The current story of the universe goes something like this...

It's a rap

Moments after the Big Bang, the seed of everything within the universe had already been created. The early universe also witnessed a great cosmic battle as antimatter collided with matter and became annihilated. The victor went on to create everything in the universe that we see around us: the stars, galaxies and ourselves.

For billions and billions of years, the universe cooled and expanded. As it did, tiny differences in the fabric of the early universe were exaggerated and became particles of dust. This dust grew into the stars and planets, forming the universe that we know today. Eventually, the attractive forces between all these celestial bodies will overpower the force of expansion, perhaps causing an inward movement: a Big Crunch.

In the early 1980s, Alan Guth at the Massachusetts Institute of Technology, proposed a modification of this picture of the Big Bang. According to Guth's Inflationary Theory, after the initial explosion, the universe went through a period of rapid acceleration before it started to slow down. This approach resolves certain problems found with the standard Big Bang model, although some issues remain, as we shall see later.

Nevertheless, cosmologists are confident that they have the universe all wrapped up. They even construct computer models that can 'build' a universe; such is their confidence in their knowledge of the universal laws.

Towards the end of the 20th century, it seemed as if our most fundamental questions about our universe had been answered. We knew where we were from, where we were and where we were headed. As the century drew to a close, data from cosmological observations began to throw doubt on this model. Cosmology entered a period of turmoil, which it is still in today. It is also one of the most exciting times in scientific history, because the rules are being rewritten.

Einstein's biggest blunder

In 1998, several teams around the world were examining data from distant supernovae. They were looking at a property called redshift. This tells them how far away something is to Earth.

If you have ever walked beside a road and heard a car rush past, you will know that it makes a different noise as it is approaching you from when it is moving away from you. The different noise is due to the wavelengths radiated by the car becoming longer as it moves away. The noise then appears to be of lower frequency. The police use this principle, called the Doppler effect, when testing the speed of cars; they send out radio waves, and then measure the frequency of the waves that bounce off the car.

Cosmologists use a similar principle when measuring the distance of galaxies from the Earth. Light radiation from distant galaxies has taken so long to reach our planet that their wavelengths have shifted into the red part of the electromagnetic spectrum.

What they found in 1998 was very surprising and revealed that we may not have everything sussed after all. As expected, these distant supernovae are moving away from us. However, instead of slowing down, as we would expect, they are speeding up.[1,2] We are living in a runaway universe! What is causing this unexpected behavior? Something must be opposing the gravitational forces pulling objects together, which should be enough to slow down the expansion of the universe.

This unexpected finding led to a revival of one of Einstein's ideas that he had abandoned and called his biggest blunder. Anyone who has ever fudged their work will be glad to hear that even Einstein did the same. In fact, physics contains a few 'fudge factors' that allow equations to fit how we *think* the universe should operate.

In Einstein's day, people thought the universe was static and neither expanding nor contracting. However, this is not what Einstein discovered in the mathematics of general relativity. So he added a fudge factor known as the cosmological constant in order to make it fit the existing static model of the universe. This factor would oppose the gravitational attraction of the contents of the universe that made it collapse inwards. Einstein added a constant, an antigravity force that would oppose the force of gravity and keep the universe in a steady state.

A few years later, Edward Hubble made his discoveries and showed that the universe was actually expanding. No fudge factor was needed to oppose the gravitational pull of the galaxies. Einstein called the cosmological constant his biggest blunder.[3]

Yet, as always with Einstein, our opinion of him is so great that even when he thought he was making a mistake, we view it as the brilliant move of a genius. When it was realized that the universe is actually accelerating away and not slowing down, a new factor opposing gravity was needed. The cosmological constant was revived as it represented the 'pushing away' force!

But what was responsible for the universe running away like this? The visible matter that we see should cause the opposite effect: a slowing down of expansion of the universe. Cosmologists came up with the imaginative name of *dark energy* to describe this exotic pushing force.[4]

The starlite desperation

As it happens, the label of dark energy did not take a huge imaginative leap; we already had a term called *dark matter*.[5] We have known for some time that we are unaware of most of the content of the universe. In fact, about 98 per cent of the universe is unknown to us. We can see visible matter, the type that appears in stars etc. But calculations tell us that this is a woefully small amount compared to the vastness of space and the mass that the universe should contain. We know that it should contain more mass, because we can witness its effects in terms of the gravity it produces. Nobody can see it; it appears to be missing.

Cosmologists have called this missing matter *dark matter*. We see the effects of dark matter indirectly in the formation of galaxies; something shapes them through a gravitational pull. Dark matter appears around a galaxy in the form of a so-called *dark matter halo*.

At first, it was thought that the dark matter might be responsible for the runaway universe, creating a force opposing gravity and blowing the universe apart. However, there did not seem to be enough dark matter in the universe to be responsible for that sort of effect. So, cosmologists creatively invented the term *dark energy* for the mysterious repulsive force that is causing the expansion of the universe to accelerate.

One of the contenders for dark energy is the energy of the quantum vacuum (QV). We have discussed the QV in detail in Chapter 7. As we recall, empty space is not empty at all, but filled with virtual particles popping in and out of existence. The QV is a potential source of energy and was considered, at first, to be the source of dark energy. Trouble is, when all the potential energy of the vacuum was added up it turned out to be limitless and that just did not make sense.[6]

When certain aspects of the QV were excluded from the calculations, the figure was still too large, a factor of 10^{123} too large. This is seen as one of the biggest mismatches in physics, described by Nobel Laureate, Steven Weinberg as "the worst failure of an order-of-magnitude estimate in the history of science."[7] If the vacuum energy is really so large, surely it would be blowing the universe apart at so fast a rate that you would not even be able to see the light from your own hand in front of your face? As we have discussed, this situation has led to physicists like Sean Carroll suggesting that the vacuum energy is that large, but is hidden from us in hyperspace.[8] The real cause of dark energy remains mysterious at the present moment.

Bang bang

Big Bang theory has never been without its hitches. It relies on the extremely delicate balance between the amount of matter within the early universe and the rate of its expansion. There is always the danger of collapse due to the mutual attraction between the contents of the universe. This balancing act is sometimes expressed as a ratio called Omega. For the universe to have evolved as it did, Omega has to have a value of one, or very close to it.[9] This has resulted in what is known as a flat universe, meaning that out of all the shapes that the universe could have taken, it had to be flat.

It is only the flat universe, which contains a balance between the density of the matter contained in it and the rate of expansion, which could have behaved in this way. Russian scientist, Alexander Friedmann, who may be seen as the father of modern cosmology, made these conclusions ten years before Edward Hubble provided the proof that the universe was expanding. The trouble is, a flat universe is extremely unstable; how has it managed to survive billions of years? This puzzle is known in cosmology as *the flatness problem*.[10]

Another issue plaguing cosmologists about the Big Bang is called the *horizon problem*.[11] With our modern telescopes we can view deep into space to see areas of the universe that are 24 billion light years apart. These areas are similar in consistency and temperature, with similar distribution of galaxies etc. However, the universe is only about 12 billion years old and light has not had time to travel from one side to another. Why is the universe so homogenous?

In the early universe, light was traveling at a finite speed from the original source that 'banged.' As it spreads out, the limitation of its reach is called a horizon. This is similar to how we can see limits of the Earth's surface as a horizon when we look around us.

It follows that the area of the universe reached by one horizon has no communication with another area of the universe reached by another horizon. Light would not have had time to reach all these different areas. The universe should have many areas that have developed differently in those early days, when each part was separate from another. These parts would have developed independently from each other, leading to patches of the universe that look very different from each other even now. Except this is not what we observe; we see that the universe looks very smooth.

Figure 13 - The Horizon problem

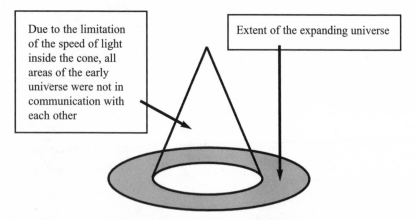

Due to the limitation of the speed of light inside the cone, all areas of the early universe were not in communication with each other

Extent of the expanding universe

Both the issues of the flatness problem and the horizon problem are solved to a certain extent by Guth's Inflationary Theory.[12] The rapid expansion of the early universe would have allowed for all parts to be in communication. Guth also realized that this early inflationary state would allow for the expression of a force that opposed gravity, like the cosmological constant described earlier. This would dominate the early days of expansion, but then gravity would kick in and the rate would slow down.

With solutions to conundrums such as these, it is no wonder that Inflationary Theory has boosted the reputation of cosmology. But is it true; is Inflation the true picture of the early universe? Nobody really knows for sure. Even if Inflation Theory is correct, it is not without its hitches. The question remains as to what started this period of rapid expansion. It also requires some carefully chosen parameters; the conditions of the universe appear to have to been handpicked with great precision.

Why does the universe require those quantities? Why did it start in the first place? Neither the simple Big Bang model, nor Inflationary Theory can answer these problems. There are some stirrings of alternatives to Inflationary Theory by Cambridge physicist, Neil Turok, and others.[13] One of these solutions, though radical indeed, provides us with the basis of the rest of our adventure through *Punk Science*.

Anarchy in the UK

The United Kingdom has often hosted the spirit of rebellion, perhaps as a response to neat little cucumber sandwiches and afternoon tea. It was within these shores that a group of physicists, led by Joao Magueijo of Imperial College, London, came up with a radical alternative to Inflationary Theory. The idea seemed to drop out of the sky whilst Magueijo was nursing a hangover, a nice demonstration of the principles behind genius described in previous chapters.

He suddenly asked; what if the speed of light was variable? In the early universe, what if light traveled faster than it does now? If this were the case, it would have had time to traverse the entire universe, making everything as smooth as we see it today. This theory is called Variable Speed of Light (VSL) and has been met with both praise and cries of heresy for daring to contradict Einstein's most sacrosanct law.[14]

The constancy of the speed of light has been enshrined in physics ever since Einstein published his paper on Special Relativity in 1905. Within a few elegant pages, he stated that the speed of light is the same for all observers no matter what speed they are traveling. Everything moves relative to this one constant of Nature, which stays the same. The actual speed is about 300,000km per second. The famous experiments by Michelson and Morley, who actually set out to prove the existence of the ether, measured the speed of light as being constant, thus disproving the existence of ether and greatly influencing the young Einstein. Since then, we have become so confident of our measurements of light's speed, that we have redefined the meter as the distance that light travels in a vacuum in 1/299792458 of a second.

The constancy of the speed of light is now a fundamental aspect of modern physics; to question it seems insane. Yet, Magueijo does not just stop there. Using the Kaluza-Klein model of an extra dimension of space, he explains how the light that we measure could actually be a projection from a higher dimension. Light could be curled around in an extra dimension and we catch it at an angle as it curls around, thus giving us the illusion that light is the speed that we think it is.

Magueijo and others, such as Giovanni Amelino-Camelia, have realized that the speed of light could change at very high frequencies.[15] In a 2002 interview with journalist, Robin Wright, Magueijo states that it would actually make more sense if light were infinite![16]

Magueijo, although rebellious, is a mainstream physicist. He is suggesting that light could be infinite and that we simply see a shadow of a higher dimensional process. He and others have said that the speed of light could be higher at higher frequencies, thus giving an alternative to Inflation in the hot early universe.

So far, in this chapter, we have described some of the current problems in cosmology and briefly described a theory that may solve some of them: VSL. We have now reached the edge of mainstream physics and are about to enter into new territory. What happens when we combine the idea in VSL with the key idea of the entire book: that consciousness is fundamental to reality? The result is something that I call *Conscious Relativity*.

Conscious Relativity

This concept provides the foundations for the rest of this book and for the understanding of the new vision of the cosmos, which is to follow. In a way, it is simply a new look at Einstein's theory of Special Relativity, but the combination of Magueijo's comments and the previous ideas in this book, creates a new perspective.

According to Special Relativity, nothing can go faster than the speed of light and the speed of light is the same for all observers no matter how fast they are moving. If you stop and think about it, this is rather counterintuitive; we are used to catching up with something if we speed up towards it, such as chasing after a friend you have spotted in the street so that you can talk to her.

With light, it is a different story. No matter how fast you move, you never catch up with it and strangely, even if you are traveling at

299,999 km/s yourself, if you were to measure light as you are hurtling along, light would still be 300,000km/s: the same as it would be if you were to trundle along at 2km/hour. Apparently, Einstein originally dreamt about this bizarre behavior of light whilst still a teenager. The contents of his dream went on to become one of the mainstays of modern physics.

Yet how can light behave so differently to objects in our everyday reality? Special relativity actually includes a subtle caveat that provides us with a clue. It says that nothing with *mass* can travel at the speed of light. As an object approaches such a speed, it also approaches infinite mass. It therefore never actually reaches light speed, no matter how fast it moves. The heavier it gets, the less it can move and so on, until infinity.

However, light does not have mass. Light does not seem to be an object as such, but a type of movement or energy. In the days of Einstein, the particle of light, the photon, was the only known particle to have no mass. Since then, we have discovered that the neutrino is also massless and is known to move at the speed of light. The caveat of mass never breaking the speed limit remains extremely important, but we now know that massless objects may do so.

Not only is the photon massless, it also exists out of space and time. How can something have a speed and be out of space and time? I believe that light is not actually something moving at all. What we measure as the speed of light is actually the limitations of our perception of this dimension of reality.

Light, as Magueijo says, is limitless.[17] It is simply expressed in the different vibrations of all the different dimensions. As many researchers across the world are now realizing, the speed of light is related to the frequency of vibration you happen to find yourself at. The higher frequencies in the early universe or in higher dimensions appear to have a higher speed of light. It is really simply an expression of the vibrational limit of perception for each dimension.

Hence, you can never catch up with a photon. You are not actually catching up with a 'thing' at all, but a limitation of vibration of consciousness. Within this limitation, consciousness takes on the form that we are familiar with, the world of electrons and other particles with mass. Beyond this limitation, mass does not exist.

Looking back to Einstein, this idea is actually present all along because he speaks of the speed of light relative to the observer. The observer, something that is perceiving, or consciousness, is already written into Special Relativity. We can rewrite the speed of light as our perception limit or Perception Horizon.

Beyond the Perception Horizon

It is now time to move beyond the Perception Horizon. When we do, we start to find the secrets to creation itself. By now, you may have realized that we have been ignoring most of our universe, that which lies beyond our Perception Horizon and out of our three-dimensional reality. Most of our universe lies in higher dimensions, in vibrations that are too subtle for us to see.

This is not the realm of mass and, because we are used to dealing with solid objects, we have totally missed this point. We try to describe the universe in terms of the familiar three-dimensional realm. Hence, most of the universe remains invisible to us. Except to the mystics: those who have received what is known as enlightenment. They are the ones who can shift their perception into these realms and catch glimpses of this subtle light, which has been described in esoteric traditions throughout the world and all history. They have this ability, because the part of them that is consciousness does not have mass and is able to move beyond the limitations of this world. This ability is within all of us, but some simply have not realized it.

We can now understand why 97 per cent of our universe is a mystery to us. We have named it dark matter and dark energy. In reality, these are the realms of light beyond the Perception Horizon. If we could perceive it, we would know that what we have called dark is not dark at all, it is brilliantly light. And the brightest of all objects is what we previously called a black hole. This is where we go next in our exploration of creation.

References to Chapter 11

1. Perlmutter S et al. Discovery of a supernova explosion at half the age of the universe and its cosmological implications. *Nature*. 1 January 1988; 391: 51-54. xxx.lanl.gov/abs/astro-ph/9712212.
2. Riess AG et al. Observational Evidence for an accelerating universe and a cosmological constant. *Astronomical Journal*. September 1998; 116:3:1009-1038. xxx.lanl.gov/abs/astro-ph/9805201.
3. Kraus LM. Cosmological Antigravity. *Scientific American*. January 1999; 35-41.
4. Battersby S. Dark energy. *New Scientist*. 5 April 2003; 30-33.
5. Peterson J. The Universe in balance. *New Scientist*. 16 December 2000; 26-29.

6. Chown M. The Fifth element. *New Scientist.* 3 April 1999; 29-32.

7. Ibid.

8. Carroll SM, Mersini L. Can We Live in a Self-Tuning Universe? *Phys. Rev.* 2001; D 64:124008; hep-th/0105007.

9. Magueijo J. *Faster than the speed of light.* (Arrow) 2004.

10. Ibid.

11. Ibid.

12. Ibid.

13. Khoury J, Ovrut BA, Steinhardt PJ, Turok N. The Ekypyrotic Universe: Colliding branes and the origin of the Hot Big Bang. *Phys.Rev.* 2001; D64: 123522 http://arxiv.org/abs/hep-th/0103239.

14. Magueijo J. *Faster than the speed of light.* (Arrow) 2004.

15. Amelino-Camelia G. Double Special Relativity. *Nature.* 2002; 418: 34-35. http://arxiv.org/abs/gr-qc/0207049

16. William R. Speed of Light (*abc.science*) 2000. http://www.abc.net.au/rn/science/ss/stories/s212674.htm [cited Dec 2005].

17. Ibid.

Chapter 12

Back in Black

In the previous chapter we have examined the current model of cosmology and looked at some of the problems that have started to arise within it. What follows is a new and radical description of the universe. It builds on everything that we have discussed before, but goes on to describe a unifying principle of the universe that is elegant, simple and coherent.

Furthermore, a range of observational evidence will be given, which not only gives credence to the model put forward, but also explains some of the mysterious observations seen in our universe, such as high-energy cosmic rays. The model also makes testable predictions, some of which have already proved to be correct. It is called the Black Hole Principle (BHP).

Throughout this book, we have been discussing how the mystical process is the method by which information is obtained from the QV, which holds a holographic store of information. In Chapter 10, we looked at how this process has been vital to the great leaps in science that have occurred over the ages. The principles we are about to explore were also partly obtained with this method of insight, but they have been combined with information found in the domain of academic science. The result is a complete blending of insight with evidence.

Insight without evidence remains in the domain of esoteric knowledge and mysticism. We live in an age where this is not acceptable. Our modern society needs scientific proof through observation and experiment in order to truly accept a model of the universe.

Similarly, remaining purely in the materialistic paradigm cannot solve the big questions in science. Once we free our minds from their restraints, we are able to piece together the true workings of the universe. We can then make sense of the observations that seem anomalous to us. Nature may be absurd, but Nature is also elegant and simple and can be revealed to us if we are ready to listen.

A brief history of black holes

We have mentioned the Black Hole Principle as being central to this book, but what exactly are black holes? Most people have heard about these fascinating objects via science fiction, which contains dramatic depictions of spacecraft being sucked into the center of a black hole by a relentless gravitational pull.

Surprisingly, we have only recently confirmed that black holes actually exist.[1] They were originally a concept that sprung from Einstein's theory of General Relativity that describes how matter and energy bend space-time. People soon speculated as to how far this process could extend. Could space-time become so bent that areas of infinite density are possible?

It was an Indian scientist, Subrahmanyan Chandrasekhar, who realized that a star above a certain mass could collapse, at the end of its lifetime, to an area of infinite density.[2] This mass is known as the Chandrasekhar limit. The result of the catastrophic collapse of such a star would lead to a black hole, a term invented by John Wheeler in 1967.[3] The center of a black hole is an area of infinite density and, therefore, infinite gravity. This led to the notorious image of a black hole sucking in nearby objects to their perilous fate with infinite gravitational pull.

The center of a black hole is called a *singularity*: an area of infinite density and space-time curvature. At such a singularity, the laws of physics break down, rather like the start point of the Big Bang. Not even light can escape from the gravitational pull of the black hole, which is why it is black.

Luckily, these relentless objects are hidden behind an event horizon, which acts as a membrane between the black hole and the outside world. For anything unlucky enough to fall into the *event horizon*, their fate is sealed; the infinite gravitational pull will draw them into the central singularity with no possibility of escape.

The dark and fearsome reputation of black holes remained unaltered until the 1970s, when Stephen Hawking started working on a puzzle. He realized that if black holes did nothing but suck, an imbalance would occur. Objects entering the black hole would be lost forever and with them, the information that they contain. This would then lead to an increase in information on the inside of the black hole, a quality reflected in the area contained within its event horizon. Physicists call this increase in information an increase in entropy. Hawking realized that if the black hole has entropy it must have temperature and therefore must emit radiation. But black holes are not supposed to emit radiation.

In a move that altered the picture of black holes forever, Hawking proposed that they actually slowly evaporate over a long period of time.[4] He combined the principles from quantum theory, describing very small objects, with those of large objects in cosmology to put forward something that is now known as Hawking Radiation.

Cast your mind back to the annihilation-creation process discussed in Chapter 7. According to quantum physics, this process of creating and destroying antimatter and matter particles from light and back again is occurring everywhere in space, even around a black hole.

Hawking realized that at the event horizon of a black hole, it is possible for one of the pair to fall in and the other to escape, thus emitting weak radiation. It is unlikely that we will ever see this happen, as the radiation is too weak for us to detect. At the end of the life of the black hole, it is likely that it will explode, giving out a final massive emission of X-rays and Gamma rays, which are forms of light with higher energy and shorter wavelengths than visible light.

Until recently, Hawking believed that although this radiation could occur, information could never come out of a black hole. He famously rescinded this decision at a high-profile conference in Dublin in 2004.[5] As we shall see, he is not the only one who is questioning the dark reputation of black holes. Since the turn of the Millennium, other physicists have questioned the received wisdom regarding black holes, suggesting that they are not the savage destroyers we once thought they were.

The new black

Even as recently as 20 years ago there was little consensus on whether black holes actually existed. The whole concept started off as a logical conclusion of Einstein's equations rather than from actual observations. However, in recent years, our telescopes have been detecting objects that fit the description of black holes. They have turned out to be more common than first thought, leading some to rethink their role in the universe.

How can we actually see a black hole? They are supposed to be black because no light can escape from them. If light does not escape from them, how can we see them? We are able to detect black holes through a number of telltale signs that allow us to view them indirectly.

a) Density – as expected the black holes are extremely dense. The Hubble telescope has indeed found such objects.

b) Accretion Disc – Material around a black hole including stars, are accelerated to great speeds. The nature of this spinning material is a sign that a black hole is at the center. Some people think that this material becomes so hot that it emits material.

c) Brightness – ironically we can spot these so-called 'black' objects by their brightness. Objects such as quasars emit gamma rays and fast-moving electrons in pulses. The process behind this is poorly understood, but it is now thought that each quasar has a black hole associated with it. Some people think that these emissions are the results of a star that has succumbed to the fatal pull of a black hole and this is its dying gasp.

If these are the telltale signs of black holes then to our surprise, we can see that they come in different sizes. Newly discovered objects such as microquasars are like their larger cousins except scaled down.[6] The same characteristics apply and at their center they have a mini black hole. These objects have been spotted in our own galaxy, suggesting that black holes appear in different sizes throughout our universe.

What is also the subject of intense speculation is the fact that black holes are popping up in one particular place: in the center of galaxies. Our nearest neighborhood galaxies and even our own Milky Way, all display the telltale central bulge indicating the dense central mass at its core: a black hole.[7]

One galaxy with a central black hole may have been acceptable under our old view of black holes, but so many have been found within our own cosmic vicinity that it is now reasonable to believe that every galaxy has a black hole at its core. But how is this possible? Black holes are supposed to be the end points of stars. As such, they should be highly unusual as the universe just isn't old enough for so many suitable stars to have run out of fuel and collapsed into a black hole. This should be the exception rather than the rule. So just what is going on?

One possible explanation must be that black holes have some role in actually creating galaxies. This has led to a new buzzword in black hole cosmology: co-evolution.[8] This implies that galaxies and black holes somehow evolve with each other. Suddenly we are being forced to examine the possibility that black holes are not destructive monsters after all, but creative creatures responsible for shaping our galaxies and therefore the fate of even our own planet.

This creative role forms the basis for understanding the BHP. Conventional physics has taken us this far. In order to truly understand the way in which black holes create our universe we need to combine some of the principles found earlier in this book with the modern observations of black hole behavior.

Let's examine that behavior in more detail by examining a medium-sized black hole, that which is associated with a microquasar.

A mini adventure

Since their discovery, microquasars have provided an opportunity to gain information about black holes. As England's Astronomer Royal, Martin Rees says, "Black holes of different masses behave in qualitatively the same way. Almost everything about them simply scales up or down with the black hole's mass."[9]

Microquasars were first discovered within our own galaxy due to the emission of gamma rays like their larger cousins, quasars. Quasars are known to be bright objects and emit the type of gamma radiation that has the precise energy that is produced by the electron-positron annihilation process. Microquasars have the same patterns, but are much smaller and their processes occur at much faster speeds.

One of their more bizarre characteristics is that they periodically emit jets of very fast moving electrons, so fast that initially they appeared to be breaking the light barrier. This superluminal travel turned out to be an optical illusion, with the true speed being more like 92 per cent of the speed of light. Furthermore, the jets are emitted in a narrow beam, which is proving difficult to explain. Stranger still, the bursts can occur suddenly and then rapidly fall away. This sort of process has earned microquasars the nickname of *the great annihilators* reflecting the involvement of the electron-positron annihilation process.[10]

Physicists are stumped as to what could be creating this behavior.[11] Some theories say they are the result of a star being sucked into the associated black hole, causing some of its material to be ejected very rapidly.[12] Some say that the magnetic field outside the black hole is being whipped up into a frenzy by its rotational energy and emitted.[13] The accretion disc around a black hole containing gas and material is often blamed, as some believe the high speeds of rotation around black holes allows material to become so hot that it is ejected into space from near the vicinity of the black hole.[14] However, the geometry of the ejections indicate that they are from the black hole itself and not the accretion disc. They lie perpendicular to the black hole center.[15] Although some do mathematical contortions to try and prove a case that the accretion disc can cause this sort of outcome, perhaps the math is being forced to fit the observations.[16]

As previously stated, cosmologists are examining microquasars that occur within our own galaxy to provide them with insights as to the behavior of black holes in general. In a similar fashion, let's use the example of the microquasar to explain the Black Hole Principle.

The Black Hole Principle

We now have all the elements in place to understand the Black Hole Principle. To do this we need to recap on some of the principles we have discussed throughout this book. If we recall, some physicists are concluding from quantum physics that consciousness is fundamental to reality. In Chapter 8, we saw how the universe exists as many dimensions of consciousness and how some of these dimensions are invisible to us. In Chapter 11, we discussed how the speed of light may not be the speed limit of the universe at all, but simply the limit of the three-dimensional world and of our perceptions.

Above this limit lies what we previously called dark matter, which we now know to contain the light of higher dimensions. The darkest places of the universe have traditionally been black holes, which contain a core of infinite density, a singularity that is beyond the laws of physics. A black hole is surrounded by an event horizon, beyond which nothing can return.

In the 1970s Stephen Hawking proposed that black holes emit radiation through the annihilation-creation process of matter, antimatter and light that occurs in the quantum vacuum in the vicinity of the event horizon. Recently we have realized that black holes exist at the center of every galaxy. They are also found within our galaxy in objects called microquasars, which mysteriously emit jets of fast particles at almost the speed of light. These objects show signs of the annihilation process.

We are now ready to totally reverse what we know about black holes. Black holes are not destructive; they are the source of creation for the universe. At the center of the black hole is the singularity, which we can now redefine as an infinite source of light. From this infinite source, light makes its journey, stepping down through the higher dimensions that lie beyond our perception, until it reaches the edge of our reality. This is the event horizon of the black hole, delineating what lies above and below the speed of light.

At the event horizon, the splitting of light occurs into matter and antimatter. The matter, in the form of the electron, is emitted in fast-moving jets. Because they have only just reached this dimension from higher dimensions, they are still going at tremendous speeds when they enter our dimension, almost at the speed of light in fact.

Figure 14 – The Black Hole Principle

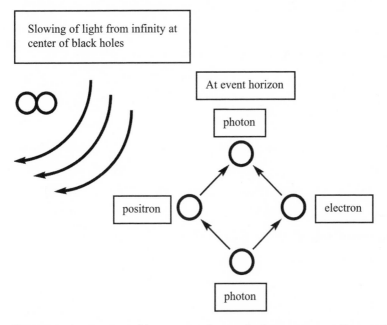

Because we are unable to see beyond the event or Perception Horizon, we see these jets as appearing out of nowhere, or try and explain them in terms of three-dimensional processes.

But that is not all there is to the creation process, nor all there is to explaining what we see emerging from black holes. When light hits our dimension from higher ones, it also produces a component of antimatter. To examine what happens to this component, we need to fall through the looking glass and enter the mirror world.

References for Chapter 12

1. Battersby S. Masters of the Universe. *New Scientist.* 1 April 2000; 32-36.

2. Miller AI. *Empire of the Stars.* (Little, Brown) 2005.

3. Wheeler JA. Our Universe: the known and unknown. *American Scientist.* Spring 1968; 56:1:1-20.

4. Hawking S W. The Quantum Mechanics of Black Holes. *Scientific American.* January 1977; 236: 33-40.

5. Hogan J. Hawking cracks black hole paradox. *New Scientist.* 17 July 2004; 11.

6. Henbest N. The Great Annihilators. *New Scientist.* 1 April 2000; 28-31.

7. Minkel JR. Bye Bye black hole. *New Scientist.* 22 January 2005; 29-33.

8. Britt RR. The New History of Black holes: 'co-evolution' dramatically alters dark reputation. *Space.com* 28th January 2003. http://www.space.com/scienceastronomy/blackhole_history_030128-1.html [cited December 2005].

9. Henbest N. The Great Annihilators. *New Scientist.* 1 April 2000; 28-31.

10. Ibid.

11. Ibid.

12. Gehrels N, Piro L, Leonard JT. The Brightest Explosions in the Universe. *Scientific American.* December 2002; 53- 59.

13. Ibid.

14. Blaes O. A Universe of Discs. *Scientific American.* October 2004; 23- 29.

15. Chicone C. Mashhoon B. Tidal acceleration of Ultrarelativistic

Particles. Astron.Astrophys. 437 (2005) L39-L42
http://www.arxiv.org/abs/astro-ph/0406005.

16. Livio M. Pringle JE King AR. The Disk Jet connection in Microquasars and AGN. Astrophys.J. 593 (2003) 184 http://uk.arxiv.org/abs/astro-ph/0304367.

Chapter 13

Finding Alice

We are familiar with the world of matter, which makes up the world around us. The world of antimatter is more exotic, but not totally unheard of in our society. As we have discussed before, antimatter is now widely used in brain imaging. It has even starred in a best-selling book by Dan Brown, *Angels and Demons*.[1]

We are only able to detect antimatter for a fleeting moment before it disappears. It was first identified in cosmic rays, having been predicted by Paul Dirac. According to the picture of the universe in the Big Bang model, the early universe was filled with antimatter and matter in equal proportions, but for some reason, matter annihilated it and went on to dominate the universe. It is not clear why this should have happened, as it has left the universe in a state of asymmetry. This is not wholly satisfactory for physicists who would rather see a symmetrical universe.[2] As we shall see, the

BHP allows for a very different fate for antimatter, possibly solving this dilemma.

In the 1970s, Professor William Tiller of Stanford University created a greater understanding of the properties of antimatter, which in turn led us to greater understanding of the behavior of black holes. Tiller examined Maxwell's equation of electromagnetism and made some interesting conclusions.[3] In only four equations, James Clerk Maxwell described all the properties of the force of electromagnetism, including how it is related to light. They are elegant, concise and versatile: a very pleasing achievement in physics.

Despite this, Tiller realized that a certain interpretation had been neglected. These were the solutions that gave rise to imaginary numbers. Imaginary numbers in mathematics, as opposed to real numbers that we use commonly use, are those such as $\sqrt{-1}$. Most people's memories of high school mathematics, however vague, will contain the concept that a minus number multiplied by a minus number gives a positive number. Thus squaring a negative number will always give a positive answer. Hence $(-1)^2$ or $(-1) \times (-1) = +1$

$\sqrt{-1}$ is therefore unable to exist as a real number: hence the term imaginary number. Although this may seem to be a very esoteric concept, it is actually quite useful in mathematics. When Tiller examined the imaginary solutions to Maxwell's equations, he realized that they could have very real applications. Combining this with Dirac's work led him to formulate a new model of the universe, which he describes in the book, *Science and Human Transformation*.[4] In this, he reveals the hidden properties of a mirror world. I have adapted the following graph and table from this text.

Figure 15 Energy-velocity diagram illustrating the different qualities of the universe above and below the speed of light and in positive and negative energy (Adapted from *Science and Human Transformation* by William A. Tiller)

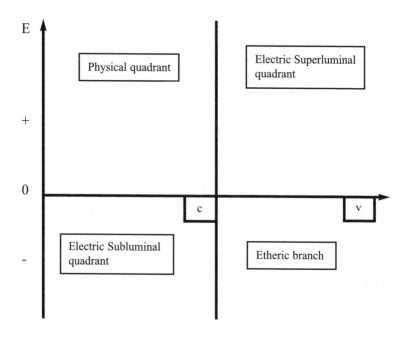

He divided the universe into four spaces. The middle dividing line represents the speed of light. We live in the world of the upper left quadrant where particles have positive mass and exist below the speed of light. However, it is perfectly possible for a world of negative mass below the speed of light to exist. In fact, this is an idea expressed in other areas of physics. William Bonner, of London University, has also explored the laws of gravitational physics to find that they allow for negative mass.[5] Some physicists are even actively looking for it.[6]

However, Tiller also realized that another region was allowed, that of beyond the speed of light. This region contains two types of mass: positive *imaginary* mass, which is in the top right hand corner of the graph. There is another region above the speed of light, that Tiller calls the etheric, that consists of negative mass. This exists in the bottom right hand corner of the graph.

Tiller proposes that there is a mirror universe that exists in a region just next to our world, but the light barrier separates it from us. This idea has not only been proposed by Tiller, but also the like of Nobelists, Tsung Dao Lee and Cheng Ning Yang who realized that symmetry could be restored to the world if a mirror universe exists. This is where we might find the missing right-handed neutrinos mentioned in Chapter 8. In fact, it is postulated that neutrinos actually oscillate between our universe and the mirror one.[6] The following table is adapted from Tiller and shows some of the characteristics of the physical and mirror world.

Physical	**Mirror**
Positive space-time	Negative space-time
Positive mass	Negative mass
Electromagnetic radiation	Magnetoelectric radiation
Inherent vibration of v<c	Inherent vibration of v>c
Gravity	Antigravity

The world is therefore divided into regions. The region we live in is that of below the speed of light and positive energy. It has positive mass and positive space-time. Then there is the region above the speed of light. It contains negative mass and negative space-time.

In the previous chapter we discussed how light is actually infinite but expresses itself in different dimensions and zones according to the rate of vibration of that region. The inherent vibration of our zone is c whilst the one of the mirror universe is c^2. That is the speed of light squared.

The c^2 region is actually the true region of antimatter, which is why we do not detect it for more than a few fractions of a second because it cannot stay in our c region for very long. It belongs in the mirror universe. Antimatter has actually existed alongside our world all along, but because it has been beyond our perception horizon, we have not been able to detect it.

Tiller goes on to explain the process of manifestation from pure consciousness to what we call 'physical'. It is hard to find a modern language to convey what this means as science only tends to consider physical processes. However, in esoteric language this may be seen as the pathway from the spirit realms. As consciousness is fundamental to the universe, it follows that there is a state of the universe that is unmanifest and formless. This is the region in the center of a black hole.

In order to create the world that we see around us, this un-differentiated light has to 'descend' through the dimensions to become our world. It expresses itself in different vibratory rates. Most of these dimensions are difficult for us to comprehend. They exist out of the linear modality, so we find it hard to articulate anything about them. The last two regions do have linear aspects to them. They are those of the c^2 region, the mirror world, and our region, below the speed of light.

Figure 16 The movement of light from the higher dimensions through to the mirror universe and into the physical world

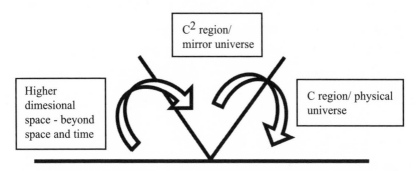

It is only when discussing these regions, that it makes any sense to speak of time or speed. All other dimensions either exist out of timeframes or experience time in ways we cannot comprehend. These last two regions are entwined with each other. When all states of the universe are viewed as a whole, they cancel out and neither region exists. But from our perspective of consciousness, both regions exist, with the c^2 region existing at a higher vibrational rate than our world.

As light makes its journey from the center of the black hole to our world, it enters into the c and c^2 region. From a linear perspective we can say that it enters the c^2 region first, before becoming the c region. At the event horizon of a black hole, according to Hawking, a positron splits into matter and antimatter. We have previously interpreted the event horizon as occurring at the speed of light and the limitation of the perception of this dimension. We can now view the event horizon as also where positrons appear and enter the c^2 region.

If we are viewing the process in a linear fashion, we can say that light comes from the black hole, reaches the c^2 region and forms antimatter, before reaching the c region and forming matter. This is the pathway that Tiller describes as the manifestation of matter, but applied to the Black Hole Principle. Engineer, John Milewski, makes the explicit link between Tiller's work and the creative process occurring in black holes, saying that black holes are the source of superlight or light traveling at c^2.[9]

Figure 17 The movement of infinite light from the black hole to the c2 region and the c region

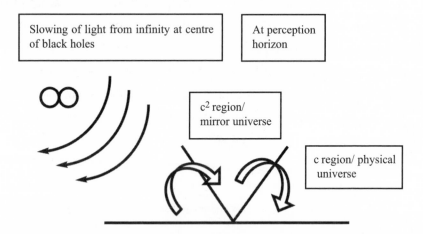

Slowing of light from infinity at centre of black holes

At perception horizon

c^2 region/ mirror universe

c region/ physical universe

So far, we have discussed the principle of the mirror universe in terms of manifesting matter. What if we were to travel in the opposite direction and convert physical matter into the stuff of the mirror universe? Could this be the basis of the famous equation $E=mc^2$?

When matter from our world gets converted into the realms of the mirror universe, it releases the energy that was there all along, but not previously available. This energy has the inherent vibration of c^2. The region of c^2 also featured in both Einstein's and Maxwell's equations. As described in Chapter 8, the mathematics of both elegantly emerge from Riemann tensors used in Superstring Theory. The c^2 region is already entrenched within our current descriptions of reality. The c and c^2 region actually co-exist and are intimately entwined with each other, therefore any description of our reality is likely to include the vibratorary rate of the mirror universe. We shall discuss this concept of co-existence in further detail later.

Figure 18 The diagram shows two zones: positive space-time and negative space-time. Where the two zones interface is the mechanism of manifestation and the reason why particles behave both as a wave and as a particle. As matter is converted back into energy it takes on the inherent vibration speed of c2. Hence the energy released by this procedure is c2 as described by Einstein's famous equation E=mc2

(v=velocity)

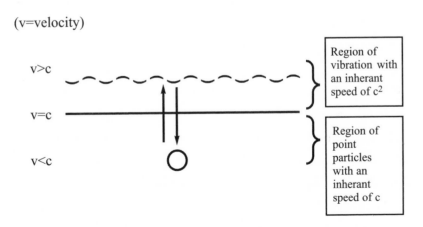

Finding Alice

So now we have explored Tiller's world of antimatter and the mirror universe we can apply this to the black hole situation.

Where is the antimatter from the Big Bang? We are taught that it was annihilated. It was not. It exists beyond the Perception Horizon of this dimension. In the section on black holes, we described how the light of infinity comes out of the black hole, expressing itself through the higher dimensions before it gets to the event horizon and creates matter.

We see this in microquasars that emit electrons at 92 per cent the speed of light.[10] This is because at this point, electrons have only just slowed down to our reality. As they enter our reality, they slow down and create all that we see around us. We have observations that show that these jets do indeed contain particles that are decelerating.[11]

What happens to the other half of the picture? According to Hawking, at the event horizon, a positron and electron are produced. We have discussed Tiller's conclusions about the true nature of antimatter such as the positron. It has magneto electro radiation, antigravity, negative imaginary mass, negative time and the vibration of c^2.

This superluminal region exists in the region of what we currently call dark matter, except now we know it is not dark, but exists in regions beyond our perception. That mirror matter and dark matter are equivalent is a conclusion made by some physicists such as Robert Foot of the University of Melbourne, Australia.[12]

From this, we should be able to make predictions about what is seen around black holes. If light comes to the event horizon and splits into two regions of both our universe and the mirror universe, we should be able to see evidence of this around black holes.

Predictions and proof

a) Matter being created. This is indeed what we see coming out of a black hole – fast moving electrons.[13]

b) Antimatter being created – there is evidence that antimatter pours out from the center of galaxies including our own, which appears to be issuing an "antimatter fountain."[14]

c) Dark Matter/ Superbright matter– Dark matter halos are found around the centers of galaxies.[15] We now know that dark matter is not dark at all, but superbright, existing at vibrational frequencies beyond our measurement or perception.

d) We can infer that dark matter is present by the way that matter behaves around it due to its hidden gravitational influence. In fact, it is said that dark matter actually shapes the galaxies. Some of this dark matter is made up of antimatter existing in the c^2 region. We have reached the principle that the dark matter/ antimatter c^2 region, shapes the visible c region, a principle we shall revisit later on.

e) We know that strong magnetic fields exist around a black hole.[16] These may be the effects of the magneto electric radiation occurring in the superluminal regions.

These observational findings fit our predictions. The light of infinity reaches the event horizon but splits into the antimatter and matter. The positron antimatter occupies the vibration of c^2, which is the region that is just faster than ours. This is too fast for us to see or measure, but still exists within space-time. It exists at a faster vibration and has the properties of antigravity and magnetoelectric radiation. It too, is found around black holes and we have found evidence of it.

Tiller says that the gravitational force associated with matter is gravity and with antimatter in the mirror universe, antigravity. The two forces oppose each other. If these forces are being produced on a large scale throughout the universe, due to there being many black holes, what effect does this have on a universal level?

Think back to Chapter 11, discussing current problems in cosmology. We mentioned how, since 1998, we have known that the universe is not only expanding, but accelerating.[17] The force of antigravity is overpowering the force of gravity. The cause of this gravitational push is mysterious, hence the terms dark energy and matter. However, this would fit with the findings that antimatter is associated with antigravity. Because it is vibrating at c^2 speed, it is more energetic than the c region.

Therefore the c^2 region "out-powers" the c region. Antigravity wins over gravity. Due to the vibrational speed, it is beyond the Perception Horizon, hence we cannot perceive this antigravity force or measure it. Is this the force behind the accelerating universe and the dark energy that is pushing the universe apart? Does the antigravity force exerted by the mirror universe cause our observations of distant supernovae to be accelerating away from us?

Ray of Light

Another feature associated with black holes is that of gamma ray bursts. These are flares of gamma rays: light of a very short wavelength. These streams of light are seen flaring from space. They are a mystery to current cosmologists, especially the fact that they are emitted around black holes, which does not fit the old, destructive picture of black holes.

The accepted theory amongst astronomers is that they are the result of explosions caused by the collapse of very large stars: the collapsar model.[18] Yet, as many more gamma rays are found, this model seem less likely to explain each situation. Why do the rays appear in jets accelerated to close to the speed of light?[19] Many explain this effect as being due to magnetic fields, but as Keith Mason, of University College London, says on the matter, "the truth is it's still a real puzzle."[20]

In our new model of black holes, we can now describe how this is occurring. The key is the dynamic balance between the two forces of creation of particles and creation of light.

We have said that at the event horizon of this dimension, matter is created and at the event horizon of c^2 antimatter is created. But the BHP is not static; it is cyclic. Sometimes light becomes matter and antimatter and sometimes the balance shifts the other way and two particles cancel out to become light. When this happens, a photon of light is created. This is emitted from the black hole as a gamma ray burst.

Both gamma ray bursts and electrons are emitted periodically. This is because the two principles of annihilation and creation are in dynamic balance. There is no set point where it comes to a rest. That is the point of life; it is a dance. The dynamism is constant and it is never static.

This dance and balance of movement, of being neither one nor the other, is well described in the mystical traditions. Perhaps one obvious example is the symbol for Taoism: the symbol for yin and yang. This shows two forces that are forever entwined and not one nor the other.

According to mystic traditions, the universe is one of dynamism. So too, are black holes caught up in the dance. When the dance moves one way, it creates matter and antimatter, when the dance moves the other way it creates light.

Sure enough, this fits with the observations we have of the light coming out of black holes in the form of gamma rays. It has the precise energy that is created when the annihilation process occurs.[21] Furthermore we have growing evidence that it does so in pulses, sometimes emitting gamma rays and sometimes electrons or X-rays.[22] X-rays are also part of the electromagnetic spectrum of light and are caused by high-energy electrons. As high-energy electrons lose some of their energy, they emit this form of light, which has a short wavelength, but not as short as a gamma ray. We use this type of light for routine medical imaging.

Why X-rays are produced by black holes is unclear in conventional physics, but according to the BHP, they could be the result of the high-energy electrons that are emitted from black holes. Therefore, as the dance of black holes moves one way and then the other, we see oscillations between gamma rays and X-rays. Sometimes these oscillations have periods of a definite rhythm, which are baffling cosmologists.[23] The emission of X-rays used to be called an 'after glow' of gamma ray bursts, but it soon became clear that these were also highly energetic and were not just a side-effect.[24]

These types of patterns do not easily fit the picture of gamma ray bursts being the dying gasps of a star being sucked into a black hole.

Why are there so many of these bursts all over the sky, when such an event should be relatively rare? In fact, gamma ray bursts have been discovered from all over the universe and not just concentrated in our galaxy.[25] If anything, gamma ray bursts appear more often in stellar nurseries where stars are born and not when they die. To make things more confusing, gamma rays with the type of energy that comes out of a black hole have been found in our own Earth's atmosphere.[26] What is going on?

These mysterious oscillatory patterns in the emissions around black holes also do not fit the idea that gamma rays are the result of an explosion. An explosion would be highly energetic at the beginning and then die away. This mismatch has led to all sorts of strange ideas, such as black holes 'burping' after eating a star, in order to produce these oscillations.[27]

This oscillatory picture gives further credence to the dynamic balance idea; the oscillations are created as the black hole goes one way or another. The fact that these periods of rapid oscillations are sporadic would also point to a process that is not due to any physical process, like an explosion. In fact it may be due to the very process that creates physicality.

The oscillations have also been noted in some clouds of high velocity gas near the center of our own galaxy. These clouds have been seen to breathe: moving one way and then the other, like a vast inspiration and expiration.[28] This is an observation that is puzzling astrophysicists, but it fits the BHP from which we would predict that the area around a black hole is dynamically moving.

We are starting to build up evidence that is pointing to no less than a new view of the cosmos. We shall explore this further in the next few chapters, revealing not only an explanation for gamma ray bursts, but also perhaps a new theory of everything.

References for Chapter 13

1. Brown D. Angels and Demons. (Corgi adult) 2003.

2. Cartlidge E. Half the Universe is missing. *New Scientist.* 4 September 2004; 37-39.

3. Milewski JV. *Superlight, One Source one force.* 17 November 1996; http://www.luminet.net/~wenonah/new/milewski.htm. [cited December 2005]

4 Carlton JB. Tiller WA. *Index of Refraction Measurements for Superluminal Radiation.* Jan 1976; 9th Annual Medical Symposium, ARE Clinic, Phoenix, AZ.

5. Tiller WA. Science and conscious transformation. (Paviour) 1997.

6. Wesson P. The Light Stuff. *New Scientist.* 20 November 2004; 31- 33.

7. Chown M. Spot the Stargate. *New Scientist.* 29 September 2001; 11.

8. Chown M. Shadow Worlds. *New Scientist.* 17 June 2000. 36-39.

9. Milewski JV. *Superlight, One Source one force.* 17 November 1996; http://www.luminet.net/~wenonah/new/milewski.htm. [cited December 2005]

10. Henbest N. The Great Annihilators. *New Scientist.* 1 April 2000; 28-31.

11. Chown M. Black holes drive speedy particles to new highs. *New Scientist.* 12 June 2004; 8.

12. Chown M. Shadow Worlds. *New Scientist.* 17 June 2000; 36-

39.

13. Henbest N. The Great Annihilators. *New Scientist.* 1 April 2000; 28-31.

14. Reich ES. When Antimatter attacks. *New Scientist.* 24 April 2004; 34-37.

15. Battersby S. The New Dark Age. *New Scientist.* 25 January 2003; 28-32.

16. Blaes O. A Universe of Discs. *Scientific American.* October 2004; 23- 29.

17. Chown M. The Fifth Element. *New Scientist.* 3 April 1999; 29-32.

18. Minkel JR. Bye Bye black holes. *New Scientist.* 22 January 2005; 28-33.

19. Gehrels N, Piro L, Leonard PJT. The Brightest Explosions in the Universe. *Scientific American.* December 2002; 53-59.

20. Clark S. A Bubble ate the Universe. *New Scientist.* 12 March 2005; 29-32.

21. Chown M. Has dark matter been found at last? *New Scientist.* 4 October 2003; 8.

22. Gehrels N, Piro L, Leonard PJT. The Brightest explosions in the Universe. *Scientific American.* December 2002; 53-59.

23. Blaes O. A Universe of Discs. *Scientific American.* October 2004; 23- 29.

24. Gehrels N, Piro L, Leonard PJT. The Brightest explosions in the Universe.

Scientific American. December 2002; 53-59.

25. Wijers R. *Gamma Ray bursts.* Physics Web. April 1998.

http://physicsweb.org/articles/world/11/4/9/1 [cited December

2005]

26. Smith DM, Lopez LI, Lin RP, Barrington-Leigh CM. Terrestrial Gamma-ray flashes observed up to 20 MeV. *Science*. 18 February 2005; 307: 5712:1085-1088.

27. Schilling G. Do black holes play with their food? *Science NOW*. 18 August 2005; 4.

28. Richter P, Wakker BP. Our growing breathing galaxy. *Scientific American*. January 2004; 28-37.

Chapter 14

The Endless Sea

In previous chapters, we discovered how black holes appear in different sizes. They manifest as super massive black holes in the center of galaxies, as well as mini black holes that appear all over our galaxy. We have also explored how black holes are now being recognized as creative and that they bring the light of infinity into our dimension.

What if it doesn't stop there? What if black holes are at every level of reality and even as small as an atom? Surprisingly, even mainstream scientists are considering this idea.

On the level

In 1999, *New Scientist* announced that tiny black holes could be produced inside a laboratory, even suggesting that black holes may exist inside of us.[1] They were describing the black hole atom, which is so dense that it collapses and forms a core of infinite density. Black holes were originally defined as the end-point of massive stars, but within this new description, it is the presence of an infinite core that counts. When defined in this way, black holes could be anywhere. As long as an object contains an area within it that is infinite and transcends space and time, it can be defined as a black hole.

A number of physicists have also compared atomic particles, such as electrons, with black holes. French physicist, Jean Charon, suggested that every electron is a 'bearer of spirit', containing a region that is infinite and exists out of space and time.[2] Even Brian Greene notes, in the best-selling book, *The Elegant Universe*, that black holes are similar to elementary particles inasmuch as they have no identifiable internal structure: they can be completely characterized by their mass, force charge, and spin angular momentum.[3]

So black holes occur at every level of the universe, from the very large - in the centers of galaxies, to the very small - inside atoms and somewhere in between. Do black holes occur at every level of reality? Suppose that every level of the universe is a creative black hole, forming a fractal pattern that goes on to infinity. That same pattern is seen at both small and larger levels of the universe. Each and every part of everything creates the universe at every level. Each part is a black hole, bringing light from infinity, creating matter and antimatter.

This is a radical statement, which if true, has many implications for our universe. It is far from simply being a pretty idea; there are actually many observations that fit this model. In fact, some would say the data fits this model better than the current models we find in physics. Cosmologists often have to contort the observable data to fit acceptable theories. This is not required in the new model of the BHP, as it provides an entirely new conceptual framework.

Furthermore, since my initial publication of the BHP in January 2004, I have discovered others who have independently arrived at very similar conclusions.[4] Notably, physicist Nassim Haramein also describes the universe as a holographic black hole fractal with creative black holes at every level. Together with physicist, Elisabeth Rauscher, he has published a peer-reviewed paper that contains the mathematical basis for this model.[5]

Although various parties have produced models that differ in language and content, the essential elements are the same. It is an example of the type of situation described in Chapter 9, in which the same experience can be interpreted in different ways, especially if it is of a multidimensional nature. However, there are many similarities between these descriptions and we may conclude that we are uncovering a universal principle.

In this chapter, I will present the evidence that the BHP is the principle of creation at every level of the universe, solving many puzzles that face physicists today. This includes a way to unite all the forces of Nature and why there are so many subatomic particles. In other words the BHP leads us to a *theory of everything.*

It also helps to explain esoteric ideas that have never had a scientific explanation before, such as the concept of chakras, as well as seemingly more prosaic phenomena, such as the mechanism behind lightning seen during thunderstorms. However, before exploring all these levels of the BHP, we need to discuss one of its main signatures: the spiral.

Spiral architect

One of the ways to recognize that the same principle is occurring at every level of reality is to identify a process that is common to all. One of these processes, or motifs, is the spiral shape. We have already looked at how the spiral is associated with black holes in the form of an accretion disc. As we shall see, the spiral is crucial to Nature; it is the signature of the universe and therefore the BHP.

We have both inferred and direct proof that the spiral is the preferred shape of creation. Let's start with the most obvious black hole spiral: the accretion disc. As previously noted, discs of spinning debris and material exist around a black hole. It is the speed of this spin that gives us an indication of the size of the black hole. The accretion disc provides some puzzles for physics.

According to the classical description of black holes, these objects are capable of sucking in all nearby material. Why is the material of the accretion disc spared? Physicists usually answer this question by saying that the angular momentum within the rotating disc is holding it in place. However, on closer analysis, there is not enough momentum to keep the material within the disc from dissipating. What is holding the disc together if it is not the physical forces that we know about?[6]

In the previous chapter, we looked at how black holes are actually creative. If black holes have the ability to create, this could explain why they are surrounded by discs of material. The material seen in the accretion disc is either material that has just been created by the black hole, or material that is adopting a certain pattern due to the forces generated by the black hole at the event horizon. These are the gravitational effects of the matter and antimatter, which attract and shape material into the observable galaxy formations.

As we discussed in the last chapter, antimatter has a gravitational pull on physical material. Some cosmologists believe that dark matter is made up of antimatter, although this is controversial.[7] For the purposes of this book, it is scientifically legitimate to attribute some, if not all of dark matter to the presence of antimatter. It has been well documented that dark matter has a gravitational pull on matter and appears to shape galaxies.[8] If we attribute some of dark matter to antimatter, we can say that antimatter too has an effect on shaping matter.

According to the BHP, light from infinity enters the higher dimensional regions before reaching the c^2 region and c region. The c^2 region shapes the c, or matter region, as it is vibrating faster than the c region. The c region then takes the shape that the c^2 region has taken, which is the spiral; hence we see spirals around black holes. The spiral is therefore, a common shape for galaxies, because they are created around a central black hole. We actually have direct observations of electrons and positrons emission from the center of the Milky Way in the form of a double spiral.[9]

Why does light form the spiral shape in particular? It may surprise you that spiral geometry has long been known to occur throughout Nature.

Phi factor

Although you may not have noticed this, Nature has a strong affinity for one particular pattern. It is seen in leaves, in pine cones, in snail shells and even in ourselves. All of Nature demonstrates the same geometric design.[10] It is called the *golden mean* or the phi ratio.

This is an irrational number, like the number pi, which is more familiar. This means that it cannot be expressed neatly as a fraction or as a whole number, but only rounded off to a few decimal places. Hence the phi ratio can be expressed to three decimal places as 1: 1.618.

All living creatures display this ratio in their structure, including humans. Hence the length of your forearm in relation to your hand displays this ratio and so on. This is a fact that has been well known throughout history; some famous buildings are purported to display the phi ratio, including, some say, the pyramids at Giza.[11]

In the 12th century, Leonardo Pisano Fibonacci discovered a mathematical series of whole numbers. Each new number is found simply by adding the previous two numbers: hence 1,1,2,3,5,8,13 and so on.

The ratio between two of the consecutive numbers approximates to phi. If we take the ratio of 5 to 3 we get approximately 1.6 and so on. The higher up the series we go, the closer the approximation to phi. There are many amazing mathematical properties of this series that are worth exploring. The book, *The Golden Ratio* by Mario Livio, is an excellent start for such an exploration, demonstrating just how interesting this series is and seemingly fundamental to Nature.[12]

The phi ratio can also be used to create fractal patterns, either via computer simulations or occurring naturally. A fractal is an infinitely repeating pattern; the same shape occurs at each level. We see fractal formations in Nature, such as in fern leaves. Fractal patterns have also entered popular culture as a form of art.

Fractal patterns consisting of phi ratio geometry are ubiquitous in Nature. It appears to be the signature of the universe and can be found at all levels from snail shells to the solar system, as we shall explore later.

Because of its fractal nature, infinity is 'written in' to the pattern; the pattern repeats infinitely. Does the light of infinity also display these patterns when entering the lower dimensions? We do indeed see spirals around black holes suggesting that this process, along with the rest of Nature, displays phi ratio geometry.

We can modify our black hole picture in the following way. Light travels from infinity and spirals towards our perception horizon. As it does, it also reaches the mirror universe in the c^2 region, just out of our perception. Not only can we find aspects of this concept in mainstream science, it also fits actual observations.

Joao Magueijo, of Imperial College, also discusses the idea that the light in our dimension is a reflection of spirals of light in higher dimensions.[13] We have already discussed how accretion discs are spirals and found around black holes. Electrons and positrons have been seen to spiral out of the center of the Milky Way galaxy.[14] Gamma rays coming from black holes are known to be twisted.[15] Conventional wisdom suggests that magnetic fields are responsible for twisting them, but they would have to be very strong and it is not known why they are present.

Light forms a spiral as it makes its way step-by-step through the dimensions. Every step follows golden mean proportions and forms another step on the spiral. Each dimension helps shape the dimension immediately below it. Eventually the c^2 region helps to shape the c region, as it is just one step 'above' our world. We may never know what lies beyond the Perception Horizon. However, from what we know about the observable parts of the universe, we can make inferences about the rest. Although we cannot see spirals in higher dimensions, it is likely that phi ratio geometry and the spiral pattern occur there just as in the rest of the world.

We are currently finding new evidence that phi ratio geometry is ubiquitous in Nature. Recently the world of nanotechnology witnessed a demonstration of this, when tiny nanoparticles were seen to form spirals in sets that followed the Fibonacci sequence.[16] Not only is phi ratio geometry displayed at such small scales, we have evidence of it occurring at very large scales also.

Latest results from the microwave radiation measurements of the cosmos reveal that the universe is a dodecahedron, a shape which displays phi ratio geometry.[17] The data suggests that the universe is an infinite series of dodecahedrons: a twelve-sided shape made up of pentagons. These pentagons display golden mean symmetry.

The dodecahedron, according to mystical traditions, is the perfect shape. In fact, ancient philosophers such as Plato described the universe as being shaped like a dodecahedron.[18] This idea is also espoused by contemporary teachers such as Dan Winter and Lynneclaire Dennis.[19,20] Modern measurements are now confirming that phi ratio geometry is fundamental to the universe. When we re-examine the old texts in the light of this modern data, they seem astonishingly accurate.

Respect for the Old School

As stated at the beginning of this section, the idea of the black hole as the center of creation can also be found in ancient spiritual traditions. In the Gnostic gospels, the traditional view of creation is that the goddess of wisdom, Sophia, fell from the center of the galaxy. This account, by John Lash, is an interpretation of the texts found at Nag Hammadi, which have been damaged and fragmented. It sounds remarkably like the BHP and even features a cosmic bound similar to the event/perception horizon.

"As Sophia slipped past the cosmic bound and departed from the galactic core… When She was entirely through the membrane there came a violent shift, a swift acceleration. Her currents now began to twist and roll, throwing Her into disorientation… And Sophia fell from heaven like a waterfall of coruscating colors wound recklessly around a torqueing coil."[21]

The BHP can now shed a scientific light on what may have seemed like a fantastic myth. It is interesting that, in the gospel, the force behind creation is seen as feminine. We have discussed how the antimatter/negative mass region, shapes the matter region. Some people associate this with the feminine principle. So this creation myth actually tallies with the modern picture that is emerging. Another way of interpreting the name, Sophia, is as the word *learning*. Esoteric wisdom says that learning is the whole point of creation and that the initial unified whole had to split itself in order to learn about itself. The separation from unity achieves this goal. In the BHP we also see the split from the light of infinity into the matter and antimatter aspects of creation.

The quote also displays knowledge of the spiral as an important aspect of creation via the black hole. Now that we have discussed this pattern and the evidence for it, both old and new, we can add it to the

BHP and even apply it to situations other than the black hole.

Atomic

As we said at the beginning of the chapter, black holes come in all sizes. Some even say that there are black hole atoms. Is there any evidence for atoms displaying the BHP? The definition of a black hole atom is one that has an infinitely dense center that exists out of space and time.

Many are now familiar with the picture of the atom as something made up of subatomic particles and empty space. The nucleus is at the center with negatively charged electrons circling around the periphery. This picture of an atom has been built up by the likes of Ernest Rutherford and JJ Thompson, in the late 19th and early 20th centuries.

Before these breakthroughs, the atom was seen as solid as a billiard ball. However, this picture started to dissolve when experiments were done that probed the structure of the atom. The picture we now have of an atom has been carefully built up from a series of experiments. It is important to remember that this was a stage-by-stage process of journeying into the unknown. Each piece of experimental data allowed further structural insights, until we gained the picture of the atom that is commonly taught in secondary schools, which resembles a mini solar system. Apparently, Neils Bohr had a dream in which the atom was depicted in this way.[22]

According to this model, levels of discrete energy, which you may know as being called *shells*, surround the central nucleus. Electrons can exist at these levels and can move up and down from shell to shell. As they go to higher levels they absorb energy and if they drop down, this emits energy. The energy release occurs as a specific packet or *quantum*, which is where we get the name *quantum theory*. Sometimes we see this energy as visible light. We make use of this in daily life: in electric lights for example.

In Chapter 7, we discussed that Paul Dirac described how, when an electron moves to a higher level, it leaves a hole behind which is its antimatter partner: a positron. Is this actually an example of the BHP? As we have said before, the definition of a black hole atom is one that contains a point of infinity, which transcends space and time.

Let's take the center of the nucleus as containing the infinite singularity point. The energy shells with their different levels of energy then become the spirals of light that come into our reality from infinity. I have found it quite difficult to find a reference that definitively demonstrates that the atomic energy shells display golden mean geometry, but there are plenty of suggestions that this is the case.[23] Furthermore, there is a link with the phi ratio and the periodic table, the progression of which is dependent on the energy shells.[24] The recent discovery of the fact that nanoparticles spontaneously form into patterns displaying golden mean geometry only adds weight to the suggestion that phi is alive and well at the atomic level.[25]

This is an area that needs further investigation. However, there are other aspects of atomic behavior, which also correlate with the BHP at the macroscopic level.

We know that the electron-positron-photon annihilation process is present in the atom too. Just like in the larger black holes we see the dynamic balance between creation and destruction of light when electrons move between energy levels in what appear to be random movements. These movements are another aspect of the dance of life.

Why are there so many different elements? They are all different levels of the Black Hole Principle progressing to the next element according to phi geometry. Each type of atom represents a particular level of expression of the BHP. Hence, lighter elements like lithium are smaller black holes than uranium.

There is another property of heavier atoms, which shows a remarkable similarity to black hole dynamics and that is radioactivity. Heavier atoms such as uranium spontaneously decay over time. As they do, they produce emissions that are remarkably similar to that of the large black holes that we have previously discussed: gamma, beta and alpha radiation. Gamma radiation is the emission of high frequency light. Beta radiation takes the form of a fast moving electron. This is remarkably similar to the processes we see in quasars and the centers of galaxies with the emission of gamma ray bursts and fast moving electrons.

What has not been observed in these larger processes is the equivalent of alpha radiation, which is in the heavier form of a helium nucleus: two protons and two neutrons. However a possible equivalent process will be discussed later in the section on the sun.

We have discussed the atomic processes in terms of the BHP, what of subatomic particles such as electrons and quarks etc? Interestingly, a common pattern found in the trails left by particles after they have smashed into each other is spirals, suggesting that spirals are fundamental to their composition as well.

The particle that is seen as fundamental to protons and neutrons is called the quark, a term coined by Murray Gell-Man. They have been extensively studied in high-energy particle colliders for some years now. Interestingly, under certain circumstances they emit jets of gamma rays, similar to black holes.[26] Both black holes and quarks emit bilateral jets. Could this be evidence of the BHP in even the smallest particle – the quark?

In terms of making the analogy between atoms and black holes, this is just the beginning of this line of enquiry; there are many gaps that need to be filled in. The basic framework of the BHP may shed new light on previously discovered observations.

We can make predictions of the sorts of findings we would expect if the BHP does occur at the atomic level. These predictions would then need to be tested by direct experiment and observation in order to confirm or refute the BHP as a model for atomic behavior. A new particle collider is being built that is going to examine the universe at ultra high energies. This Large Hadron Collider (LHC) may help to test these predictions and reveal aspects of the mirror universe.

It is important to note that the BHP is not a purely linear process; it involves infinities and hyperspace geometries. We can interpret this in a three-dimensional fashion and describe light spiraling in from infinity and reaching the event horizon. However, we cannot possibly fully conceptualize the process, because we cannot visualize higher dimensional geometries completely. So in certain circumstances, the process may look different from the process described in the microquasar.

Hence in the atom, the process looks like electrons jumping up and down energy levels, whilst releasing or absorbing energy. The BHP is all these things; there are different ways to describe the process, but they have essentially common features. The

Haramein-Rauscher model describes the dual nature of creation in terms of the dual torus (which is similar to a doughnut shape). Their illustrations, available from their website, clearly show the spiral nature of this torus.[27]

Another variation on a theme is the model put forward by Dr Chaim H Tejman, who says that all levels display the same pattern of a horizontal loop of energy linked to a vertical magnetic loop which is linked to the positron.[28]

These variations, developed by different teams, highlight that a basic pattern may be interpreted in different ways, because different interpretations exist!

Other atomic properties and uniting all forces in physics

We have just described how the atom displays characteristics of the BHP.

Over the years, physicists have learnt much about atomic processes. They have uncovered a myriad of subatomic particles, some of which are just fleetingly glimpsed in the debris of particle collisions. As discussed in Chapter 8, physicists would like to find an underlying principle that unites all of these diverse particles and explains why each one has such precise characteristics. This quest has resulted in Superstring Theory, which is not without its glitches. It is also a theory that is often accused of having no experimental proof.

The BHP may provide a method with which to unite all particles. In the BHP, light spirals out from infinity and into our dimension. The various particles could be certain aspects of this underlying spiral, caught at certain angles. From our point of view, the particles have particular characteristics that are seemingly disparate. However, they are unified, because they are all aspects of this fundamental light. David Bohm is often quoted as having said that matter is frozen light.[29]

Figure 19 - Each particle is simply a snapshot of the underlying spiral of light, caught at a certain angle

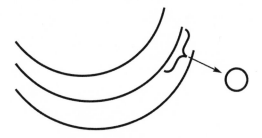

Perhaps the different particles are merely different geometric perspectives of the one spiral of light, as if we see it frozen at particular points.

Physicists are constantly exploring deeper into high-energy states and catching glimpses of exotic particles that are only seen for a fleeting moment before disappearing. Maybe they are not really disappearing, but entering a higher energy state, which is beyond the Perception Horizon. Is this where all the missing particles such as right-handed neutrinos exist: in the mirror universe? Perhaps they originate in even higher states?

Forces

Unification does not only involve particles, it involves forces too.

Surprisingly the BHP is consistent with the behavior of known forces. As discussed, physics is looking for a way to unify the electromagnetic, the strong and weak nuclear forces with the force of gravity.

We have discussed how light 'moves' from infinity through higher dimensions to our reality. This cannot be a 'movement' in the same way that we see matter move, because this is the process that creates matter. Furthermore, we have already stated that light is transcendent of space and time and simply expresses itself in different vibrations. Therefore if light does not exist in space and time, it cannot 'move' from point A to point B. Nevertheless, it is easier for us to conceptualize if we think of some sort of flow from higher states to lower.

The forces that we know of in Nature are reflections of the 'movement' of this fundamental light from infinity to our reality. When seen at certain levels, we see gravity. At the level of the atom we see the strong and weak nuclear forces. Somewhere in between is the force of electromagnetism.

Although gravity seems such a fundamental force in our lives, responsible for preventing us from floating off into space, it has proved an elusive entity in physics. Could gravity be the one force that exists on the spiral at levels beyond the perception horizon? Is the reason why it effortlessly acts at a distance, is because it is supraluminal?

It could explain why certain aspects of gravity, such as finding a particle of gravity, have been so hard. It is different from the other forces in that it is beyond our dimension. We simply feel the effects from the higher realms. Interestingly, a similar concept can be found within mainstream science today.

The Randall-Sundrum model of gravity suggests that the force is so weak because its source is actually on another brane, from another dimension and it leaks out onto our brane.[30]

John Milewski has also previously suggested that all the forces can be united by light of a very fast vibration that comes out of black holes.[31]

Because the same process is going on at every level of the universe from the very large to the very small we can now suggest that all the forces are really due to one process: the movement of light from infinity. Which force you detect just depends on which part of the spiral you are looking at.

Figure 20 – The Black Hole Principle occurs at every level of the universe from inside atoms to galaxies. The forces created by the process depend on the level of the universe

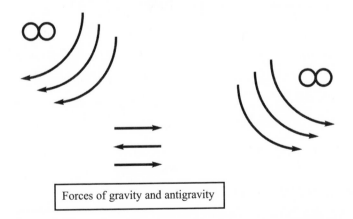

Forces of gravity and antigravity

The spiral nature behind forces is actually quite familiar. It is Faraday's discovery that the force of electromagnetism acts in a spiral fashion that resulted in the motor-driven appliances that we are so used to today. He succeeded in understanding electro-magnetism where more highly educated scholars had failed, because he followed the inductive method of making scientific leaps. He listened to Nature instead of presuming how Nature behaved.

He realized that the force of electromagnetism is curved and that it works in a circular motion. In this way, he was able to obtain electricity from a magnetic field. Everyone else thought the force behaved in a linear fashion and therefore failed.[32]

Gravity too, has spiral geometry. It is actually part of Einstein's theory of General Relativity that gravity results in a curve in the fabric of space-time: the more massive the body, the greater the curve.

A rather interesting, if seemingly trivial demonstration of the spiral movement of gravity, comes courtesy of NASA and their reporting of the curious growth patterns of moss plants. Moss plants sensitive to light and gravity were taken on board a shuttle expedition. Away from the influence of Earth's gravity and kept in the dark, the plants grew in a spiral motion.[33] This confounded NASA, but would fit our model. When the plants were taken out of the direct influence of Earth's gravity and away from a source of light, could this have allowed them to follow the predominate gravitational pattern: the spiral?

There is another curious phenomenon, which may be answered by the BHP. During a solar eclipse, the pendulums of clocks stop moving side-to-side and begin to rotate.[34] Is this due to an interruption of some of the sun's gravitational influence, leaving them free to rotate in another underlying pattern of gravity?

These examples are only a start. Much more needs to be done in this area before the forces of Nature can truly be linked to the BHP. We also need to find evidence that the strong and weak nuclear forces also fit this pattern.

We have mentioned how the behaviors of different objects of our world display the BHP at different levels. We have explored the galactic and the atomic level, but we now need to look at the levels in between: at the stars and planets.

References for Chapter 14

1. Chown M. Holes in one. *New Scientist.* 1 April 2000. 24-27.

2. Charon J. *The Unknown Spirit.* (Coventure) 1993.

3. Greene Brian. *The Elegant Universe.* (Random House) 2000.

4. Samanta-Laughton M. QBC: The Science of Auras and Chakras. *Holistic Health.* Winter 2003/4; 79:16-21.

5. Haramein N, Rauscher EA. The origin of spin: a consideration of torque and coriolis forces in Einstein's field equations and grand unification theory. *Noetic Journal.* June 2005; 6:1-4:143-162.

6. Blaes O. A Universe of Discs. *Scientific American.* October 2004; 23- 29.

7. Chown M. Has dark matter been found at last? *New Scientist.* 4 October 2003; 8.

8. Battersby S. The New Dark Age. *New Scientist.* 25 January 2003; 28-32.

9. Finkbeiner DP. *WMAP Microwave Emission Interpreted as Dark Matter Annihilation in the Inner Galaxy.* January 2005. http://www.arxiv.org/abs/astro-ph/0409027.

10. Southey W. Geometry in the Natural World. *Infinite technolo-*

gies. 2003. http://www.infinitetechnologies.co.za/articles/geome-try1.html.

11. Melchizedek D. *The Ancient Secret of the Flower of Life, Volume 1.* (Light Technology, US) 1999.

12. Livio M. *The Golden Ratio.* (Headline Review) 2003.

13. Magueijo J. *Faster than the speed of light.* (Arrow) 2004.

14. Finkbeiner D P. *WMAP Microwave Emission Interpreted as Dark Matter Annihilation in the Inner Galaxy.* January 2005. http://www.arxiv.org/abs/astro-ph/0409027.

15. Chandler DL. Twisted Secrets of Gamma ray bursts. *New Scientist.* 7 June 2003; 25.

16. Li C, Zhang X, Cao Z. Triangular and Fibonacci Number patterns driven by stress on core/shell microstructures. *Science.* 5 August 2005; 309: 909.

17. Luminet J-P et al. Dodecahedral space topology as an explanation for weak wide-angle temperature correlations in the cosmic microwave background. *Nature.* 9 October 2003; 425: 593-595.

18. Lahanas M. *Plato's model of the Universe –Space and Time.* http://www.mlahanas.de/Greeks/PlatoSolid.htm [cited December 2005].

19. Winter D. *Implosion: the Secret Science of Ecstasy and Immortality.* (Implosion group) 2004.

20. Dennis L. *The Pattern.* (Integral Publishing.) 1997.

21. Lash JL. The Gaia Mythos. *Metahistory.* April 2004. http://www.metahistory.org/Gaia_Story.php [cited December 2005]

22. Black P. *Neils Bohr Dream leads to Nobel Prize.* (Bella Online) http://www.bellaonline.com/articles/art19116.asp [cited Dec 2005].

23. Wlodarski J. The Golden Ratio and the Fibonacci Numbers in

the World of Atoms. *Fibonacci Quarterly*. December 1963; 61.

24. Javanovic R. *Atomic structure and the Pascal triangle*. http://milan.milanovic.org/math/english/atom/atom.html [cited December 2005]

25. Li C, Zhang X, Cao Z. Triangular and Fibonacci Number patterns driven by stress on core/shell microstructures. *Science*. 5 August 2005; 309: 909.

26. Gefter A. Liquid Universe. *New Scientist*. 16 October 2004; 35-37.

27. Haramein N, Rauscher EA. The origin of spin: a consideration of torque and coriolis forces in Einstein's field equations and grand unification theory. *Noetic Journal*. June 2005; 6:1-4:143-162.

28. . Tejman CH. *United Nature theory: Wave theory*. 2001http://www.grandunifiedtheory.org.il/book1.htm [cited Dec 2005]

29. Weber R. *Dialogues with scientists and Sages*. (Arkana) 1990.

30. Randall L. *Warped Passages*. (Allen Lane) 2005.

31. Milewski JV. *Superlight, One Source one force*. 17 November 1996; http://www.luminet.net/~wenonah/new/milewski.htm. [cited December 2005.]

32. Bodanis D. $E=MC^2$: *A biography of the world's most famous equation*. (Macmillan) 2000.

33. Miller K, Phillips T. Mossy Space spirals. *Science@NASA*. 16 July 2002. http://science.nasa.gov/headlines/y2002/16jul_firemoss.htm [cited December 2005]

34. Schilling G. Shadow over gravity. *New Scientist*. 27 November 2004; 28-31.

Chapter 15

42

According to what we have discussed so far, the BHP should be manifest at every level of the universe. If this is the case, our sun and every planet in our solar system should display black hole behavior, including our very own home planet.

Although the thought of our local neighborhood consisting of myriads of black holes sounds ludicrous, it is actually the area where we have the most evidence of the BHP, because we are able to make more detailed observations.

In this chapter, we shall examine the evidence for the BHP existing in our solar system and go on to discuss how it can provide a scientific explanation for aspects of esoteric knowledge, making the BHP a possible candidate for the answer to life, the universe and everything!

Black hole sun

The sun is our closest star and enables the existence of life on Earth.

Over the years, astronomers have been able to study the sun's characteristics, but finding an explanation for the sun's behavior is another matter.

The sun is fuelled by the conversion of hydrogen to helium, making it a giant nuclear reactor. This process has kept the sun shining for millions of years. However, our home star displays certain patterns of behavior that are puzzling physicists. Can we find an explanation in the BHP?

If the BHP is correct, the sun should display characteristics of a black hole such as spirals, annihilation of matter and antimatter and ejection of fast moving particles and gamma rays. Not only do we find these characteristics in the sun, but we also can learn about the BHP itself from its behavior.

Since 1859 we have known about the existence of solar flares: eruptions from the surface of the sun that can emit high-energy particles.[1] These events can produce such strong magnetic activity that they disrupt instruments stationed in the Earth's atmosphere.[2]

Interestingly, they also emit another signature of the BHP, gamma rays, which are the result of antimatter and matter annihilation.[3] We have also seen X-rays around the sun as well as electrons and positrons.[4,5] The speed that these electrons travel has been recorded as being close to the speed of light.[6] It appears that the sun is a black hole!

This could explain why the sun's surface is so hot. It is a mystery to current science as to why the surface of the sun is a million degrees higher than the center.[7] This could be explained if there is an infinite source fuelling the whole process. The center of the sun may reflect higher dimensional processes of the BHP, thus having a lower temperature in our dimension.

The behavior of the sun can give us some insights into other aspects of the BHP. We have mentioned that the universe exists as a fractal pattern of infinite black holes. The sun shows us that each celestial object also consists of black holes within it: black holes within black holes.

Within the sun there are indeed darkened areas called sunspots, which are areas of high magnetic activity.[8] We have already discussed how we associate the areas of strong magnetic activity with the BHP. These sunspots have been observed for years, but nobody has been able to figure out what they are. [9]

They are also seen to move across the sun over a period of about eleven years, a fact known to ancient peoples such as the Mayans.[10,11] High sunspot activity is associated with an increase in solar flares, which is what we would expect if sunspots are actually small active black holes of creation.[12] In fact X-rays have been seen directly streaming from sunspots, a telltale sign of the black hole creative process.[13]

The cycles and differences in numbers of spots at different times, which appear random to us, are the results of forces of creation of light or antimatter and matter in their constant dynamic balance. We also see patterns in solar flare activity due to the balance between these forces. These oscillations have actually been well documented.[14] It has even been noticed that there is a correlation between solar activity and the Earth's weather patterns and its earthquakes, a topic we will return to later.[15]

The sun also demonstrates another aspect of the BHP: that the particular particles involved do not have to be positrons, electrons and photons. The principle of cycling between antimatter and matter could express itself in a myriad of ways, depending on the level of the universe being discussed and the angle of the spiral.

The sun emits neutrinos, which are massless particles that hardly react, making them difficult to detect. They leave the sun traveling at almost the speed of light. They exist in three different states, electron, muon and tau. Experiments have shown that neutrinos cycle in and out of all three states as they travel. This has solved a forty-year old mystery as to why we can only detect a third of the number of particles that we should, as only the electron state of neutrino can be detected.[16] What people are trying to figure out, is why. This activity may be another manifestation of the BHP, but more work on this is needed.

The sun also emits heavier particles, including high-energy helium nuclei: alpha radiation.[17] Could these be the equivalent of the alpha radiation in the atom? In a black hole at the level of the center of a galaxy, we are possibly unable to detect such processes if they are occurring at all. The sun's radiation is close enough for us to observe and may be the analogy for atomic alpha radiation that we are looking for, giving us a new perspective on the BHP.

Our local sun is not the only star that displays black hole behavior. A young star has been spotted within a 'star development center' or nebula. Intriguingly, it displays the characteristic bipolar jet emissions seen in quarks and black holes.[18] These stellar jets are known to be very fast, at least as fast as sound. The current explanation of this behavior is that the jets are due to a violent event, the collapse of the accretion disc or the force of angular momentum.

All of these explanations require exceptional circumstances in order to occur. Is Nature really that complicated? Why are super fast jets with similar bipolar patterns seen in so many objects, from black holes to quasars to stars and even quarks? The BHP gives an elegant, simple explanation that requires no special circumstances. It provides us with a deep underlying principle that negates the need to concoct unusual violent events and extrapolate them to fit all similar observations.

Generation X

Now we leave the world of the sun, to explore the rest of the solar system. Surely no black holes here, right? Wrong! It is not hard to find curious anomalies in the behavior of our neighboring planets, which may be explained by the BHP.

In pictures taken with the Chandra telescope, that specifically looks at X-rays, Jupiter shows distinct regions of X-rays coming from the poles.[19] In Saturn, the X-rays are at the equator.[20] Both patterns could be just different expressions of BHP. It has been noticed that the X-rays from Saturn are similar to the X-rays from the sun, leading some to speculate that the surface of Saturn is reflecting the sun's radiation. Yet, puzzlingly, the planet's ring system does not reflect the rays at all.[21]

This paradox can be solved by the BHP. Saturn itself is producing the X-rays via the process of creation in the BHP and forces associated with this process have formed the ring structure around it.

With Jupiter, the poles are the creative sites, leading to different characteristics for that planet. One of these manifestations may be the difference in the cores of the two planets: Saturn has a rocky core and Jupiter a soft one.[22] This is an unexpected finding, as current theories of planetary formation say that they are the result of the accumulation of debris. As Jupiter is larger than Saturn, it follows that Jupiter should have a denser core, but this is not what has been observed. This is an example of where old theories do not actually fit observations and the refinement of the BHP may lead to the elucidation of all the possible patterns of planet formation.

The planet Mercury also displays behavior that is deemed mysterious in the old model of planetary formation. It has a magnetic field that is much larger than is expected given the current models.[23] We currently think that the Earth's magnetic field is created by the movement of its molten core. Because Mercury is too small to have a molten core, the strength of its field is a mystery. Unless of course, it is a result of the BHP and the strong magnetic fields created due to the presence of mirror matter. Strong magnetic fields are found in the sun and also black holes. It makes sense that we would find them around planets if they all follow the same principle.

Data from the red planet, Mars, shows that it too has a glow of X-rays around it.[24] A similar glow is seen around the sun.[25] A contrived explanation has been proposed for the latter situation, leading to the comment of it being "widely speculative."[26]

Comet sense

Even comets are known to emit X-rays.[27] Until recently, it was thought that the solar wind excites electrons from the comet, which then give off energy in the form of X-rays, as well as an even layer of icy material. In a triumph of the BHP over conventional astronomy, the observations of comets actually fit the picture of comets being black holes. Comets show jets of activity, rather than melting in a smooth sheet over the surface. Furthermore, the jets are not confined to the side of the comets facing the sun. They display this activity away from the vicinity of the sun. Such results have astronomers "scratching their heads in confusion."[28]

It seems that all objects produce X-rays, from massive black holes to comets; they are all manifestations of the BHP. This is also demonstrated by the fact that objects outside of our solar system and therefore out of the influence of the solar wind, such as supernovae, have also been observed to have an X-ray halo.[29] Even objects like brown dwarfs, which are thought to be too small and cold to be active, have surprised astronomers by giving off X-ray flares.[30] Why are cold, small objects like brown dwarfs and comets giving off such high-energy emissions? The emissions are even seen in the bipolar pattern, characteristic of BHP.

The crab nebula in the constellation of Taurus is supposed to be the remains of an exploded star. It is a bright source of X-rays even a thousand years after this event. It is currently just accepted as an aftermath of the explosion.[31]

At the other end of the scale to the brown dwarfs and stars that have long gone, young protostars have also been seen to give off fast-moving X-rays.[32] Under current theories of stellar formation, these stars are too young to be so powerful; their gravity is not strong enough to be emitting particles at such a fast rate. So something else must be powering them.

Could these X-ray glows be the results of the electrons moving out beyond the event horizon of each black hole object and then losing some of their energy as light, thus causing the object to have a glowing halo? Certainly the majority of the data would fit this hypothesis better than the current ideas about what causes X-ray halos around cosmic objects.

Before we move onto to discuss our home planet, let's look at the solar system as a whole. It is known to display some interesting geometry. For example the moon is 400 times smaller than the sun and 400 times further away.[33] As a consequence of this quirk, we are able to see the sun completely eclipsed by the moon. Why does such precision exist in the solar system?

There is evidence that the solar system shows the same golden mean geometry that is seen throughout the universe. By taking the distance of Mercury to the sun as the unit of one, these golden proportions are revealed.[34] Even the rings of Saturn display golden mean proportions.[35] Are these examples of the spiral of the BHP? Is this what causes the rotation of the planets?

As Nassim Haramein points out, current physics has yet to fully explain the perpetual rotation of celestial bodies such as planets and stars, let alone subatomic particles. Rotation is written into the BHP as is the source of all motion is the infinite singularity at the center of each object.

Could the size and spin and indeed number of planetary satellites reflect where the particular planet exists on the spiral, just as in the various subatomic particles?

Terra vision

What lies at the center of the Earth has been the subject of both science and science fiction. It is only in recent years that we have been able to get an actual picture of what is going on in the center of the Earth and it is indeed the creation and annihilation process that also occurs in black holes. Antineutrinos have been detected coming from the center of the Earth.[36] It has been postulated that the center of the Earth is a large nuclear reactor of uranium, creating these antineutrinos.[37]

Part of the reason why this theory is being put forward is that nobody can figure out why the core of the Earth generates so much heat.[38] What is powering it? We have known for centuries that the Earth generates a strong magnetic field; it is a dynamo. Beautiful pictures are available which not only show the magnetic fields of the Earth, but also nicely demonstrate that they are in the shape of a torus.[39]

This magnetic field is attributed to movements of the molten iron core below the surface of the Earth. Large scale convection currents occur within the liquid, with hot areas rising to the surface of the outer core of the Earth creating complex turbulence which, when magnified, reveal many vortices resembling the surface of the sun.[40] Although imaging is not clear, initial pictures show laminar flow that may turn out to look like the sun's solar flares. The spiral is alive and well within our own planet.

The fact that the power generated by the Earth is a mystery means another explanation could provide a better fit and that could be the BHP. We have already discussed how the BHP could explain some of the surprising activities in many different objects. Our own Earth may be no exception. Just as the sunspots on the sun represent spirals within spirals or black holes at every level of the object, the Earth may also display this pattern, hence the turbulent spiral magnetic fields seen on our planet. The effects of these magnetic spirals can be seen every time we see water spin down a plughole, spinning anticlockwise or clockwise depending which hemisphere of the planet you happen to find yourself in.

Some of these spirals are particularly large on our planet and act as foci of creation for the rest of the planet. We would expect there to be particularly strong magnetic fields at these points. There could even be something even stranger going on. In *Anti-gravity and the World Grid,* David Hatcher Childress describes areas of the planet, known as *vile vortices.*[41] These could be areas of high earthquake activity or even include what is known as the Bermuda triangle.

If we remember, the BHP involves the creation of both matter and antimatter components with associated gravity and antigravity. Could the vile vortices, where planes and aircraft have been reported to disappear, represent areas where the balance between the two forces sometimes goes too far towards antigravity and these craft effectively levitate out of the Earth's atmosphere or, even more exotically, get converted into negative mass?

Interestingly, journalist Nick Cook has uncovered evidence that antigravity technology has already been developed by certain military groups.[42] At the heart of this technology is the use of vortices. Our Earth may be a black hole, producing matter and antimatter in a central annihilation-creation process and forming the Earth's magnetic field.

The BHP does not just stop at the central black hole of the Earth: it is black holes all the way down. The black hole motif appears many times on the Earth. Look again at our weather systems. They are all spirals! Could the BHP be responsible for the Earth's geological shifts? Could earthquakes be the equivalent of gamma ray bursts or fast-moving electron emissions arising from the center of the Earth?

Although we have not (yet) measured gamma rays from volcanoes, we have actually found them within the Earth's atmosphere. These are known as Terrestrial Gamma-ray Flashes or TGFs.[43] They have been detected in the Earth's upper atmosphere by the latest telescopes and are surprising astronomers who did not expect to find activity of this nature within our own environment.

TGFs are just as energetic as the gamma ray bursts that are seen coming out of black holes.[44] These too, occur in cycles just like their galactic counterparts. Astronomers suspect that they are also concentrated into narrow jets, similar to those from black holes.[45] They have also found a correlation between TGFs and lightning storms, finally giving a clue as to how such storms originate.[46] It may surprise you that, even after hundreds of years of modern science, we are still not sure what causes lightning. We do know that it consists of fast-moving electrons traveling at one-third the speed of light.

One current explanation is that lightning is caused by the ionization of the air in clouds. Yet nobody has found the sorts of electric fields in storm clouds that would do that; the ones found have been extremely feeble compared to what is required. This has led to the assumption that such fields exist; we just haven't found one yet.

But now the link has been found between TGF and lightning, we might be moving towards an explanation of this weather phenomenon. If the Earth has a central black hole, then the Earth's atmosphere should also have smaller black holes. Do these cause storms and lightning? The evidence is building that the Earth's atmosphere displays the activity of the BHP.

For some years, satellites have enabled us to see above the clouds of thunderstorms. Various phenomena have been recorded at such sites and these have been named after members of the fairy realm.[47] Hence, there are *sprites*, which are jets of high-energy electrons coming from the tops of thunderstorms. *Elves* are flat discs which move out horizontally, faster than the speed of light, (thought to be an optical illusion). Joining these are the *pixies, gnomes* and *trolls*, which are other phenomena seen around storms.

Highly energetic activity occurs both within the planet and in its atmosphere, which is not explained by current theories. Periodic jets of activity are produced by earthly phenomena from TGFs, sprites to volcanoes. The Earth's magnetic field and its weather systems show spiral patterns. The center of the planet shows signs of the annihilation process. Are we living on a black hole?

If the answer is yes, it would start to explain the patterns that we see on Earth: from earthquakes to hurricanes. All these spiraling black holes that make up our planet are in constant dynamic balance, continuously pushing and pulling. We can get a sense of how they are all connected and influence each other.

When they go one way, we get a TGF, the other a lightning flash perhaps. Or maybe a volcano eruption or a hurricane or a Bermuda triangle type incident: all depending on where the forces are that day.

The forces on the Earth do not work in isolation. Their push and pull are felt throughout the solar system and the biggest creator of these forces is the sun. Some researchers have noted that solar activity corresponds to violent weather patterns and seismic activity on the Earth. Mitch Battros is the founder of Earth Changes TV. He gives the following equation for the cause of the Earth's weather. [48]

Equation:

Sunspots => Solar Flares => Magnetic Field Shift => Shifting Ocean and Jet Stream Currents => Extreme Weather and Human Disruption

In fact, the picture is much wider, with every part of everything displaying these push and pull and forces. The larger the object, the greater the effect it has on everything else.

Zodiac mindwarp

The idea that every planet in the solar system is caught in an intricate web of forces is not an unfamiliar one! Combine this idea with the central principle of this book that consciousness is fundamental to reality and this may explain one of our most popular, but derided esoteric disciplines. The relationship between consciousness and the forces of the planets is more commonly known as astrology. Astrology is a very ancient discipline and is recorded, in the apocryphal biblical book of Enoch, as being one of the first skills that the gods gave to humanity, alongside skills such as metallurgy.[49]

We know that it was central to the belief systems of many ancient civilizations: hardly the ridiculed remnant it is today, that appears in our daily papers and magazines. The importance of astrology is still seen in Eastern countries such as India and China where it is central to life. Maybe astrology has been preserved from an ancient science that recognized that we are suspended in the forces of the planets. We are effectively caught in the push and pull between every planet in our solar system. If these forces are fundamentally conscious, when these dynamic forces move one way or the other do they have a resonant effect on our moods? By studying the patterns of the planets and the concurrent emotions, could it be possible to predict our predominant moods simply from knowing the positions of planets? Are there any other ways we can see the BHP at work within us?

References for Chapter 15

1. Lovett RA. Dark side of the sun. *New Scientist*. 4 September 2004; 44-45.

2. Ibid.

3. Mackenzie D. Here comes the sun. *Discover*. May 2004; 63-69.

4. Hogan J. Sun's halo linked to dark matter particle. *New Scientist*. 17 April 2004; 8.

5. Muir H. Celestial Fire. *New Scientist: Inside Science 161*. 21 June 2003; 1-4.

6. Ibid.

7. Ibid.

8. Mackenzie D. Here comes the sun. *Discover*. May 2004; 63-69.

9. Muir H. Celestial Fire. *New Scientist: Inside Science 161*. 21 June 2003; 1-4.

10. Ibid.

11. Gilbert AG, Cotterell MM. The Mayan Prophecies: Unlocking the secrets of a lost civilization. (Element Books) 2000.

12. Muir H. Celestial Fire. *NewScientist: Inside Science 161*. 21 June 2003; 1-4.

13. Mackenzie D. Here comes the sun. *Discover*. May 2004; 63-69.

14. Muir H. Celestial Fire. *New Scientist: Inside Science 161.* 21 June 2003; 1-4.

15. Mackenzie D. Here comes the sun. *Discover.* May 2004; 63-69.

16. Muir H. Celestial Fire. *New Scientist: Inside Science 161.* 21 June 2003; 1-4.

17. Burch J. The Fury of Space Storms. *Scientific American.* April 2001; 86-94.

18. O'Dell CR, Beckwith S V W. Young stars and their surroundings. *Science.* 30 May 1997; 276: 5317:1355-1359.

19. X-ray snap of Saturn reveals a polar puzzle. *New Scientist.* 20 March 2004; 19.

20. Ibid.

21. Ibid.

22. Battersby S. Telltale signs of a broken heart. *New Scientist.* 24 July 2004; 9.

23. Ravilious K. Mercury's magnetic tale. *New Scientist.* 7 February 2004; 14.

24. Sun gives Mars a halo of X-rays. *New Scientist.* 4 December 2004; 21.

25. Hogan J. Sun's halo linked to dark matter particle. *New Scientist.* 17 April 2004; 8.

26. Ibid.

27. Clark S. Tails of the unexpected. *New Scientist.* 10 September 2005; 32-35.

28. Ibid.

29. Chown M. Odd one out there. *New Scientist.* 11 December 2004; 33-35.

30. Rutledge RE, Basri G, Martin EL, Bildstein L. Chandra detec-

tion of an X-ray flare from the brown dwarf LP 944-20. *The Astrophysical Journal.* 1 August 2000; 538:L141-L144.

31. Muir H. Crab throws light on Titan's big air. *New Scientist.* 17 April 2004; 14.

32. Young star's X-rays a mystery. *New Scientist.* 12 March 2005; 17.

33. Bennet A. Solar geometry. 1999. http://solargeometry.com/Overview.htm [cited January 2006]

34. Ibid.

35. Meisner G. Phi and the Solar system. *Golden Number.net.* 2005. http://goldennumber.net/index.htm

36. Battersby S. Fire down below. *New Scientist.* 7 August 2004; 26-29.

37. Glatzmaier GA, Olsen P. Probing the Geodynamo. *Scientific American.* April 2005; 32-39.

38. Ibid.

39. Childress DH (ed) *Anti-gravity and the World Grid.* (Adventures Unlimited Press) 1987.

40. Cook N. *The Hunt for Zero point.* (Century) 2001.

41. Kitchin C. Earth's mini gamma-ray bursts. *Astronomy Now.* June 2005; 74-76.

42. Ibid.

43. Ibid.

44. Gosline A. Thunderbolts from Space. *New Scientist.* 7 May 2005; 30-34.

45. Kitchin C. Earth's mini gamma-ray bursts. *Astronomy Now.* June 2005; 74-76.

46. Battros M. About Mitch Battros. *Earth Changes TV.*

http://www.earthchangestv.com/aboutmitch.php [cited Jan 2006]

47. Charles RH. (translator) *The Book of Enoch.* (SPCK) 1994.

Chapter 16

Between Angels and Insects

So far, we have discussed how evidence for the BHP is present in galaxies, atoms and even in the planets of the solar system. Can we see the BHP occurring within us? If the BHP exists as a fractal pattern throughout all of creation, it should also be evident within ourselves. We have already discussed how our bodies display phi ratio geometry, reflected in the ratio of hand to forearm and forearm to arm etc. It is not just our limbs that show these ratios, they are evident throughout our bodies. This fact has recently gained publicity in the best-selling book, *The Da Vinci Code* by Dan Brown, which discusses the Fibonacci sequence and the fact that our bodies display phi ratio geometry.[1] It is also discussed in many websites and even a film, if the reader wishes to research this further.[2,3]

So if our bodies show this aspect of the BHP, are there any other characteristics that we can observe? If we think back to the central theme of the BHP being one of creation, we can start to see that the same signatures of manifestation are present in our bodies too.

The 'central black hole' of the body is likely to be the umbilicus, as this is the center of creation of the embryo. Some authors do indeed assert that the embryo grows in a spiral displaying phi ratio geometry.[4] The umbilical cord is indeed a spiral of blood vessels. The same phi ratio can be seen in many organs of the body.[5]

This may explain why the right and left sides of the body are asymmetric: a fact that puzzles scientists but seems rather basic to our body.[6] The asymmetry of the body reflects the unfolding spiral within it. This is easily seen in the shape of the heart.[7]

Another structure of the human body that displays many spirals is the brain. It is consideration of this fact, in the context of the BHP, that may give us new insights into conditions such as epilepsy. It has been noted that people who have epilepsy may show unusually high electrical activity in the brain, which is apparent on EEG recordings. This electrical activity is caused by the discharge of electrons throughout the brain. Such chaotic activity may be responsible for the person with epilepsy experiencing a seizure.

The brain therefore can display a periodic release of electrons. A particular form of epilepsy is called temporal lobe epilepsy, because the activity seems to originate from that particular part of the brain. There are certain structures in the temporal lobe that have been singled out to be the foci of activity, namely the amygdala and hippocampus. These structures have the characteristic spiral shape.

Could this be an example of the BHP and the light of infinity entering our dimension through the brain? It is interesting that before a seizure, some people with epilepsy have reported feelings of transcendence: a sense of being out of space and time. This has led to the hippocampus being labeled by neuroscientists as the *God spot,* because they can reproduce these types of experiences by applying external electrodes to the hippocampal region.[8]

Their work may have identified a black hole center in the brain, which is not only a good connection point to infinity, but may also be causing epilepsy. The current medical model still does not have a definitive picture of what causes and triggers epilepsy.

By considering such a mechanism, we may be able to find answers in the future that help people with the condition. I did find at least one scientific reference, which has linked solar flare activity to seizure rate and thus suggests that the push and pull forces that suspend us all may influence seizure rate. It is a topic that needs further investigation.[9]

Wheels on fire

The BHP could shed light on a subject that hardly ever comes under scientific scrutiny: that of chakras. Scientific quarters often dismiss the chakras as being no more than a New Age concept. The word *chakra* is derived from the Sanskrit word which means wheel. According to esoteric tradition, chakras are spinning centers of light in the body. The traditional view is that chakras create the body. They are represented as different colors; these represent their different spins and their different frequencies. Traditionally, the different chakras are responsible for creating the various organs.[10]

Although this concept is now ridiculed in the West, this was not the situation in the past. The chakras were probably originally seen directly by mystics in the East via direct conscious experience.

Could chakras actually exist? They are dismissed in reductionist science, because they cannot be measured or found by dissecting the body. Are chakras black holes?

We have now realized that the rotating spiral structure is one of the hallmarks of creation. Chakra healing, in its various forms, usually consists of repairing chakras or bringing them into balance. This supposedly will result in an improvement in health. This idea is consistent with the BHP; the different chakras create different organs. The chakra is another way of creating from infinity

Figure 21 – The Black Hole Principle in the chakra

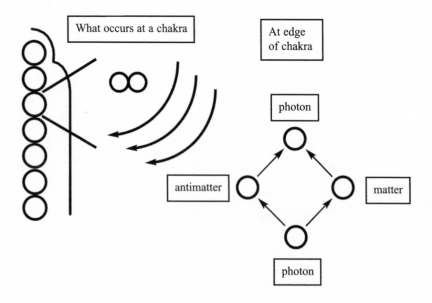

Most of the 'structure' behind chakras is not in our dimension, but lies beyond the Perception Horizon. Usually only mystical people can perceive them. This is why many people are skeptical about chakras existing; there is little physical proof. Measurements using

instruments from our dimension will not detect information from chakras.

However, we can make inferences about the chakras by measuring around them. As discussed in Chapter 9, researchers such as Professor Valerie Hunt at UCLA have taken EMG measurements from the areas of the body where chakras are supposed to be and found corresponding piezoelectric currents.[11] These are very weak electric currents, which Hunt feels are simply reflections of higher dimensional processes.

According to the BHP, at the edge of the Perception Horizon of a black hole, a positron and electron are emitted. When discussing the black hole process in the chakra, we see that the matter component, the electron, goes on to making the body. Just as in galaxies, the antimatter component enters the c^2 region. This is the mirror image of the body but in a higher frequency and shapes matter.

The c^2 region around the body is vibrating too fast to be seen by everyone. This is what is traditionally known as the aura. People who work with auras know that changing the aura results in a change within the body, without the body even having to be touched. This is a common factor in many healing modalities. This would fit with the idea that the aura is the antimatter region and therefore helps shape the body.

People also teach that positive intent makes a difference to a healing session. This may be a demonstration of the fact that consciousness is entwined with physical reality. Various clinical studies relate positive intent with an improved healing outcome, suggesting that our own consciousness does indeed have an influence on manifestation, via the BHP.[12]

Antimatter and emotions

Antimatter may also be the region where certain emotions are held in the body. I was inspired to consider this concept having heard the work of Dr John Demartini, an American chiropractor and wisdom teacher. He has developed a method of resolving emotional issues called *The Quantum Collapse Process*.[13]

He compares emotional healing to the matter-antimatter annihilation process. According to Demartini, we tend to have a polarized perception of situations; they are either good or bad. In the deeper reality, no such polarities exist and situations are neither good nor bad. This is similar to the way antimatter and matter are actually polarized expressions of light. They appear to be separate entities and can act as such, but at a deeper level of reality, they are aspects of light: 'frozen light' as David Bohm has said.[14]

In every situation, the deeper reality is always present and there is neither good nor bad, we just have to shift our awareness in order to see it. Actually every reality contains the healed reality; it is just our perception that sees the polarity and therefore judges the situation. Demartini likens the shift in our consciousness to become aware of the healed reality as similar to combining the antimatter and matter regions and turning them back into light.

If the antimatter region surrounds us in the form of an aura, could this represent our subconscious buried emotions? As we discussed in Chapter 9, our lives not only reflect out conscious thoughts, but our subconscious thoughts as well. The process of emotional healing involves our gaining conscious awareness of these subconscious emotions so that we become aware of where we have judgment and polarity.

As we do become aware, we move out of polarity and judgment about the situation and it no longer has a hold over us. In fact, we often forget what the issue was in the first place.

Demartini likens this to moving the situation from one of charge, polarity and mass – all properties of antimatter and matter, to one outside of space and time with no charge or mass, like a photon. Emotional resolution could actually mean uniting our matter aspect with our antimatter aspect to become light. Life could be a series of annihilation and creation processes as we move from one situation to another. We never rest in the healed reality for long; we simply move onto another.

This would entirely fit with the BHP. The BHP is a balance between the two directions of creating matter and creating light. There is never a set point; there is always dynamic equilibrium. So it is with our lives, just as we think we have got everything figured out, another situation arises that requires us to heal.

We have discussed how people change frequency as their journey unfolds. This is the mechanism by which this occurs. This can also be seen as personal alchemy: turning base material into gold, i.e. light.

A truly brief history of time

Throughout this book, we have touched on the aspect of time. For example, in Chapter 6, we discussed how remote viewers are able to see events in the future before they have happened. This suggests that events are predetermined.

The BHP allows for a new understanding of time. The ancient sages have always maintained that we live in an Eternal Now: that the universe is timeless. In the scientific era of reductionism, people believed in universal time. It was thought that the passage of time was the same no matter where you were in the universe.

Einstein's theory of relativity changed all that. We understood that the passage of time is affected by how fast you are traveling, for example when traveling near the speed of light, time moves much more slowly. When relativity is taken to its logical conclusion, time does not really exist. Yet the human experience is that time does exist. We perceive a past, present and a future. A child grows from boy to man, a tree grows from a seed and a cup that falls and smashes will never be whole again and so on. The passage of time is fundamental to our everyday experiences. However, according to ancient wisdom and modern science, the passage of time is an illusion.

The BHP allows for us to have our cake and eat it; we can experience the passage of time and the Eternal Now. According to the BHP, black holes contain regions that are in space and time as well as in the timeless reality of infinity. Because each and every part of the universe expresses this Black Hole Principle, all parts of the universe are both in space-time and infinity, at the same time. A timeline exists, but there is also the Eternal Now. Both exist.

At the edge of the Perception Horizon, light splits into antimatter and matter components. The three are eternally bound in a continuous cycle, being neither light nor matter nor antimatter. The antimatter and matter components are 'real', but are rather like viewing light through one aspect. They are separate from light and not separate at the same time.

This idea of this dual existence, of something being both one thing and another, has become familiar to us since the dawn of the quantum era. In quantum physics, a particle is both a wave and a particle at the same time. So are the aspects of creation; we think we can know reality, but reality is elusive and cycles from one state to another.

As we have mentioned before, William Tiller revealed that the component of antimatter exists in negative space-time and at the c^2 vibration, whilst matter exists at the c vibration.[15] The two worlds are mirror images of each other and intimately entwined. In fact, the antimatter gives rise to the matter region. This leads to an extraordinary conclusion. Everything that happens in our world with matter and positive space-time has already happened in the negative time antimatter region.

The antimatter region contains a type of blueprint that shapes our world. It contains all the information for everything to exist in the positive timeline region. Remember that when we are in either the c or the c^2 region, it is as if we are looking at light, through a certain aspect. Just as a prism splits light into different colors, light has been split into different regions, the c and c^2 region. The underlying truth is that all is light.

So it is with the mass and charge and time of the antimatter and matter. When combined, they cancel out. So really time does not exist in the big picture, it is as if consciousness itself is looking through a window, which gives the illusion that time exists. This window is our world, with all the events that occur within it. In the deeper aspect of our reality, all the events are happening at once, they are therefore both in a timeline and out of one, *at the same time.*

This idea of the deeper reality being timeless is explored in physicist Julian Barbour's book, *The End of Time*.[16] According to Barbour, time is a series of *Nows*, emergent from timelessness, which give us the impression of a passage of time. He even suggests that each Now is self-aware and linked to the quality of consciousness. His ideas have been highly influential on physicists such as Lee Smolin, one of the originators of Loop Quantum Gravity.[17]

The BHP is finally in a position to answer questions about free will and destiny. Your life has already happened in the negative timeline region and is simply following a pattern shaped by the antimatter region. This idea will leave many people uncomfortable, as it seems to remove the element of choice in our lives.

However, remember that we are all both antimatter, matter and light at the same time. We exist both in time and out of time at the same time. Part of everything and everyone is eternal and exists beyond the Perception Horizon. It is this part of you that is in the Eternal Now of mystical teaching. This is what is traditionally known as the higher self. When you choose, you choose from the eternal self that exists out of space and time. From this perspective, events do not occur in a sequence. This is the region of transcendent consciousness that is just on the edge of scientific discussion. The choices you experience in your life have truly occurred here, transcendent of your birth and death. The blueprints for our life events exist in the mirror world in negative space-time and we simply travel through them in positive space-time.

This may lead someone to question the point of a life where the choices have been made for you. The point of life is the experience, those daily thoughts and our reactions to events. It is as if the great oneness is playing a game with itself and pretending to be separate in order to learn about itself.

Never mind the bleep…here's Punk Science!

It is only in the c and c^2 regions that a sequence of events exists. The sequences run both forward and backward in time. It may be possible for some people to tune their consciousness to the c^2 region and see events that have 'happened' in the future. This could be the mechanism behind remote viewing and other forms of clairvoyance: seeing a future that has already happened. The studies in remote viewing have been done in a scientific manner and do indeed suggest that the future has already happened.

Many people believe that we choose our reality in each moment. This view is one that features heavily in teachings that may be considered 'New Age', but also in the philosophical considerations of quantum physics. As we recall, at the quantum level of reality, particles exist in a state of infinite reality, it is our observation that collapses this nebulous existence into something more tangible. Some have interpreted this as saying that we have infinite choice in each moment of our lives, even that each choice has been made by a parallel you, in a parallel universe. The film that has popularized the idea of infinite choice in each moment, *What the Bleep Do We Know*, features physicists such as Amit Goswami and William Tiller.

The BHP shows us that the sea of infinite choice that is glimpsed in quantum physics is actually the region that exists out of space and time. When below the Perception Horizon, which is complexed with its mirror world, the choice has already been made. This is why quantum physicists often criticize the idea that we have infinite choice and create our own reality, saying that the 'real world' does not act like the quantum world.

The parallel worlds are actually the infinite choices that are presented to our infinite selves. They occur in mathematics, but not in the reality that exists in space and time. Within our reality, our lives are predetermined; there is no parallel 'you' making another choice. This also means that the choices we make are always the 'right' ones because our infinite selves have already chosen them.

This is the view taken by contemporary philosophers such as Story Waters and it helps to create acceptance of the reality that is in front of you instead of trying to choose your way out of it, which is paradoxically disempowering, because it implies that you are a victim of circumstance.[19] Waters teaches that you have already chosen that reality as you are limitless. We may dislike some of the aspects of our lives, but we have chosen them from our limitless, infinite selves in order to give ourselves the right circumstances to learn within a particular life.

As people travel on their spiritual journey, they often encounter a stage of development when it seems that linear, ego self creates reality. We seem to manifest our intentions. Although this works, it appears to be a prelude to a time of surrender when there is no longer any need to create, as the individual realizes that everything has already been created by themselves anyway. It is not so much our consciousness that creates reality, but consciousness itself that creates and we are a part of it.

Time's arrow

Ironically, the idea of a predetermined future is a strange return to the Newtonian world. Perhaps Newton's mystical abilities actually took him to this level. Even Einstein disliked the idea of chance realities that quantum physics introduced and said "God does not play dice."[20]

It also solves the paradox of causality and time travel. According to the theory of relativity, time travel should be possible, which would lead to situations where you could go back in time to kill your own grandfather, creating a paradox.

The BHP shows that it is impossible for matter in the c region timeline to travel in time. Non-physical aspects such as consciousness are able to travel in time, but are unable to interact with anything in the physical dimension. So your mind is able to see the past and the future, but not change the physical events. This is what is experienced in remote viewing and past-life regression.

BHP finally reconciles the possibilities of time with the actualities of experience. Within physics, there is a debate as to why time only runs forward in the way we experience it in our daily lives. We do not see a cup that has fallen off the table and smashed piecing itself back together again, it remains broken although the possibilities of physics say that time can run backwards and the cup can become whole again. The BHP solves this problem, because time runs differently according to which perspective you find yourself at. Hence, the arrow of time will always run forward from the perspective of the c region, yet in higher dimensions, timelessness exists.

The goddess of negative time

The idea of being both within a timeline and out of time finally reconciles our everyday experiences with the conclusions of quantum physics and relativity.

The BHP requires the existence of this rather strange region of c^2 vibration of negative space-time. To my utmost surprise I found that this concept is not new and exists in both ancient and contemporary esoteric teachings.

The c^2 region is associated with the feminine principle. This is a conclusion made by physicists such as Dale Pond.[21] The c region is one of positive male principle action, whilst the c^2 exerts its more powerful force through a type of negative action.

An example of this sort of feminine negative action is seen in women when they give each other the advice "Make him think it's his idea." (A good depiction of this is seen in the film, *Mona Lisa Smile* with Julia Roberts.)[22] Women have often been taught to control situations, but not by direct action. Of course, not all women behave in this way, nor is it a behavior exclusive to women.[23] It simply gives us an example of what negative action looks like. This is seen as a feminine way of shaping reality by indirect action; a negative pull of attraction to shape events.

Women also give birth! This is in agreement with the idea that matter must come through the feminine region before entering the world from infinity: the principle found in ancient teachings.

The Secret Book of John is one of the Gnostic gospels that were rediscovered at Nag Hammadi in 1945. It was excluded from the Bible by the early church fathers, presumably because it did not support their doctrine. In the book, John records a description of creation given by Jesus. It reveals the elements of the c^2 region.[24]

Ch 3.3-10 "Its Thought became active and she who appeared in the presence of the Father in shining light came forth. She is the first power: she preceded everything, and came forth from the Father's mind as the Forethought of all. His light resembles the Father's light; as the perfect power, she is the image of the perfect and invisible spirit... Foreknowledge comes from the thought of the invisible virgin Spirit."

In the above passage we can see that the Father is the pure light of infinity, the "virgin spirit" is the invisible mirror world, which is not quite as bright: the c^2 region. The foreknowledge that precedes everything is a reference to negative time.

A lady called Carrie Harris, who attended one of my lectures, reflected on the possibility that the Holy Trinity of Christianity, the Father, the Son and the Holy Ghost, could be the infinite light, the matter and antimatter region. The teaching of three in one and one in three reflects the constant cycling between states.

Anthropologist Migene Gonzalez-Wippler identifies the Holy Spirit as being the *Shekinah* of Kabbalistic teachings: the female principle that presides over creation in the material realm.[25]

The same theme is found in Eastern teachings. Physicist Wayne Wang found the similarities between the physics of the holographic universe and the *Tao Te Ching* so startling that he makes an explicit link in his book *Dynamic Tao*.[26] In this book, originally written by Lao Tzu in 500 BCE, the manifest world is described as *Yo*, the mirror world as *Wu* and the infinite singularity as the eternal Tao.

In another of the Chinese teachings, the *Ta Chuan*, the themes of negative and positive space and time becomes more explicit. This quote describes the manifest and mirror universe as male and female and their entwined relationship.[27]

"The process of *Ch'ien* completes things through the male.

The process of *K'un* completes things through the female.

Chi'en knows the great beginnings.

K'un makes and completes all things."

In a more contemporary spiritual text, the Kryon books channeled by Lee Carrol, the term antimatter is used.[28]

"Where is antimatter? It's... in a slightly different time frame."

Astonishingly, it also describes a version of the BHP. However it is not only in esoteric texts that we find the concept of negative timelines, it is also present in modern physics. We have already discussed how negative time is entirely possible mathematically. The concept is part of the theory of loop quantum gravity and answers the question of what happened at time zero.[29] If you follow the positive timeline back to time zero, you enter the negative timeline and a mirror universe. So the idea of a negative timeline is actually part of mainstream science.

There must be more to life – revisited

We have discussed how the material realm is formed from infinite light via the creation of a mirror realm that shapes it. This mirror realm contains the blueprint for the events and creations in material reality. Now when we revisit some of the questions that arose in Part II, we get a new set of answers as to what shapes embryos and how evolution occurs.

In Part II, we raised the issue that biologists do not have a definitive answer as to how an organism gains its three-dimensional shape. The shape actually already exists as a blueprint in the c^2 region. This informs the dumb molecules as to how to organize themselves. Just as dark matter shapes the galaxies, so are living organisms shaped by the dark/ antimatter region. Everything in our universe has its mirror component that already exists.

This could also explain the results obtained by Harold Saxton Burr when he examined the electrical field around the unfertilized egg of salamanders and found the shape of an adult salamander.[30] Just as in the chakra, the piezoelectric field around the egg is a representation of information that exists in the c^2 region, which has a negative timeline. The salamander already exists in negative time, even though the egg has not even being fertilized. The molecules within the egg grow into the salamander shape with the c^2 region as its blueprint.

Evolution itself exists in a timeline, becoming more ordered and sophisticated from a less ordered state. The process is following a blueprint, which is fuelled ultimately by infinity and is therefore limitless in its energy. We shall expand on this theme in the final chapter.

DNA as a black hole

The BHP involves phi ratio geometry, which often manifests itself as a spiral. There is an obvious place where a spiral exists in the body, in DNA. The pioneering work of Dan Winter shows that DNA too displays phi ratio geometry.[31] Is DNA a black hole?

In our previous discussions on DNA we have shown that DNA is purely responsible for creating proteins. In other words it is responsible for adding to the matter component of a cell. We now know that matter must be complexed with an antimatter component; both are in a continuous cycle with light.

As we know from the work of Psychoneuroimmunology, by Bruce Lipton and Ryke Geerd Hamer, perception of the environment affects the production of cells.[32,33] An abnormal increase in cell production results in cancer. Hamer made the link between receiving an emotional shock and the development of cancer. An emotional shock causes a fragment of consciousness to be stuck in space and time. Unless emotional resolution occurs and the antimatter and matter components are turned into light, part of that person's consciousness remains stuck. This tips the dynamic balance of the DNA black hole spiral towards producing antimatter and matter. This leads to more cells being produced and less of the annihilation process.

Amazingly we have experimental data that confirms that less light is produced by cells when a person has cancer. Fritz Albert Popp has been studying photon emissions from living organisms.[34] Few such photons are emitted so his instruments have to be very sensitive. When people are healthy they give out emissions of light, which pulse in waves. Is this the equivalent of the cyclic gamma ray bursts in DNA?

When someone gets cancer, Popp found that the emissions of light decrease and the cyclic pulses disappear.[35] This is what we would expect if the balance of the BHP were predominately in the realms of matter and antimatter. It also hints at the importance of being in the dynamic flow of Nature, as becoming stuck in one perspective or another may lead to disease.

In this chapter we have examined how the BHP relates to our

own lives. Now we are ready to look at the big picture: the whole shebang.

References for Chapter 16

1. Brown Dan. *The Da Vinci Code*. (Corgi adult) 2004.

2. Meisner G. *Golden Number.net*. http://goldennumber.net/ [cited January 2006].

3. Aronofsky D. (Director) *Pi*. DVD (Pathe Distribution) 2004.

4. Melchizedek D. *The Ancient Secret of the Flower of Life, Volume 1*. (Light Technology, US) 1999.

5. Ibid.

6. Ainsworth C. Left right and wrong. *New Scientist*. 17 June 2000; 40- 45.

7. Winter D. *Implosion: the Secret Science of Ecstasy and Immortality*. (Implosion group) 2004.

8. Ramachandran V. *Phantoms in the Brain*. (Fourth Estate) 1998.

9. Spottiswoode SJP, Tauboll E, Duchowny M, Neppe V. Epilepsia. 1993; 34: 2: 56-69.

10. Gerber R. *Vibrational Medicine: New Choices for Healing Ourselves*. (Bear and company) 1996.

11. Hunt V. *Infinite Mind*. (SOS Free Stock) 1996.

12. Bunnell T. the Effect of 'Healing with Intent' on Pepsin enzyme activity. *Journal of Scientific Exploration*. 1999; 13:2:139-148.

13. Demartini J F. *The Breakthrough Experience*. (Hay House) 2002.

14. Weber R. *Dialogues with scientists and Sages*. (Arkana) 1990.

15. Tiller WA. *Science and human transformation*. (Pavior) 1997.

16. Barbour J. *The End of Time*. (Phoenix) 2000.

17. Smolin L. *Three Roads to Quantum Gravity*. (Phoenix) 2001.

18. Vincente M, Arntz W, Chasse B. *What the Bleep do we know?* [DVD]. (Revolver Entertainment) 2005.

19. Waters S. *The Messiah Seed, Volume 1*. (Limitlessness) 2004.

20. Born M, Einstein A. *The Born-Einstein Letters*. (Macmillan) 1971.

21. Pond D ed. *Universal Laws Never Before Revealed*. (Infotainment world Books) 1995.

22. Newell M. (director) *Mona Lisa Smile*. [DVD] (Columbia tri-star home video) 2004.

23. Icke D. *The Biggest Secret*. (Bridge of Love) 1999.

24. Meyer MW. *The Secret teachings of Jesus: Four Gnostic gospels*. (Vintage) 1996.

25. González-Wippler M. *Keys to the Kingdom*. (Llewellyn) 2004.

26. Wang WL. *Dynamic Tao and its manifestations*. (Helena Island Publisher) 2004.

27. Karcher S. *Ta Chuan: the Great Treatise*. (St Martin's press) 2000.

28. Carrol L. Kramer J. (Ed) *A New Dispensation*. (Kryon writings) 2004.

29. Gefter A. The world turned inside out. *New Scientist*. 20 March 2004; 34-37.

30. Burr HS. *The Fields of life*. (Ballantine books)1972

31. Winter D. *Implosion: the Secret Science of Ecstasy and Immortality*. (Implosion group) 2004.

32. Lipton BH. *The Biology of Belief*. (Mountain of Love) 2005.

33. Hamer RG. *Summary of the New Medicine*. (Amici de Dirk) 2000.

34. Popp FA. Biphoton emission of the human body. *Journal of Photochemistry and photobiology.* 1997; 40:187-9.

35. Popp FA et al. *Coll.Phenomena.* 1981; 3:187.

Chapter 17

The whole shebang

Table of the Black Hole Principle expressed at different levels of the universe

Level	Annihilation process or evidence of antimatter	Spiral/ evidence of phi ratio?	Infinity/ out of space and time at center?	Ejection of gamma rays	Ejection of X-rays or fast moving electrons
Universe	No	Yes	Possibly	No	No
Galactic cluster	No	Yes	No	Yes	Yes
Galaxy	Yes	Yes	Yes	Yes	Yes
Micro-quasar	Yes	Yes	Yes	Yes	Yes
Solar system	No	Yes	No	No	No
Sun	Yes	Yes	No	Yes	Yes

Planets	No	Yes	No	Yes	Yes
Earth	Yes	No	No	Yes	No
Weather systems	Yes	Yes	No	Yes	Yes
Human	No	Yes	No	No	No
Chakra	No	Yes	No	No	No
Atom	Yes	Yes	No	Yes	Yes
Subatomic particles	Yes	Yes	Yes	Yes	No
DNA	No	Yes	No	Yes?	No

The above table shows the components of the BHP that have been found at various levels. It shows there is evidence for the antimatter process in supermassive black holes, for example. If no evidence has yet been found for a process at a particular level of the universe, then we can only make predictions that this will be found at a future date. The theory of the BHP may be modified or even superseded by a later theory with the benefit of further data.

For now, we have an interesting unifying concept to explore that does indeed fit the patterns that we see in Nature. The BHP fits our current data and we can consider it to be a reasonable picture of the universe. If the BHP is true, then creation occurs at each and every level of reality. The seemingly solid world we see around us is simply an aspect of infinite light. In this infinite world there is no beginning or end to creation, just a continuous spiral from the singularity of each black hole center, coming to the edge of the Perception Horizon and becoming the material and mirror worlds.

Yet we are told that the beginning of creation occurred with a massive explosion, a Big Bang. The first few seconds of the early universe have all been mapped out; it underwent a period of rapid expansion that we call inflation. Since then, the universe has been expanding, accelerating away, perhaps to culminate in a contraction or Big Crunch. Surely creation has already happened and we have appeared after the party is over?

In actuality, the Big Bang theory is increasingly being questioned; the evidence is accumulating that it does not fit our observations. Nor does it explain why events such as gamma ray bursts are seen throughout the universe. It seems that the era of Big Bang may be drawing to a close.

There is a current rise of dissent about Big Bang theory amongst cosmologists. Some have organized themselves into The Alternative Cosmology group and are protesting that too many fudge factors and assumptions have to be made in the Big Bang theory. They published an open letter in *New Scientist* in April 2004 in order to draw attention to the fact that research funding is not given to people working on theories other than Big Bang, which has led to a scientific restraint on the development of alternatives.[1]

They argue that the dominance of Big Bang theory has led to cosmological data being dismissed because it does not fit. Every new piece of evidence that is incorporated into Big Bang needs the addition of new adjustable parameters: fudge factors. They compare this situation to that of Ptolemy who believed that the planets of the solar system revolved around the Earth in a circular fashion and were not elliptical. So when observations did not fit this theory, he kept adding more and more circular orbits called *epicycles* to make the observations fit. Big Bang theory is also accused of failing to make predictions that have later been successfully backed up by observations.

These are powerful accusations and probably only represent a fraction of the level of dissent on this subject. Certainly there are numerous websites that describe alternative theories of cosmology, but these are currently seen as being on the fringe of science. It is worth discussing some of the current issues raised with Big Bang theory and also why cosmologists have deemed the theory to be proved by cosmological data in the first place. As we shall see, this very same data, when interpreted in a different way, gives support to the BHP.

Faded stars or new hopefuls?

According to Big Bang theory, the universe expanded from a point of singularity. All parts of the universe moved away from all other parts. At the present moment, we cannot measure light outside of the c region, so we have to wait for light to travel to us from distant parts of the universe. By the time it reaches us, it may be a few billion years old. If the universe is 13.7 billion years old, the light from distant galaxies should be showing us relatively young stars and galaxies. We should be looking into their early history, when they had not had time to mature.

However, this is not what we see. Even in the light from distant galaxies, we see that they are very well developed.[2] If the universe is only as young as we think it is, why do these galaxies look so old?

The way that we measure these distant galaxies is with the technique of measuring redshift that has been described in Chapter 11. Could we be misinterpreting this redshifted light? Is this why our observations of the universe do not fit our theory? One of the more prominent members of The Alternative Cosmology group, Eric Lerner, suggests that redshift is due to a mechanism other than the expansion of the universe.[3]

Another maverick theory, put forward by Lyndon Ashmore, is the Tired Light theory that suggests that redshift is due to photons of light from distant galaxies having lost energy whilst traveling across space due to interactions with electrons.[4]

We also have the opposite problem in that there are many more young stars than expected. Where we expect to see stellar nurseries that have long fizzled out, we see new stars being created within them.[5] Everywhere we look we see the evidence of continuous creation.[6] New stars are always forming and many black holes are unexpectedly active and emitting material. These observations do not fit a model that places such acts of creation in an early, hot, dense universe. However, a mixture of old and young stars throughout the universe is exactly what we would expect to see if the BHP were true, as each part of the cosmos is in continuous creation.

Cosmic microwave background radiation

One of the recent triumphs of cosmology has been the mapping of the cosmic microwave background (CMB) radiation with the Wilkinson Microwave Anisotropy Probe (WMAP) satellite. As we recall, the accidental discovery of the background microwave radiation by Arno Penzias and Robert Wilson in 1965, has been seen by many as the proof of Big Bang theory.

This has led cosmologists to confidently say that we have a standard model of cosmology.[7] However, there are glitches in the CMB data that could be severe enough to send cosmologists back to the drawing board, according to *Scientific American*.[8]

Not only does the pattern of the data show some important omissions compared to the expectations of the standard model, it also shows some curious alignments.[9] Checking and rechecking has so far confirmed that the CMB is aligned with aspects of our own solar system including the pathway of the sun. According to predictions, these alignments should not exist.

Maybe the CMB is not actually coming from 'out there', but is an effect of the continuous creation process at every level of the universe. If that is the case, then alignments with processes within our solar system are to be expected.

There is a particular observation that may shed some light on this issue. Large numbers of microwaves have been found pouring out of the center of the Milky Way. These are typical of those seen when high-energy electrons and positrons circle around magnetic fields! This has their discoverer, Douglas Finkbeiner of Princeton University, wondering if the annihilation process is responsible for the microwaves.[10]

So if our own galaxy is producing microwaves by annihilation, isn't it possible that every galaxy is producing them and therefore every black hole? The production of microwaves could be occurring at every level of the universe and be an aspect of the BHP. This would leave our universe with a background of microwave radiation, exactly what we do indeed find. This also explains why the CMB has persisted so long; it is being continuously created.

So the reason why the data shows up an alignment with our solar system is that we are recording the microwaves produced from within it. The findings of 1965 were correct, this is the signature of creation. However the inference may be wrong, creation may not have occurred just 13 billion years ago, but in every single moment.

Gamma ray bursts and X-ray emissions

We have already explored these subjects in depth as part of the explanation of the BHP. However, these subjects are worth mentioning here, as these phenomena are not fully explained by current models of cosmology. As we recall, highly energetic gamma ray bursts have been observed for some decades. The energy contained within them is so enormous that current theories of cosmology can only explain them as powerful explosions or collisions. There is no other possible mechanism within the current paradigm that deals only with physical matter. Teams around the world are currently searching to find gamma ray bursts as soon as they happen because they are looking to find debris and after-glows left over from an explosion. The discovery of after-glows has confirmed that these gamma ray bursts can reach us from the far reaches of the universe.

All sorts of exotic theories have been put forward to explain these bursts. One is that they are the dying gasps of neutron stars, objects known to have enough gravity to be able to power these observed rays.[11] If gamma ray bursts are the results of stellar processes then we should be able to see a concentration of them within our own galaxy. This is not what we see.[12] These energetic processes are occurring all over the universe. This has flummoxed cosmologists because if the cause of the bursts is at a great distance, then the energy has been sustained during the time it takes to travel here. Yet no objects are known to produce that kind of power without violating Einstein's laws.[13]

We may not be able to find a physical process that creates gamma ray bursts, but non-physical processes that create the physical may be responsible. As the BHP is powered by infinity, which causes the creation of the physical world, there is no shortage of energy available!

The same goes for X-ray emissions. They have been found coming from various objects in our universe, sometimes un-expectedly. They are also seen all over the sky, which has prompted a search for their source. It is currently believed that these X-rays are the dying gasps of stars entering black holes that we have yet to identify.[14] The BHP predicts the appearance of X-rays and gamma rays bursts all over the night sky, as the process is happening in a fractal fashion at every level of the universe.

Dark energy and dark matter

If Big Bang theory did not really happen, why do we see distant supernovae accelerating away from us? Surely this is a sign of the universe expanding? This expansion of the universe has been attributed to a force opposing gravity: antigravity. As we have previously described, the region of antimatter in the mirror universe is associated with the force of antigravity. This may be the reason why we cannot detect the force accelerating the expansion of the universe; it lies out of our region of space-time. This is why it appears dark to us and we cannot detect it.

The energy of the antimatter, antigravity region exists in the c^2 region and, according to the BHP, this force is being created all over the universe when light splits into its constituents. Antigravity has more energy than gravity and is spread across the universe. This is why the attraction of physical objects to each other by gravity is overridden and distant objects are therefore accelerating away from us, driven by forces that exist outside the realm of matter.

The creation of planets

Another problem with current models of cosmology is the lack of an exact mechanism behind the creation of objects such as planets.[15] As we recall, the current model states that planets originate in fluctuations in the otherwise smooth state of the early universe. However, nobody truly knows why these fluctuations should exist.

These early fluctuations are supposed to have caused clumps of matter to accumulate creating a gravitational pull that attracts more matter, until a solid planetary core has been built. However, many agree that this process is simply not enough to cause the creation of the planets. The main problem is how the dust particles stick together during the early part of the process. What we do observe around a forming planet are the bipolar jets that are characteristic of black holes.[16] These bipolar jets have also been seen around forming stars as well.[17]

Another aspect of planets and other bodies is perpetual rotation. How do so many objects in the universe, from black holes to planets to atoms, continuously rotate? What is fuelling this movement? How is the energy provided? According to the BHP, the universe is continuously spiraling itself into existence from an infinite core. Every part of the universe has access to infinity, so does not have to worry about ever running out! This is what sustains perpetual motion.

There are some parallels with a leading theory in physics, Loop Quantum Gravity, which says that the fabric of the universe is a series of evolving spin networks.[18] Space-time is the result of these geometrical spin networks.

In fact, the influential mathematician, Kurt Gödel, concluded that the whole universe is rotating, but this was dismissed as nonsense.[19] The universe is continuously spiraling itself into existence. We are inside the universe and everything in it is in perpetual rotation from stars to planets to galaxies. It can appear to us that the entire universe is not rotating, but we can only judge rotation when it is relative to something and at this level, we have nothing to compare it to! Gödel showed us the mathematics and the Haramein-Rauscher model has reiterated this.[20] The perpetual motion of the universe and everything within it is fuelled by infinity. The question is; what is infinity?

To infinity and beyond

The incorporation of the infinite is the crux of the BHP. Every single part of everything in the universe is in touch with the infinite. Within every spiral, the eye of the storm remains unmoved and still. Each singularity at the center of every black hole in this fractal universe is not only in touch with every other singularity, it is the same singularity.

If this is making your head spin, don't worry. These are difficult concepts that seem so removed from our linear daily world. In fact, the idea of infinity is precisely something that is unknowable. We can never conceive of the totality of the universe; it is unknowable.

This is an unpalatable fact for today's scientists, who are desperately looking for a description of the universe that will incorporate everything. Really, this cannot be done; we can only go from one description to the next. Hence Newtonian mechanics was superseded by relativity, which is probably also about to be replaced. Every time a new theory arises, we see the last one as simply an approximation to reality.

When I received my vision in 2003, whilst sitting on the branch of a tree, it made me feel humble to realize this. I have provided much evidence in this last segment for a new *theory of everything*, but I am fully aware that this is only another approximation until the next leap in consciousness.

In the course of writing this book, I have been amazed at how physicists have often used fudge factors, so that infinity does not enter their equations. At a physics conference in 2005, I was shocked to hear Michael Green say that Heisenberg had actually realized that the universe was a sea of black holes with infinity at each core.[21] This was the original picture of the quantum vacuum and the basis of Heisenberg's uncertainty principle. We can now view the quantum vacuum in terms of the BHP and redefine it as a sea of black holes in constant dynamic creation and destruction. Heisenberg had the answer, but disliked the concept of infinity, so thought that he was mistaken.

Feynman used a process to remove the infinities in quantum electrodynamics.[22] It seems unpalatable to physicists that infinity is the answer; they dismiss it as nonsense. I once heard Michio Kaku say that he wanted to find an equation for the theory of everything that is elegant and an inch long. ∞ is the symbol for infinity. It is elegant, less than an inch long and is the answer to everything!

An equation describes a relationship to something else. By

definition you are splitting the whole into parts that can be related to one another. With infinity, there is no relationship, it cannot be defined, and it is boundless and formless. We can never truly conceptualize or define the infinite.

Infinity is unknowable, but physicists believe that this is not so: that one day their minds can conquer everything. The fact is, all we can do is gain insights on parts of infinity in relation to the infinite. We can never truly understand infinity. It is beyond our comprehension and knowledge.

As we have seen throughout this book, when consciousness is seen as fundamental to the universe some of its secrets are revealed. Is the originator of the universe an infinite mind that gives rise to everything within the universe? Is this the mind of God?

To be fair, physicists are also playing with concepts of infinity. The singularity exists at the heart of every black hole. The Randall–Sundrum model describes membranes of infinite dimensions, Magueijo discusses infinite light.[22,24] There is another rebel band of cosmologists, based in Italy, who say that the universe expresses itself as a fractal.[25] Although not yet mainstream, their approach may become popular as alternatives to Big Bang theory become more visible.

This concept of infinity being the source of all and forever unknowable solves another issue with Big Bang theory. Where did the universe come from, what banged in the first place? Current theories have the universe coming into existence out of nowhere, violating all the laws of physics anyway. Physicists have currently resigned themselves to not asking the question of what came before the Big Bang. Some even say that it is irrelevant. With the BHP, the universe is continuously spiraling into existence. Although this does not answer the question of why and what started it all, it may turn out to be a more elegant picture of creation than a Big Bang.

Last action hero

These concepts will be difficult to come to terms with for many. We don't want to hear that the *theory of everything* is unknowable. We want to understand and define in the terms that we are used to.

I believe that this is the major stumbling block to science today; despite the conclusions of quantum theory describing a nebulous universe, many still believe that the answers to the universe lie in physical processes. I believe that this is why science is currently approaching a standstill. The physical universe has been explored; reductionism is drawing to a close. As people move on in their evolution and discover their spirituality, their consciousness shifts and they see the universe in a different way. This is about to be reflected in our science.

I do not mean to be critical of men, but for a female on the outside of physics, the language used has a feeling of it being in an action movie. This may hold clues as to why the true nature of the universe is being missed; if you think in these terms, you are going to look for your answers in these terms. Hence the language used is often the language of violence - annihilation, black holes devouring stars, gamma ray bursts as explosions and the search for the smoking gun of the Big Bang. We currently view the universe as a violent place.

A step back from this violent paradigm shows us that antimatter did not get eliminated in a battle with matter, but instead co-exists with it. Our planet contains many people who believe that the only way to exist is to annihilate each other. According to our current thinking, peaceful co-existence is not possible. The BHP shows us that something can be both one thing and another, at the same time. The BHP moves us from a state of separation, duality and opposition into one of cooperation, peaceful co-existence and harmony.

This is the way of the sacred feminine, which does not mean female, but the principle of the universe so neglected that is a part of all of us. I do not think it is a coincidence that at the same time of writing this book, which discusses the c^2 region associated with the feminine principle, many people are reading the *Da Vinci Code*, which discusses the biblical figure of Mary Magdalene.[26] As the author, Dan Brown, points out, the deeper story is that we have lost the aspect of the sacred feminine; some would call this the Holy Grail.

Is it time now to discover that this co-existence is not just an unrealistic ideology that has nothing to do with the real world? This is the way our universe works, both the feminine and masculine are harmoniously entwined and co-creating each other.

It is the ignorance of this principle that has kept so many so blind for so long: unable to interpret the data before them with any coherence. Unless someone is healed within themselves with respect to their own inner sacred feminine, they cannot conceive of it. This is tragically rare for it requires a gentler listening to inward processes and a stillness not encouraged by the business of modern life.

Understanding the sacred feminine principle is part of the path to wholeness, not only for humanity's evolution, but also for the advancement of scientific knowledge.

References for Chapter 17

1. Lerner E. Bucking the Big Bang. *New Scientist*. 22 May 2004; 20.

2. Chown M. End of the beginning. *New Scientist*. 2 July 2005; 30-35.

3. Ibid.

4. Ashmore L. Ashmore's tired light theory. *Lyndonashmore.com*. 5 February 2005. http://www.lyndonashmore.com/tired_light_front_page.html [cited January 2006].

5. Zepf SE, Ashman K M. The Unexpected youth of globular clusters. *Scientific American*. October 2003; 26-33.

6. Barger AJ. The Midlife Crisis of the Cosmos. *Scientific American*. January 2005; 32-39.

7. Shanks T. That's all folks. *New Scientist*. 14 February 2004; 19.

8. Starkman GD, Schwarz D J. Is the Universe out of tune? *Scientific American*. August 2005; 36-43.

9. Ibid.

10. Finkbeiner DP. *WMAP Microwave Emission Interpreted as Dark Matter Annihilation in the Inner Galaxy*. January 2005. http://www.arxiv.org/abs/astro-ph/0409027.

11. Britt RR. Black hole swallows neutron star, observations suggest. *Space.com*. 14 December 2005. http://www.space.com/scienceastronomy/051214_star_collision.html [cited January 2006].

12. Gehrels N, Piro L, Leonard PJT. The Brightest explosions in the Universe. *Scientific American*. December 2002; 53-59.

13. Amelino-Camelia G. Double Special Relativity. *Nature.* 2002; 418: 34-35.
http://arxiv.org/abs/gr-qc/0207049

14. Why does the Sky glow? *Universe.Nasa.gov.* 3 August 2005. http://universe.nasa.gov/press/2005/050803a.html [cited January 2006]

15. Chown M. Pulling Power. *New Scientist.* 29 September 2001; 32-34.

16. Chown M. Lone Planets make it just like stars. *New Scientist.* 29 November 2003; 10.

17. O'Dell C R, Beckwith SVW. Young stars and their surroundings. *Science.* 30 May 1997; 276: 5317:1355-1359.

18. Smolin L. Atoms of Space and Time. *Scientific American.* January 2004; 56-65.

19. Gott JR. *Time Travel in Einstein's Universe.* (Phoenix) 2001.

20. Haramein N, Rauscher E.A. The origin of spin: a consideration of torque and coriolis forces in Einstein's field equations and grand unification theory. *Noetic Journal.* June 2005; 6:1-4:143-162.

21. Green M. *The Synthesis of relativity and Quantum theory in String theory.* 11 April 2005. Plenary presentation at the Institute of Physics: a century after Einstein, University of Warwick.

22. Feynman RP. *Q.E.D. The Strange theory of Light and Matter.* (Penguin Books Ltd) 1990.

23. Randall L. *Warped Passages.* (Allen Lane) 2005.

24. Magueijo J. *Faster than the speed of light.* (Arrow) 2004.

25. Baryshev Y, Teerikorpi P. *The Discovery of Cosmic Fractals.* (World Scientific Publishing Company) 2002.

26. Brown D. *The Da Vinci Code.* (Corgi adult) 2004.

Part V

Applications of Punk Science

Chapter 18

The Spirit of the New Reality

So far in this book, we have traveled to the ends of the cosmos and back into black holes, atoms and chakras, covering topics as diverse as the Gnostic gospels and quantum theory.

What remains to be explored is how all this relates to our daily lives. Does *Punk Science* belong purely in the realms of navel-gazing, or are there practical applications to be gleaned from it that can enhance our everyday lives? In this section, we shall be exploring the applications of *Punk Science* and how we are already entering a new reality.

American idiot

The early 21st century has been a time of global turmoil. The attacks on the twin towers of September 11th 2001 and their aftermath, have led to a mistrust of world leaders.[1] This is highly apparent in the case of the president of the US, George W. Bush. Anti-Bush campaigns have been seen throughout the world. He has become a focus of collective human hatred. By discussing his example, we can learn much about the current state of human consciousness and how we are moving into a different paradigm.

The response of Bush to the September 11th attacks included the statement to the world, "You are either with us, or you are with the enemy."[2] These words reveal a consciousness steeped in separation and division. It is a concise demonstration of the Newtonian mechanistic paradigm. In the pre-quantum era, it was scientifically valid to believe objects, such as human beings, were distinct and separate from each other.

We now realize that it is not possible to describe a person as truly being 'other' and distinct from ourselves. Science has revealed that so-called enemies are intimately connected, as all people of this planet are actually part of one whole when viewed at a deep level. If our very subatomic particles are linked through time and space, then separation cannot really occur.

Coinciding with the increasing understanding of the science of non-locality is the rise of the number of protests against war. The reality of the connectedness of human consciousness is becoming the dominant paradigm. We are less able to view the children of other countries as unfortunate targets in war; we see them as our own children. We are moving into an era of knowing the scientific truth of non-locality within ourselves.

In protesting against the war, many continue to create separation and duality. In doing so, they continue to create an external enemy. World leaders such as Bush have become the focus for public hatred.

Yet the same principle of non-locality and connection must apply here too. Uncomfortable though it may be for some to accept, at a deep level, Bush is a part of each of us; we are all connected.

Whether you think of him as a hero, a cruel dictator or even a shape-shifting reptile, he is also a part of this holographic universe.[3] As every part of the universal hologram contains the information of the whole, Bush too, holds the consciousness of each and every one of us. He holds up a mirror for us to see exactly what is within ourselves as a collective global race! In a way, we can see Bush as a great teacher, for he is showing us our own souls in such a public way.

As this new scientific vision enters our lives on all levels, it must change the very fabric of our society and our politics. In the holographic non-local universe, there is no true separation, only unity. It is this understanding, when truly absorbed into the public consciousness, that will transform our world.

The business of *Punk Science*

There are few subjects on this planet as emotive as money; it often changes the way people behave. For example, when faced with daily financial realities, many give up on their dreams. When it comes to business, idealism often disappears. Likewise, many believe that esoteric knowledge is wholly separate from the 'real' world of making money: that different rules apply.

However, if the ideas in *Punk Science* are really universal, they should apply to financial realities as well as everything else. Already a movement exists amongst leading business thinkers that recognizes the need to apply ideas in new science to the way we work. They are realizing that 'business as usual' often belongs to the old Newtonian way of thinking. Hence, lack of connection, competition and mechanistic thinking are apparent in many organizations.

Author and filmmaker Michael Moore describes an example of the consequences of this disconnectedness in the film, *The Corporation*, in which he discusses how people in his hometown often do not realize that their manufacturing of automobiles will result in environmental pollution.[4] As people wake up to the ways of interdimensional, interconnected consciousness this will naturally lead to the creation of new business models.

One of the ground-breaking books linking new science with business, is Margaret J Wheatley's *Leadership and the New Science*.[5] She highlights how current organizational consciousness is largely stuck in a Newtonian mechanical, disconnected world and not engaging in post-quantum paradigms. The Newtonian worldview deals with solid objects and certainties, which translates into a belief that the world is static and can be easily controlled.

Wheatley stresses the need to move into the post-quantum world with its inherent uncertainties. She describes the importance of remaining fluid and present with your current reality. This has direct analogies with the BHP, with its dance between the forces of creation of light and matter. Wheatley recognizes the need to play with the dance rather than hold on to false certainties: "We can realize that, like all life, we know how to grow and evolve in the midst of constant flux."

A central idea of *Punk Science* is that consciousness is fundamental to physical reality, also a theme of Wheatley's, who says that informational processes are fundamental to the universe and create physical form. She has also recognized that systems always work in a fractal nature. This self-similar organizing behavior is often evident at every level of an organization from the shop-floor employee to top management. Thus organizations are examples of fractal consciousness, as seen throughout the universe.

One of the key features of the BHP is the spiral. We have discussed how the spiral is key to manifestation and is apparent at every level of life, so why not at the level of an organization? I spoke with Morel Fourman, CEO of London-based Company *Show Business*, which provides organizations with transformational tools.[6]

He has realized that a healthy system is the result of the balance between wisdom and material output. Too much wisdom with not enough material output and the system is not self-sustaining, as it does not produce enough resources to maintain itself. Too much material emphasis and not enough wisdom and the company will start to flounder due to lack of coherence. This has obvious analogies to the BHP and the importance of fluidity in the system between the creation of light and the creation of antimatter and matter.

Furthermore, Fourman has realized that the spiral is essential to the process of manifestation. In what he calls the Global Transformational Vortex, he outlines which elements are needed for a system to transform and for it to be self-sustaining. Inputs into a flagging system, such as values-based resources, consultants who are in touch with true wisdom and wisdom-based models can lead to a transformed system. Crucially he sees the inputs in terms of a spiral, so that seemingly disparate aspects are actually adding to the whole. He has, therefore, naturally discovered the truth of the BHP within the context of his life and is using it successfully within a business model.

The idea that financial realities follow the spiral pattern has been previously explored with some interesting results. There is evidence of the stock market following the Fibonacci series. In the 1930s, accountant Ralph N. Elliot realized there was a link between market indices, such as the Dow Jones, and the mathematical Fibonacci series.[7] These patterns are known as Elliot Waves and have been linked to everything from Major League Baseball to hemlines in fashion. It seems that the signature of the universe is evident in unexpected areas our lives, if we care to look.

The punk path of leadership

When someone starts to live according to the principles of new science, this can lead to enormous shifts. These profound changes are becoming more common in humanity, some call it *living in the new paradigm* or *flowing with the Tao*. A beautiful account of one man's navigation of this journey is Joseph Jaworski's *Synchronicity: the inner path to leadership*.[8]

In this extraordinary tale, weaving Jaworski's professional life with his personal journey, it is clear that a new way of living is emerging. Jaworski's own life began with apparent Newtonian certainties when he worked as a top lawyer, but his life turned out to have never been that certain anyway. After a personal wake-up call, he started on a new path: one of listening to the blueprint of his life already in existence.

One of the most striking moments in the account of his journey is when he passed his future wife for the first time in a busy airport, yet instantly recognized this stranger as belonging to his life. It is such a beautiful example of the way people start to change so that they no longer operate from the old causality model: their consciousness is in tune with the future, in which their life has already happened.

As more people shift in awareness, this type of event is becoming more common, resulting in changes in the way we experience our daily lives. Jaworski founded the American Leadership forum. He experienced immense flow during this process: synchronous meetings and coincidences. He realized that this journey started with a different type of commitment to the one he knew before. Previously, his success lay in being highly disciplined and pushing himself to succeed. However, the new type of commitment allows for the unfolding of events rather than forcing their creation. Order already exists in our lives; we simply have to recognize that it is so.

As we have previously discussed, physicist David Bohm discussed how the universe has an implicate order. A meeting with Bohm was pivotal to Jaworski and helped him to form a conceptual framework for the new interconnected universe he was starting to experience. His book illustrates a new way of living and how all aspects of our lives become totally integrated when we align with our deepest sense of self.

"We begin to listen to the inner voice that helps guide us as our journey unfolds. The underlying component of this kind of commitment is our trust in the playing out of our destiny. We have the integrity to stand in a 'state of surrender,' ... knowing that whatever we need at the moment to meet our destiny will be available to us. It is at this point that we alter our relationship with the future."[9]

Although Jaworski does not express it as such, he has encapsulated an important principle, not only for leadership, but also for all aspects of life. There is a moment in a person's development when they realize that their life is not caused by their past, but is caused by the future! They become aware that their future blueprint is already in existence and undergo a surrender process, where they no longer need to strive to create their reality, they realize they have already created it from the part of them that is beyond space and time. They become aware of the c^2 region and beyond. Collectively, we are moving into awareness of these realms. As we do, our old ways are being replaced by a new sensibility about life in which concepts from new science are playing a key part.

Lost prophets

Personally, the most startling discovery whilst writing this book was the fact that ancient texts, such as the Gnostic gospels, contain the Black Hole Principle. This implies that the original religious philosophies included a highly advanced, scientific cosmology. It is only in the later years that science and religion split, partly because the true interpretation of these texts became forgotten.

The Gnostic gospels contained principles of the universe unknown to most modern scientists. The Gnostic gospels are considered by some people to be the writings of the very early Christians and to be closest to the true Christian message.[10] It is thought that certain controversial passages caused the early Roman church leaders, such as the Emperor Constantine, to censore them, perhaps ordering every copy of such scriptures to be destroyed.

Hence the texts found at Nag Hammadi are perhaps our only surviving copy, hidden by someone hoping to save this knowledge for future generations. The Gnostics practiced methods of directly knowing the universe or *gnosis*. This effectively means obtaining information from the Quantum Vacuum in the manner discussed in this book. The established church leaders saw this practice of directly experiencing the 'divine' as dangerous and followers of these types of traditions were energetically eliminated.

The fact that the Gnostic gospels contain information about cosmology that is now proving to be correct tells us that the very seed of what we now know as religion was never separate from scientific exploration at all. The information obtained by the skills of long-forgotten adepts with multidimensional skills needs to be interpreted with a similar consciousness or they remain as allegorical stories.

When the Gnostic gospels say that creation occurs as a spiral from the center of a galaxy, this has been interpreted through the ages as a mere fanciful tale with no basis in real science. In actual fact, someone is reporting the information gained directly from the universe. The language of the times may have substituted goddesses for particles, but the principle of creation is unmistakably the same.

At the very core, everything from Taoism to the Vedas to Christianity contains a deeply scientific description of the universe. The fact that ancient knowledge is being validated as correct by modern methods may help to heal the rift between science and religion.

The *Punk Science* of healing

An obvious application of *Punk Science* is in the burgeoning field of complementary medicine and this is where I begun my quest. As a physician, I found it disturbing that some of the less toxic treatments available in the world of complementary medicine, such as Reiki, were not being used as an adjunct to orthodox medicine. I had a deep sense of failing my patients. I was doing my job as a doctor, but the knowledge I had as a person went much deeper.

Such experiences sparked a need in me to communicate the findings of new physics and highlight the mechanisms behind practices of complementary medicine and thus help integrate them into the current orthodox medical model. Though I eventually found much more than I expected, many of the principles of *Punk Science* are indeed useful in finally providing a mechanism behind some of the esoteric concepts in complementary therapies.

The concept of distant healing was explored in Chapter 6 in terms of physics that has been known about for some time. The newer Black Hole Principle could finally explain the subtle system of the body: a concept that is common to many complementary therapies. Hence the chakras and meridians of the body can now be seen as stages on the pathway of the manifestation of physical matter from the infinite. They are not measurable by physical instruments, because they lie beyond the Perception Horizon. Originally, information about concepts such as chakras and meridians probably came from mystical adepts. Far from being the primitive ramblings of a forgotten people, they are the mark of human sophistication.

The modern application of such concepts must be appropriate to the modern context. *Punk Science* provides the scientific mechanisms for such practices, which are necessary for acceptance in our modern era. It is not a lack of clinical trial data that is preventing complementary medicine from further integration, as these trials are taking place; it is a lack of understanding of their mechanisms. Without this understanding, medical professionals have no conceptual framework with which to understand some complementary medicines and therefore reject them, despite positive trial data.

As recent scandals in the pharmaceutical industry associated with drugs such as Lipobay and Vioxx prove, adequate trial data does not ensure patient safety.[11,12] Yet medical professionals feel more confident of these simply because they feel they understand the physical mechanism behind their actions. If they were provided with a scientific understanding of complementary therapies, this might dispel some of the fear associated with them. Certainly, this would be more in keeping with public demand; such is the popularity of complementary medicines that health insurance companies are increasingly offering them as part of their policies.[13]

A beautiful mind

The understanding of mental health is perhaps one of the most controversial topics in *Punk Science*. I have highlighted a sore point for modern medicine: the lack of a clear scientific mechanism for the symptoms of mental health.[14] In this book, I have suggested a link between the implications of modern physics and the symptoms of mental health. I am not the only person to have made this link.

I interviewed Dr Andrew Powell, the Chairman of the Royal

College of Psychiatrists' special interest group in spirituality.[15] He has written several papers on how concepts in the new physics can be applied to psychiatry.[16] During our interview, he spoke of keeping the balance between the higher and lower realms. When the consciousness of a person moves too far into the higher vibrations, that person can become ungrounded and display pathological and harmful symptoms. When the person is too grounded, the richness of the higher realms is totally missed and the person is unaware of their own human potential. It struck me how his description of the dynamic balance of mental health is another example of the dance of forces of the BHP.

Although Powell and his colleagues are making the connection between new science and psychiatry, I feel we are still a long way off from having a coherent, scientific description of mental health. The ideas contained in *Punk Science* may initiate dialogue on this issue.

Indigo evolution

The spiral motif is not only applied to specific organisms, it can also be applied to evolution as a whole. Surprisingly, conventional scientists are unsure about whether the human race is still evolving.[17] Logically, evolution should be a continuous process. In recent years some people seem to have answered the question of whether or not we are evolving.

In 1999, Lee Carroll and Jan Tober published a book called, *The Indigo Children* in which they collated reports from various psychologists and other experts from around the world who have independently noticed a change occurring in children.[18] They also reported the observations of a clairvoyant, Nancy Ann Tappe, who noticed that these children were more likely to have the color of indigo in their auras and hence these children were called Indigo children. Since then, there have been others who have come forward with labels for children such as crystal, rainbow and star children, some of whom are perhaps wishing to claim a stake in a growing trend.

However, this does not negate the fact that something is happening to the human race. What exactly is occurring is a complex question, as all people and children are individuals and have unique gifts. People are noticing different sensory abilities in these children and skills that they do not need to be taught.

More children are naturally speaking with telepathy, seeing auras, displaying gifts of healing, remembering past lives and seeing spirit guides. The talents that used to take many years of spiritual practice are now being effortlessly demonstrated in some four-year olds. Some argue that these gifts are nothing new and societal conditioning previously prevented people from displaying such talents.

Although the subject is controversial, there does seem to be some consensus that more children are aware of other aspects of reality and are continuing with this conviction into adulthood. As this occurs in greater numbers, humanity is in for some changes!

Why is this change occurring? If the spiral motif and golden mean geometry is displayed at every level of nature, could evolution itself be following the same pattern? Is consciousness itself evolving in a spiral and currently making its next leap? Certainly the idea that human consciousness is expressed in a spiral fashion is found in a very successful model called spiral dynamics.[19] Proponents of this model are currently advising government bodies as to how to improve communications between people at various levels of the spiral.

Consciousness itself could move through stages in a spiral fashion. As it does, human beings displaying different behaviors are created. Hence the modern behaviors are different from those of people in Middle Ages Europe and so on. The Indigo children may be the next expression of the human condition. As this occurs, we need to make necessary changes in our public systems such as in education.

We don't need no education

Punk Science calls for a shift in perspective, moving us to an understanding that every part of our universe is continuously creative. We have previously been living in a paradigm of the Big Bang which tells us that all the action is over, that creativity happened in the past.

This paradigm affects how we live our lives and how we teach our children. Author, lecturer and reverend, Matthew Fox, speaks of creativity as the human encounter with the divine.[20] It is part of our fundamental nature to be creative, yet this is not what we encourage in our society.

Frustration is growing in our educational systems, which are based on forcing facts into young people until the inner creative human impulse is all but forgotten. We tend to admire those who remain creative and find their genius, whether it is acting, singing, gardening or cooking.

The truth is, we all have our own creativity, our own divine force within which is our unique interaction with the quantum vacuum that results in our personal expression of genius. However, this creative impulse tends to be overridden, resulting in a society which views people as economic units.

It is in our educational systems that people tend to be conditioned out of being creative as an individual. If we shift our worldview to recognizing that creativity did not start and end billions of years ago, but is alive in every moment and that we, as conscious beings, each have our unique spark of this principle, then maybe education will become a process of drawing out the creativity of each person, of being deeply present and listening to that human soul and assisting them to find their own genius within. As mystic teacher, Yannis Pittis points out; this is how people were taught in Ancient cultures.[21]

"In ancient India, Egypt and Greece the station of the teacher and the priest were highly revered. Children were watched and observed carefully in order to identify their natural inclinations. Subsequently, their education was tailor made to suit their particular character.

Their educational system was designed to awaken the latent talents of the student, and encouragement was given to place them in service for the good of the whole community. New avenues of self-expression and study were initiated to unfold new abilities that as yet had not been actualized by the student."

In the new worldview discussed in *Punk Science*, our place in the universe can be re-evaluated and this has a profound effect on how we view ourselves and the fundamental nature of our creativity.

It's the end of the world as we know it (and I feel fine)

The totality of this book contains the seed of a new vision of reality.

This revolution is being led by the changes in human consciousness itself and being reflected in our science. As we have made science into our ultimate voice of authority, when science describes a different world, we have to take note.

This has far-reaching implications: from understanding the paranormal, to altering political realities, to understanding the very fabric of the cosmos. Although this book may be challenging for some, the intent behind this radical voice is simply to open up possibilities for our world. I hope you have enjoyed your journey through *Punk Science* and perhaps it has even changed your view of reality. Perhaps it has not touched you at all. In the immortal words of John Lydon of Public Image Limited, "I could be wrong. I could be right."

References for Chapter 18

1. Sullivan A. The Year we questioned authority. *Time*. December 26 2005. 124.

2. Transcript of President Bush's address September 20, 2001. *CNN.com*. 21 September 2001. http://archives.cnn.com/2001/US/09/20/gen.bush.transcript/ [cited January 2006].

3. Icke D. *The Biggest Secret*. (Bridge of Love) 1999.

4. Achbar M, Abbot J. (directors) *The Corporation*. [DVD] (Metrodome distribution) 2005.

5. Wheatley MJ. *Leadership and the New Science*. (Berrett-Koehler) 2001.

6. Author's interview with Morel Fourman. September 2005.

7. Casti J. I know what you'll do next summer. *New Scientist*. 31

August 2002; 29-31.

8. Jaworski J. *Synchronicity: the inner path of leadership.* (Berrett-Koehler) 1998.

9. Ibid.

10. Pagels E. *The Gnostic Gospels.* (Penguin books) 1990.

11. Bayer denies Lipobay cover up. *Pharmafocus.* 26 February 2003. http://www.pharmafocus.com/cda/focusH/1,2109,21-0-0-FEB_2003-focus [cited January 2006].

12. Vioxx; an unequal partnership between safety and efficacy. *Lancet.* 9 October 2004; 364:9442: 1287-1288.

13. Budworth D. Don't get the needle -get insurance. *The Sunday Times.* (UK) August 21 2005; 8: 4.

14. Else L. The Spirit doctor. *New Scientist.* 19 November 2005; 50-52.

15. Author's interview with Dr Andrew Powell. October 2005.

16. Powell A. Spirituality and science; a personal view. *Advances in Psychiatric Treatment.* 2001; 7:319-321.

17. Douglas K. Are we still evolving? *New Scientist.* 4 September 2004; 27-28.

18. Carrol L. Tober J. The Indigo children. (Hay House) 1999.

19. Beck DE, Cowan C. *Spiral dynamics: Mastering values, leadership and change.* (Blackwell publishing) 2005.

20. Fox M. *Creativity: where the divine and human meet.* (Jeremy P Tarcher) 2003.

21. Pittis Y. Philalethia Centre. http://www.philalethia.net/ [cited January 2006].